PRAISE FOR *TRU*

'A brilliant distillation of the way the world is moving today, where the moral compass is important and authenticity isn't a catchphrase. It was happening before the Covid-19 pandemic, but all over the world, people are confronting the mismatch between their consumption behaviours and the world they say they want to live in, and actions speak louder than words. This book takes no prisoners and is important because it positions action in the laps of the leaders who are responsible and frankly discusses the challenges of genuine leadership at a time when the corporate world has realized that if we wait for politicians our fate is bleak. Now is the time when corporate leaders have to rise to the challenge of recalibrating attitudes that are now superseded by the imperative of leading as both citizen and corporate leader. This book chronicles a moment of profound change and provides a roadmap to help all those who would learn from those who have gone before and wish to give the best version of themselves to those they serve, their fellow citizens and their companies. Utterly riveting.'
Sir Tim Smit, Founder, Eden Project

'Those brands that succeed moving forwards will be those living and breathing a clear purpose authentically, which makes this book an essential and timely read for marketing leaders.'
Peter Markey, Chief Marketing Officer, Boots plc

'A really timely and helpful book, packed full of global examples, references and handy checklists. It is a refreshing mix of common sense and sound research to ensure that any organization knows how to observe the truth, the whole truth and nothing but the truth in everything it does if it's to succeed now and into the future.'
Rita Clifton CBE, Deputy Chairman, John Lewis

'As more and more companies activate their purpose and consider how best to connect with key audiences, *Truth Be Told* shows them how to be successful. An indispensable playbook for every PR and marketing professional committed to driving positive change.'
Paul Polman, Co-founder, IMAGINE

'Businesses and brands have come to understand the power – even necessity – of a clearly articulated purpose has recently become well understood, but nailing it is harder than it sounds. *Truth Be Told* provides a roadmap for business and communications leaders to identify an authentic, credible and inspiring purpose.'
Kim Sample, President, The PR Council

'Founding strategies and communications on purpose-based truth is a shortcut to success – *Truth Be Told* offers a clear pathway to make this effective.'
Sophie Devonshire, Chief Executive, The Marketing Society

'In a world of fake news, it is more important than ever for brands to be "Truth Tellers" and to tell their brand stories authentically. This book is brilliant at helping brands achieve this important ambition moving forward.'
Fred Cook, Director, USC Center for Public Relations, USC Annenberg

'Many books, blogs, and articles have been written about purpose and purpose-led organizations recently. This book is the result of two well-respected communications professionals and provides many interesting insights and observations about one of the most challenging business topics of our time. A must-read for those who want to make a true difference in building meaningful reputations and brands.'
Andre Manning, Managing Director, Logeion (Dutch Association for Communications Professionals)

'This is an incredibly worthwhile and valuable book, packed with substance and insight. The authors make sense of this unprecedented moment in society and business and provide a clear path forward for you to distinguish your organization as a leader. They powerfully illuminate the intersection of purpose, stakeholder capitalism and communications and tell us how to "create external value for the values you hold internally". This is not a book about how to run an effective marketing campaign — it is something much more profound. Read it!'
Rob Flaherty, Chairman, Ketchum

'Authentic purpose, clear values and ethical culture are now critical for enduring business success. This book provides a timely challenge to marcoms professionals to help deliver this.'
Professor David Grayson CBE, Chair, The Institute of Business Ethics

'In a paradoxical and uncertain world, the best (if not the only) way to thrive is by finding a purpose. John O'Brien and David Gallagher explore – and bring clarity around – the main verticals and ideas surrounding purposeful business and stakeholder capitalism. A must-read for executives, entrepreneurs, investors and everyone interested in understanding how to link profit with human-centric social impact. A hugely insightful read for journalists as well, as truth-seekers and communicators. A brilliant book!'
Elizabeth Filippouli, Journalist, Author and Founder of Global Thinkers Forum

Truth Be Told

How authentic marketing and communications wins in the purposeful age

John O'Brien
David Gallagher

KoganPage

Publisher's note

Every possible effort has been made to ensure that the information contained in this book is accurate at the time of going to press, and the publishers and authors cannot accept responsibility for any errors or omissions, however caused. No responsibility for loss or damage occasioned to any person acting, or refraining from action, as a result of the material in this publication can be accepted by the editor, the publisher or the authors.

First published in Great Britain and the United States in 2021 by Kogan Page Limited

2nd Floor, 45 Gee Street	122 W 27th St, 10th Floor	4737/23 Ansari Road
London	New York, NY 10001	Daryaganj
EC1V 3RS	USA	New Delhi 110002
United Kingdom		India

www.koganpage.com

Kogan Page books are printed on paper from sustainable forests.

ISBNs

Hardback	978 1 3986 0018 8
Paperback	978 1 3986 0016 4
Ebook	978 1 3986 0017 1

British Library Control Number

A CIP record for this book is available from the British Library.

Library of Congress Control Number

2021930186

Typeset by Integra Software Services, Pondicherry
Print production managed by Jellyfish
Printed and bound by CPI Group (UK) Ltd, Croydon, CR0 4YY

This book is dedicated to John's parents who taught him truth needed to be told, and to David's parents, who instilled the importance of listening as the means for understanding.

CONTENTS

ABOUT THE AUTHORS – TWO
JOURNEYS TO TRUTH

John's path to truth in marketing

I was the product of a family of small business owners in a rural market town in the British Midlands in the early 1960s. Both my parents had their own shops, as did my grandparents, and several other relatives were businesspeople and smallholders. In two of the shops, at an age too small to be seen over the counter, I would stand on a step to watch the shop whilst whichever family member or member of staff went off to make the tea. As I grew, so did my awareness of the efforts my family put into the businesses and their local marketing, from adverts in the local newspapers, a picture ad at the cinema, thematic window displays, as well as involvement in the local business chamber, charity events and community activities. The shops were a bustle of activity; not just customers, but also employees, sales representatives, local suppliers bringing goods in or neighbours popping in for a chat. The shops were a part of their local communities and a community in itself. My family responded to local circumstances, met market demand and used simple messaging, alongside their front-of-house behaviours, which built trust and reputation. The oldest business was a shop started by my great-grandfather in 1908 and which is still operated today by a former employee under the same name; for over 100 years it has served local people with the same sense of character and goodwill which local businesses are best placed to embody. That surely is sustainable success in business.

Having left school, and after a few short years in banking, I actually took a diversion, attending the Royal Military Academy at Sandhurst, gaining my commission and going on to serve 10 years as an infantry officer. That experience embodied within me a strong sense of personal purpose, as aligned with the organization. This in turn was based on strong ethics and a set of behavioural values. When I left the Army in 1994, I found myself applying such principles at the interface of business with society, including 10 years as the Prince of Wales's director of programmes at his responsible business network BITC (Business in the Community), which gave me unparalleled experience working with and advising major global and UK business leaders on initiatives covering over 20 countries. Then in 2010, having become disillusioned by the relative failure of Corporate Social Responsibility (CSR) to change business behaviour in the wider sense, I embarked upon creating a post-CSR proposition, helping contribute to much of the now accepted language and thinking around ethical purpose in business. Having built my own business, I joined Omnicom in 2017 to co-lead their ethical purpose consortium of agencies, leading to a further expansion of applying purpose strategy thinking into global marketing and communications.

Coming from what can be described as an unconventional path into the world of brand, advertising, PR and digital communications, brought a different perspective to that of my colleagues and broadened out the possibility of how one amplifies the power of purpose, using the influence of communications. If I draw a line between my family businesses, the last 25 years' experience, and what I see today, it is this: business of any scale is first and foremost about people and the communities within which it operates. To build long-term success, you must meet the expectations of those people and do so in a way that can be trusted but at the same time be profitable to support the ongoing business needs. Marketing is about telling that story well and that story needs to be truth.

I now split my time between Omnicom, co-leading ONE HUNDRED, a consortium of cross-specialist agencies, and a portfolio of non-executive business advisory and voluntary charitable roles. I can be found at: www.johnobrien.world; LinkedIn: www.linkedin.com/in/johnobrienwritlarge/; Twitter is @Johnwritlarge

And David: same place, different road

It's somewhat remarkable we landed at the same place, at the same time, with such similar thoughts, given the very different paths we have taken. I have spent the last 25 years in a 'big agency' environment, working my way through various roles within the largest group of communications and PR specialists in the world, advising giant companies, famous brands and powerful government institutions on all kinds of major announcements, changes, and campaigns, not to mention a few serious crises. These assignments took me to dozens of countries and required me to become familiar with hundreds of businesses and organizations across just about every industry, sector and media environment; so many differences, so much nuance to every situation, and yet one feature common to every single engagement – a fundamental desire to communicate something of importance, of value, to the world.

Of course, not every assignment actually included substance of importance or value. Often the brief to us was to find something meaningful to say about a product, or a new corporate direction, or tired old government initiative, and while we often managed to succeed, it was clear we were starting at the wrong end of the process. How much easier it would be to establish why something is crucial, before worrying about how to make it sound important.

Looking further back, my first professional experiences were instrumental in shaping my later views on purpose and meaning. After gaining a journalism degree from the University of Texas, I found myself looking for editorial odd-jobs in Washington, DC, eventually landing a jack-of-all-words role at a mental health advocacy organization. This and a similar, later job at a major diabetes research association had all of the usual resource-related challenges associated with non-profits and charities, but they both enjoyed a powerful, priceless asset: a clear and defining sense of mission. One focused on improving the lives of people with mental health problems, the other toward funding research and services for people with diabetes – and both organized every single effort under these unambiguous aims.

If forced to date my very earliest memory of 'work' and what my future might hold, there's an old photo of me at age four or five, in the print shop of my grandparents' small-town newspaper in central Oklahoma (probably not the safest place for a small child, in hindsight). I remember asking my grandmother who set the type and sold the ads, what the newspaper was for. 'We tell people about things that happen when they can't see it for themselves,' she said. And what if you get it wrong, I wondered? 'We try very hard not to,' she said. 'It all has to be as true as it can be – or we'll hear about it!'

Thinking of these experiences as a whole, themes emerge. The most successful communications or marketing projects I've supported served a clear, meaningful purpose from the start. These projects were undertaken not as one-way projections of 'key message' or product features, but as part of ongoing conversations with a wider community. These communities in turn included participants well beyond shareholders and end-users, earnestly engaging all who had a stake in that overarching aim. And they were all as true as they could be.

I spend the majority of my time heading international growth and development for the Omnicom Public Relations Group, alongside volunteer advisory roles for the McCombs School of Business at the University of Texas, Mothers 2 Mothers, and the London School of Hygiene and Tropical Medicine. I can be found at: Twitter @TBoneGallagher; LinkedIn: https://www.linkedin.com/in/david-gallagher-4a23394/

CONTRIBUTORS

In the process of researching this book we spoke and corresponded with dozens of colleagues, clients past and present, and even the occasional competitor or two, all of whom were generous with their expertise and experience. Comments quoted directly have been approved for publication by the following contributors:

Nick Andrews, Claire Barry, Farzana Baduel, Richard Bagnall, Stephanie Bailey, Girish Balachandran, Fabrice Barron, Sir Peter Bazalgette, Maxim Behar, Marjorie Benzkofer, Pascal Beucler, Stephanie Capuano, Lee Hartley Carter, Sandrine Cormary, Malcolm Devoy, Scott Guthrie, Jon Harris, Sabine Huckmann, Shafaat Hussain, Will King, Paul Lindley, Jim Macnamara, Alex Mahon, Jessica Mendelowitz, Jim Moser, Melanie Norris, Lee Nugent, Catherine Overko, Lindsay Pattison, Tim Race, Manfredi Ricca, John Rosling, Petra Sammer, Emma Sergeant, Mark Stouse, Iqbal Wahhab, Richard Walker, Rosalinde van de Wall, Steffan Williams, Charles Wookey, and Prince Zhang.

FOREWORD

In January 2020, many of the world's business leaders embarked on their journey towards 'stakeholder capitalism'. During the World Economic Forum's 50th Annual Meeting in Davos, companies from every sector, and all parts of the world, committed to the 'Davos Manifesto 2020'. It stated that the purpose of a company is to 'engage all of the company's stakeholders in shared and sustained value creation', and that the best way to do so is 'through a shared commitment to policies and decisions that strengthen the long-term prosperity of a company'.

The Manifesto in this way marked a milestone: it made explicit that companies should do more than chase short-term profits, and focus on a broader purpose instead. But mere weeks after the conclusion of the event, the question of how to best deliver on these long-term goals in the face of short-term pressures became extremely pertinent. The COVID-19 pandemic plunged our world into the most challenging times we've faced in generations. In many Western societies, citizens rose up against systemic racism. And the climate crisis started to cause ever more environmental damage, from the wildfires in Australia, to the cyclone Amphan in West Bengal.

For the business leaders who had committed to stakeholder responsibility just months earlier, these events required them to 'hit the ground running' on finding and delivering on their stakeholder purpose. In addition to protecting their revenues and business activities, they needed to help protect all their stakeholders – employees, suppliers, customers, and society. And, amidst these multiple crises, they needed to clearly communicate their actions. This wasn't going to be easy in any circumstance, but it was important to get this right, because the long-term prosperity of their own businesses, and that of society as a whole, depended on it.

Truth Be Told is a handbook for executives who want to know how they can communicate their stakeholder actions and their broader purpose to the outside world, including in uncertain and tempestuous times like these. Its premise is clear: communicating on your virtuous actions will only be effective if your words are supported by meaningful actions on the ground. The right order of action is to first, truly commit to stakeholder responsibility and redefine your purpose; second, reassess your business activities against this light, and course-correct where needed; and third, communicate about your accomplishments to the outside world.

A brief history of stakeholder capitalism

Before you read this book, it's important to know that companies haven't always committed to this purpose-driven, stakeholder-oriented form of capitalism. Globally, capitalism has appeared in three main forms. The first is 'shareholder capitalism', embraced – until recently – by many companies and economists. It holds, as Milton Friedman said, that 'the business of business is business' (Newsmaker, 2010) and that its primary goal should be to maximize its short-term profits. The second is 'state capitalism'. This form of capitalism entrusts the government with setting the direction of the economy and has risen to prominence in many emerging markets, not least China.

The third is 'stakeholder capitalism'. I first talked about it a half-century ago, in the book *Modern Enterprise Management* in 1971, and in the first Davos Manifesto, signed in 1973. This model positions private corporations as trustees of society – stakeholders themselves who pay their fair share of taxes, show zero tolerance for corruption, uphold human rights throughout their global supply chains and advocate for a competitive level playing field. It's clearly the best response to today's social and environmental challenges.

The rise of shareholder capitalism, though, which was dominant until now, is not without merit. During its heyday, hundreds of millions of people around the world prospered, as profit-seeking companies unlocked new markets and created new jobs. But advocates of shareholder capitalism had neglected the fact that a publicly listed corporation is not just a profit-seeking entity but also a social organism. Together with financial industry pressures to boost short-term results, the single-minded focus on profits caused shareholder capitalism to become increasingly disconnected from the real economy. This model was no longer sustainable.

Coinciding with the launch of the decade of action to deliver the Sustainable Development Goals (SDGs) by 2030, at the Forum's Annual Meeting in 2020, global businesses prepared for a year and decade of action on some of the world's most pressing challenges: climate change and greenhouse gas emissions, rising cyber risks associated with digitization, the need for massive workforce reskilling, and the need to reduce inequities in access to healthcare, especially mental healthcare – to name just a few. And the pandemic crystallized the need, like never before, to collaborate on developing solutions to these challenges and many others facing our world.

Finding your purpose and communicating to stakeholders

The pandemic and resulting social and economic crises now present a rare but narrow window of opportunity to reflect, reimagine and reset our world to create a healthier, more equitable, more prosperous future.

As we seize upon this window, companies should do two things: first, they should realize their purpose and their role in revamping societies and economies, both in the immediate response to issues like COVID-19 and the climate crisis, as well as in the long term. And second, they should include stakeholders in the conversations that matter. This consultation process should be organized such that executives and boards can make decisions, well aware of the issues that matter to their stakeholders.

The good news is that both of these tasks can be executed. To realize their purpose, the World Economic Forum's International Business Council, comprising 140 of the world's largest companies, in September 2020 presented a new set of environmental, social and governance (ESG) metrics and disclosures, called the 'Stakeholder Capitalism Metrics'. Led by the Chairman of the International Business Council (IBC), Bank of America CEO Brian Moynihan, with support from the 'Big Four' accounting firms, these stakeholder metrics are meant to complement standard financial metrics. They can ensure that a company measures its sustainable value creation in a way that is consistent across industry sectors and countries.

The broad, cross-sector support for the metrics shows a real commitment on the part of companies to being more transparent in their communications about their non-financial performance – and already we're seeing it play out. Companies are responding to their employees' and suppliers' needs in the crisis, changing their supply chains to reduce emissions and donating to social justice organizations and launching initiatives to make their own workplaces more inclusive and equitable. And as the pandemic-induced lockdowns have required people to work, learn, shop and socialize almost exclusively at home, opportunities to communicate with stakeholders directly have been increasing.

Thanks to the digital innovations of the Fourth Industrial Revolution, businesses also have the opportunity to engage directly with stakeholders, including the public, like never before. One example comes from the World Economic Forum itself. Over the past years, we set up 'Global Future Councils', to include experts in all domains into our agenda setting. We've set up hundreds of hubs of 'Global Shapers' – young people under the age of 30 – to make sure the voices of the world's young are heard. And we built a global social media following of 25 million people and opened up our events, including the Annual Meeting in Davos, to the public, with livestreaming and social media coverage across platforms including Facebook, Twitter and TikTok. The 50th Annual Meeting in 2020 in this way was historic in its level of stakeholder participation. Many companies are making similar efforts to make sure they can consult their stakeholders as well.

However, this opportunity is not without risk. In the midst of the COVID-19 pandemic, climate-related disasters and social upheaval, we're relying on digital technology and digital communication platforms to work, learn, and even see doctors – and information can quite literally save lives. But there is also a dark side to the ubiquity of these information technologies: the risk of misinformation. This is all the more reason why businesses must communicate, openly and often, so stakeholders aren't led astray.

Stakeholder capitalism requires not only open and transparent communication, but also vigilance. Companies have a duty to combat the viral spread of misinformation that's (intentionally or not) misleading or provocative, ensure the safekeeping of their stakeholders' private data, and take action to prevent or stop cyber security threats. And, if and when something inevitably goes wrong in this new space, even more clear, transparent communication about what happened is needed, and what will be done to fix it. After all, damage can be done by rapid misinformation even when the correct information quickly follows.

The bottom line

The new world of communications is no longer just about the message your company is putting out into the world. One-way communication, from business to shareholder or business to stakeholder, isn't enough. Today, the communications environment is one in which everyone interacts with one another. Businesses have a role to play in ensuring they are having a dialogue with – and especially listening to – stakeholders, verifying information, responsibly managing and mitigating risks and, if one of those risks does come to bear, communicating even more.

To create a better world, companies must have a purpose rooted in the world around them, not just in their own operations. John O'Brien and

David Gallagher show how to do so in any company in an honest and purposeful way. I hope you enjoy reading their book.

Klaus Schwab
Founder and Chairman, World Economic Forum, Geneva

Reference

Newsmaker.com.au (2010) The Business Of Business Is Business, https://www. newsmaker.com.au/news/5603/the-business-of-business-is-business#.X66m-cj7TIU (archived at https://perma.cc/3TRQ-WPHR)

ACKNOWLEDGEMENTS

Writing a book of this kind is never the sole effort of its authors and we are extremely grateful to the many colleagues, clients, friends and connections who have shown such interest in the subject, shared their knowledge and experiences, contributed to our research and helped inform our thinking.

We must start by thanking all our colleagues across the Omnicom network, the ONE HUNDRED EMEA agency consortium in particular, and those within our sector who have supported our endeavour. The privilege of being within the world's largest multi-disciplinary marketing and communications collective brings the broadest of expertise together for our clients and inevitably helped us equally draw insights from the full range of marketing and communication specialisms, relevant to you and the thinking within this book.

Several colleagues are quoted throughout the work, but many others generously shared their observations, experiences and feedback to help craft the end result. We are particularly grateful to our close colleagues, Emma Sergeant, Fenella Grey, Jo-ann Robertson, Mark Flanagan, Jim Donaldson, Brian Crimmins, Rob Flaherty, Sairah Ashman and AnnaMaria Nalbandian, who were so generous with their time and encouragement.

Outside the Omnicom 'family' we have benefitted from the commitment to truth and purpose of many recognized leading practitioners, innovators and commentators in our sector, including Francis Ingham, Kim Sample, Stephen Waddington, Johnna Burke, Bridget Brennan, Maya Pawinska, Alex Meyers, Sarah Waddington, as well as Fiorenza Plinio of Cannes Lions and Adrian Monck of the World Economic Forum, for their particular efforts.

This book, of course, is not just for or of agency-based individuals, but is enriched massively by those clients, business founders, leaders and senior communication professionals who willingly shared their perspective and for this we thank all our many contributors.

Our global perspective not only required us to reach across our own professional networks but to throw out a wider net and we are very grateful to David Brain, co-founder of StickyBeak research in New Zealand, and Arun Sudhaman, CEO and editor-in-chief at PRovoke Media in Hong Kong, for collaborating on our quantitative research resulting in over 350 participants being empowered from around the globe to input accordingly.

A thank you also to our friends at Kogan Page – Helen Kogan for 'getting it', Chris Cudmore for 'guiding it' and Stephen Dunnell for 'editing it' – whilst without the additional research, referencing and detailed rigour of Matthew McQuiston Gallagher, we quite simply would not have hit our deadlines. A special note must also go to our proofreaders and early reviewers whose feedback was invaluable: Martyna Borys, Paula Stei, and Aina Teper.

We are rightly humbled and immensely grateful for the interest and fore-word of Professor Klaus Schwab, founder and executive chairman of the World Economic Forum, for sharing his perspective as a global thought leader and placing our own thinking in such valuable context. We present our modest contribution to help in crafting the vision of a better world as advocated by Professor Schwab and are grateful for the opportunity to do so.

If *Truth Be Told*, John shares his thanks to the late composers Ralph Vaughan Williams and George Butterworth, whose music transports him to a state of detachment from the world, where his thinking and writing is best nurtured. David is grateful for the early morning head-clearing walks on Hampstead Heath with the boisterous canine duo of Poppy and Hugo, his two most ardent supporters. In such contrasts and collective efforts, are successful partnerships made.

Finally, thank you to our wives and families for their forbearance and support at times when we were not present and for those where we may have seemed so, but our minds were on a purpose elsewhere.

As for our commitment to truth, we take full responsibility for complete accuracy in our content and for any shortcomings which of course are ours alone.

Introduction

How we came to be here

It is early morning; a pre-office breakfast and we are sitting in a trendy café/bar adjacent to several large buildings near the Tate Modern gallery on the busy and trendified Southwark Street in south London. These buildings house upwards of 6,000 people working in digital design, audience research, brand strategy, marketing, advertising and public relations; many are colleagues, some are competitors, but the majority are generally enthusiastic, highly intelligent and very creative millennials, keen to do great work for good clients.

They bustle past on their way into these bright shiny offices, but to what, exactly? Well, regardless of their specialism, these are people whose days are filled with one overarching draw on their time, namely helping clients prosper and grow through communications and marketing. They are outwardly confident and inwardly content that they are at the centre of where they wanted to be, in a vibrant city, in the creative sector, in professional roles and expressing themselves on the wider world through their clients. They celebrate the success of the latest campaign they have helped create, they look forward to the parties of PR and adland award season, and embrace their 21st-century lives.

Yet as we see them passing, we know that this new decade of the 'roaring twenties' presents an ever-increasing risk to it all, with factors and trends already transforming the basis on which business relationships are based, how people connect, and how success is measured. This leads us onto why this book is necessary and how to use it to power up your own activities. In setting down our experiences, we have created a set of principles which form the basis of a new way to do your job better. We set this out in chapters that are designed to be enlightening and thought-provoking, providing perspectives that will demand that you answer a set of fundamental questions about your role, those around you, and your business or the client you are working for. Each chapter explains the overarching principle and then sets out the observations and summarizes with questions at the end. Finally, in the concluding chapter, these are collated into a single narrative, as an *aide mémoire* to the accumulated wisdom you will have shaped yourself as you embark upon your own truthful thinking.

The path is clear, the light we shine will encourage and support you, and your interpretation will become your truth, a truth which is now more necessary than ever in such challenging and – dare we say it – 'interesting times'.

'May you live in interesting times'

Putting all irony aside, this longstanding English expression, erroneously referenced as a translation of a Chinese proverb and known as the 'Chinese Curse', is used to suggest that life is better in times that are less interesting. Of course, it is only just over 12 months ago we were becoming aware of a virus originating in China that would become universally known as COVID-19 and make all our lives far more interesting than we might have either expected or liked.

You may wonder why this is a particularly appropriate start point as the introduction to a book on business strategy and in particular marketing and communications. But the reason is quite simple; indeed, we share a whole chapter on it. It is that up until 2020, we as senior-level advisors, regular public speakers and commentators would use a phrase which suggested that the world was already interesting enough – how little we knew.

The phrase we and others regularly bandied around was 'VUCA', standing for Volatile, Uncertain, Chaotic and Ambiguous. It is a phrase fashioned originally by the US military to explain the post-Cold War threat environment and adopted by many of us to highlight the combined challenges we operated with in our business norm. It is therefore without any hesitation that we have to say that the phrase VUCA, as interpreted for business prior to COVID-19, has lost its validity as an expression of extreme business conditions. In order to make a distinction, we have opted in this book to describe the new environment as VUCA2.0. This is a re-definition because our future ability to manage, lead, cope and communicate needs to take into account not just the VUCA factors of yesterday, as they affected business, but most importantly the VUCA factors as they affect people, as individual human beings, their health, that of their loved ones, and the communities within which they/we live and do business. VUCA2.0 places us in a world where the need for this book, its collated thinking and proven processes has never been more relevant or important.

So, what could be more 'interesting' than going over the horizon, into a world of chaos, being able to assess the situation, formulate a plan and deliver it successfully? This is the challenge that everyone is facing in successfully building businesses, growing market share and delivering long-term sustainable success. It is no accident that the initial sentence here is exactly how John felt his military training prepared him and countless others to survive and indeed live through volatile operational conditions. For David, having spent his professional life in the world of public relations, so much of his time has been spent helping clients to resolve the chaos around them or to navigate the difficulties which resulted from such factors.

Together we recognized that our efforts were so often to bring clarity in interesting times, but not just to survive, which appears so often to dominate the short-term needs of business leaders, but to flourish. We wrote this book to share how our collective experiences, alongside input from friends and colleagues, can go beyond reinforcing an old business paradigm, and shine a light on the changes demanded of business now and how to communicate in powerful, resonant terms.

As we sat there on the South Bank talking, we circled all these issues at the macro level, as well as the micro-illustrations of various corporate behaviour and how they have both impacted upon our lives and those around us. As we did so we realized that one particular question, in various contexts, kept emerging as the core to all we asked. It is that most important question of *Why?* Essentially, reflecting on why we have been lucky during this period brought us to ask why we exist and why what we do matters. But breakfast can only last so long, so to put some parameters around the discussion, we were looking at what we do in our respective professional worlds, whether anything we do really matters and therefore why we do it. This can even be asked about our writing this book and so in the interests of not just raising questions, but also providing answers, it is right that we explain why we have written it, why it is needed and why it should be important to you. In doing so we will then answer the inherent question (almost) in our title *Truth Be Told: How authentic marketing and communications wins in the purposeful age.*

In the previous decade, developments in our own specialisms of ethical business purpose and public relations have changed the questions we face and the solutions we create. We share our respective perceptions of what is being demanded of business and specifically how marketing and communications is critical in meeting these new expectations. We face an ever more established purpose paradigm, where there is a growing acceptance of the fact that the perceived rationale around business has changed and this has led to a growth in 'purpose-led' campaigns and activities.

The path ahead in this book will require you to ask yourself fundamental questions about your approach to your role. It will provide insights and explanations of everything from often-confused terminology, through to societal trends, which sets it apart from any business marketing book you will have read to date. From this, a navigable process will emerge which allows you to apply the essence of how to build brand and business success through leading marketing and communications in a way you have never done before. At the core of this is our proven knowledge and personal belief that at the heart of business success for the future lies two things: a *human truth* which is the essence of the business purpose, and a truthful approach to promoting that business to the world. We can summarize these as the case for a 'Human, Truthful Business'.

How would we describe a human, truthful business? Why is it important to put a human context at the core of why you exist and how you operate? How does such a human truth then manifest itself in your branding and communications? What does having a truthful culture really do for your business's performance? How does one develop a human-centric marketing strategy? Never have so many questions been so necessary for so many.

We take these questions and others and deconstruct them, place them in historic and current contexts, craft them into clear thinking, share our proven processes and build it all into a solution-driven set of thinking that provides answers to both engage and inspire you, your teams and your customers in order to activate your brand purpose successfully.

This comes at a time, where whether you are a founder of a social purpose start-up or the CEO of a PLC, a marketing director of a FTSE 100 or an agency-based marcoms consultant, you are facing demands to change and build new success in a way which has never happened before. You can create such change by building your business's future, fusing the very best of your brand values, its behaviours, talent and culture around a powerful human, truth-based purpose. By creating something that matters to people, you will change the business by having changed their mindset. You will change customers into fans, employees into ambassadors, suppliers into partners as they see alignment between what they care about and what your business cares about. This is the excitement of what we face now.

Much has been made in recent years of the power of data and the use of artificial intelligence and other technologies to drive business forward, and for good reason. Collecting and using customer information helps leaders make better decisions, optimize spending and refine creative messaging, making data-driven marketing one of the most transformative developments in business since the invention of the spreadsheet. But while data and technology can bring us closer to human truth, they cannot replace it – not yet at least.

Human truth is a communications strategy whose age has come. The purpose is to help your business maximize its potential, achieve its specific objectives and, by reflecting your behaviours, create the success through meeting people's needs well. This should not be at all surprising because a business's success has to be based on its ability to meet a need for people. That need can be feeding them, inspiring them, entertaining them or caring for them, but it meets a human need and thereby creates the business opportunity. By placing greater understanding and emphasis of human need in both the business and its brand communications you will change the way all your stakeholders, employees, customers, suppliers and investors think about and value your business. By creating such a shift in the mindset of those your business depends upon, it will power up your business by creating a new relationship, the most powerful of factors for long-term success.

Let us also be clear about who we hope to reach. This is not a set of thinking confined to a particular specialism or job role; indeed, in the same way as we represent a wide experience and help professionally advise across all sectors of marketing and communications, the relevance of this book is broad. If you are a senior business leader or work in the marketing and communications department, then this book is for you. If you commission or create advertising, manage public relations, lead on creative design, manage the internal employee brand or the external brand positioning, this book is for you. The content of our message is too important for us all that it must not become, as John says, 'an occupation for a few, but rather a preoccupation for the many'; because having such human and truthful thinking is now a leadership imperative. Never has there been a greater demand on leaders to put authentic values at the heart of how they lead and how their business operates. In addition, every business is operating in a disrupted marketplace, with equally hungry businesses vying for market share through increasingly commoditized, product-based strategies. How do you therefore stand out, if everyone is simply pushing product qualities that are invariably similar? Let's face it, one bar of soap, broadband package or pair of trousers is very much like the next. A distinction which creates difference in the marketplace can establish greater attention in our fragmented media, building what we describe as 'external value for the values you hold internally'.

Leaders need to be mindful that many people have for some time felt corporate focus has been too much on the 'value' for profits, at the expense of the 'value' for people. Since the corporate scandals of the 2000s, it is business leaders themselves who have started advocating a shift from the short-term, aggressive, consumption-based marketplace. People are becoming more conscious of the environmental and societal credentials of businesses and their products, the values they operate under and how they treat people. This shift in consumer consciousness has grown over the last 10 years and been fast-forwarded further by the COVID-19 crisis and economic fallout. To be successful now, a business has to shift its emphasis on how it operates and how it communicates to meet an entirely different set of expectations.

At the same time, this VUCA2.0 world, which we describe in Chapter 1, offers businesses a new set of opportunities to create brand success because many people are actively seeking the type of businesses that recognize the human values and purpose we extol in this book. Although this perhaps sounds contradictory, these are people who don't necessarily feel the need to improve their lives simply through the acquisition of ever more 'things', the normal marketeer's dream; rather, these people are seeking to replace the brands they purchase with those that seem more meaningful, more aligned with their own values. Businesses that can understand this and develop a meaningful brand promise for people will create the necessary market distinction. This is where a VUCA world can confuse many but for those with such clarity it will be a rich opportunity to grow.

These questions therefore created our 'Why' for writing this book, simply because no such book has yet been written, combining our own experiences of ethical business strategists with those of global marketing experts, at a time when businesses and society need to both combine and share good thinking in order to become great again. Our purpose in bringing together our insights alongside so many of the best in business is to create something that is useful to others in their business development. We aim to extract from a world of over communication and chaos, something which provides clarity of thinking, a proven process, and a route to adoption, all designed in short to provide you with the means to identify your business 'Why?', how to unleash it and how to build a good business and a greater world.

So, in the knowledge of us answering our 'Why', let us now help you first understand and then answer yours, namely why this book is a book for you.

The reason these questions, this book and its answers, are not just relevant but should be important to you, is the current state of complexity which now exists in the world. You are attempting to navigate the VUCA2.0 world which has made VUCA1.0 an entirely superseded definition. In this world, whether you are in a specific business, or like us are in business to help others safely travel through this world, understanding VUCA2.0 and how to navigate it is critical. Clients or management come to you, as advisors, because they believe that your worldview, coupled with creativity and diverse talent, can create clarity in their strategies and resulting communications. You are a mixture of coach, aide, catalyst, provocation, surge capacity and even on occasions a comfort blanket. The difficulty, however, is that in the old VUCA1.0 world, there was a relative lack of sophistication in creating really meaningful solutions, which we have witnessed across many of the strategy and marketing efforts we see in the world. In VUCA2.0 that simply isn't sustainable, and alongside the reader who may be in the businesses themselves, this book and our insights have one overarching requirement: they must be impactful. None of us can afford anything less.

Why was the previous state of play prevalent? This was because the previous two decades had seen a gradually growing and substantial shift in what constitutes the basis of our respective professional expertise. Firstly, we witnessed a set of successive corporate scandals, which shook both confidence and trust in business and ultimately overturned the previous standard doctrine of why a business exists. Secondly, and partially due to the former, but also as much to external societal changes, there has been a seismic shift in what people expect when it comes to businesses talking about themselves, their products, services, culture and practices. This undoubtedly has led to business leaders questioning themselves and, adding to their own pressure, being asked more questions by more people. 'Why have I taken over a business which runs this way?', 'Why do my employees ask this of me?', 'Why are investors demanding this?', 'Why are we expected to comment on the news?', 'Why do my children think business is bad?'

This book's purpose is not to attempt to disentangle all of the issues that affect business in this new age, but it is written in the knowledge of what has occurred, the resulting suspicions around global supply chains, the demands in society of different styles of corporate leadership, and the varied demographic impacts from the reduction in opportunities for the young through to reduced pensions for the old. It takes, as best as any authors can, a broad range of public information, identifiable business and social trends and then, uniquely, insights from hundreds of business leaders and practitioners, from across all sectors, large and small and from around the world.

We know that in the clamour of breaking out into the new market and economic environment, the scramble of regaining growth, re-establishing brand awareness and market share, many will look backwards, not to learn, as we do here, but simply to say, 'it worked for us then – it will work for us now'. You may be lucky, you may be in a constrained, formulaic industry where the same old same old will work, but for the vast majority of us, that simply will not be the case. The VUCA2.0 world requires creativity, imagination, different perspectives.

Together our aim is to encourage you if you need, firstly to change the way you think and then, if you can, you will change the way you behave; once you do that, what you do to market, communicate and sell yourself, your business and your products will seem the most natural and obvious way.

For those who have open minds, a willingness to go beyond the norm, who can step boldly into the volatile, uncertain, chaotic and ambiguous future, quite simply – read on.

01

The world: what you need to know

The last few years have seen significant levels of disruption across the entire marketing communications sector, public relations and advertising. There are ongoing commentaries which talk about the domination of digital platforms, the power of predictive analytics, the emergence of direct-to-consumer brands, the challenges of successfully coordinating multi-channels, the rise of in-housing and, of course, ever reduced budgets. Our communities of practice, in agencies, consultancies or within companies and brands, are also feeling the impact of developments from beyond our immediate industry, from artificial intelligence, augmented reality and the internet of things (IoT). But we have witnessed, and acknowledged in our solutions for our clients, something more so, which we see as the backdrop to the sector's challenges (and that of modern business more broadly): a set of much more powerful influences.

In this chapter we show you that the start point for this reimagining is not in the first instance within your business or those you advise, but rather it is outside, in your understanding of the world. This is the world far beyond simply the market you are operating in, or your direct customers – it is a world of significant external influences.

These influences have been characterized as the Fourth Industrial Revolution by Klaus Schwab, founder and head of the World Economic Forum in Geneva; a new way of living, working and relating with each other. According to the Forum:

> These advances are merging the physical, digital and biological worlds in ways that create both huge promise and potential peril. The speed, breadth and depth of this revolution is forcing us to rethink how countries develop, how organizations create value and even what it means to be human (World Economic Forum, 2020).

So, what are these influences and how are they manifesting themselves? By way of illustration, consider the worldwide revolution of children striking for climate action; mainstream politics failing to address (or choosing to exploit) populist concerns; the distrust and legislation in some countries around social influencers; how personal data has become both a major public concern and new global commodity; a society increasingly seeing the need to reduce carbon, shift from non-recyclable plastics and grow alternative energy sources. If you add on top of these the #MeToo movement, #BlackLivesMatter, the online 'cancel' culture, persistent gender pay gap issues and the continuing wider diversity battles, you have multiple, daunting paradoxes.

1 **Growth is good, but consumption is bad**. In business, profitable growth is seen as crucial for a company's long-term survival, while the ad and marketing industry is perceived as existing to feed the consumption that drives growth. 'More is better' is increasingly at complete odds with how many consumers and particularly younger generations feel, who see the challenges of climate change and poverty as being a result of a society based on consumption. If the market model is measured on how much product is shifted, the methodology is falling out of step with consumers' thinking.

2 **Information is ubiquitous, but cynicism is rife**. People are better connected with each other, with news and information sources, and with the companies they patronize than ever before, yet (or consequently?) they are more cynical about business than ever before. Since 2008, successive scandals mean that consumers doubt what they see and trust companies even less. If our proposition is that people should trust our messages, simply because of who we are, then we are blind to their demands for more diligent, detailed information so that they can make informed decisions of their own, not just on our products but on the business overall.

3 **Quality counts, but issues matter**. Many people feel themselves unable to secure the lifestyle their parents enjoyed and at the same time see the past occupied with constraining, inappropriate behaviours. Powered by social media, people now join together to reject the status quo and rally on issues they now take personally. If you take the biggest issues of recent years, they render much of what had been our stock in trade – sex and gender stereotyping, diversity-based humour and excess – completely at odds with people's thinking and what society finds acceptable.

4   **Technology binds us, but technology separates us**. Advances in cloud
     computing, mobile connectivity and automation give people far greater
     access to each other and their own creative potential, not to mention news
     and information from every corner of the world, and yet we are feeling more
     socially isolated (Ortiz-Ospina and Roser, 2020), more politically polarized
     (Bail *et al*, 2018) and less trusting in our institutions (Edelman, 2020).

These paradoxes combined have created a world where there are ever greater expectations placed on your business and by default your marketing and communications. With such fault lines across business and society, people are looking for alternatives to get their information and how they establish trust and truths. They look to see whether their purchasing is both ethical and inherently valuable, whilst at the same time good value. So where does all this lead? Let us accept four norms that easily cover our broad range of marketing and communications activities:

We **Inform**, that is introduce something to people.

We **Persuade**, show why one thing is better than another.

We **Remind**, reinforcing existing awareness.

We **Manage** perceptions, risks and reputations.

One needs to wonder whether this accepted mantra can really serve as well in this new age. So, let us just think this through a bit further. Our industry prides itself on changing behaviours, but are we that good at changing our own? Do we, for example, actually take the time to understand such global trends, such geopolitical-societal shifts in thinking? We contend that the reason many of us feel we are facing some of the toughest and most disruptive of periods we are ever likely to see in our professional careers, is simply that we cannot grasp the need to change our thinking to meet the changes already taking hold in the world. Such a period of change is not just demanding on business generally; the harsh reality is that in the field of marketing and communications, we are facing unprecedented demands from the widest of stakeholders, far beyond what might traditionally have been the case.

As businesses all over the world consider how they successfully address such societal shifts in expectations, ongoing economic challenges, post-COVID-19 developments and the continual need for innovation to drive ongoing market success, we, those who speak for the business and its products and services, face a multiplicity of demands, requiring dramatic new thinking.

In conversation with Manfredi Ricca, Global Chief Strategy Officer at Interbrand, he said:

> For the first time since the industrial revolution, customer expectations are moving faster than the fastest businesses. This is due to contextual conditions such as hyperconnectivity, the abundance of choice, the speed of technological adoption, and our shifting frames of reference (whereby for instance we increasingly expect the process of opening a bank account to be as fast as hailing a cab or compiling a playlist).

> Like never before, organizations must therefore be in touch and in tune with people, in an ongoing dialogue with them, to capture what's changing in their minds, hearts, hopes and fears that is ultimately going to revolutionize categories. It also pertains to a desire for people to have a greater sense of their own role in life and this affects how they engage. Only by such awareness can businesses be able to leap ahead of expectations, making bold and meaningful moves that spark desire and create utility – and which we call Iconic Moves.

Against this backdrop of what many see as 'The Purposeful Age', where people seek greater purpose in their own lives and the organizations they work for and purchase from, we need new approaches to address the needs of businesses and this general trend, by reimagining the way marketing and communications can operate successfully.

This trend requires a new kind of professional who, regardless of a particular specialism, possesses a new global, purposeful mindset. This new perspective will allow individuals to build a truth-driven strategy capable of cross-functional approaches, of combining their specialism in marketing and communications with an important general knowledge, which we might describe as *informed empathy*. Both parts are essential: 'informed' is both adjective and an ongoing process about understanding the world around us, and 'empathy' underscores the need to see and feel that world through the eyes of others. Mastering this evolution as a mindset is likely to differentiate the most successful of individuals and their brands over the next decade. It is this perspective that we want you to consider in this chapter.

Some time ago, John had the opportunity of helping organize a series of events at London's British Museum, as part of an initiative of His Royal Highness the Prince of Wales's responsible business network, Business in the Community. The events invited some of the UK's most senior business leaders to share their insights around their approach to leadership. Set against the backdrop of one of the world's greatest historical artefact collections, the museum helped cast their contemporary leadership thinking onto the longer reach of history, providing context and reflection of how things change but often in many ways stay the same. One such leader was John (now Lord) Browne, who was then CEO of BP, the global energy business.

Lord Browne has a passion for Venice and in describing his approach to leading BP, as well as his thinking on business in society generally, he drew upon museum artefacts to illustrate the time when Venice was the most vibrant of cities in the world, both in trade and culture. He described the role business played in creating its pre-eminent position and where it all went wrong. The particular comment he cited as being relevant those hundreds of years ago and has remained critical to successful business ventures, illustrates the basis of this chapter. Browne cited the scene from William Shakespeare's play *The Merchant of Venice*, where one merchant says to the other, 'What news on the Rialto?' – the Rialto of course being the commercial centre in Venice. This question asked for a summary of what goods were up, what prices were down, who was saying what, who was 'in', who was 'out' and what was happening in the world generally. Browne went on to explain that once the merchants of Venice stopped asking that question, stopped questioning what was happening in the world, their fortunes and those of the city simply ebbed away.

Today, we face the exact same need to keep asking the question, 'What news on the Rialto?', albeit in other words and through different means. If you are to succeed in your role of leading marketing and communication activity, you must understand why the question is asked and what answers are indicative and influential to your own task. The appreciation of the world, global circumstances generally and your specific business environment is critical if you are to master an ability to best communicate what your business proposition is, best secure attention and grow market share. Any successful leader, either of business or of its communication activities, must be alert to what is happening around them. Critically this is because the way in which we perceive our business, our specific customer proposition and how we communicate, is absolutely as a counterpoint to the way the world sees us and how we are viewed in contrast to what else is happening and what others are doing. The world will influence your behaviours in the same way that you hope to influence the world's. Those leading the messaging to the world must have a hunger for understanding it and this goes well beyond traditional customer appreciation or knowledge of marketing techniques. The acceptance of this and the resulting impact is reflected in 2020 research from the University of Texas at Austin's McCombs School of Business, where David is an advisor. Researchers showed that today's most successful marketing strategies are not simply focused on customers, but that they communicate and promote across a wider front, looking to build relationships across whole sectors, industries and in effect the wider world.

Companies with this broad-based approach, termed 'marketing excellence' in the field, generated portfolios with up to 8.58 per cent higher rates of return than those using standard marketing approaches, according to Sebastian Hohenberg, assistant professor of marketing, with Christian Homburg and Marcus Theel with the University of Mannheim (Hohenburg *et al*, 2020).

They describe this approach as 'Seeing the Ecosystem', where a company's willingness to look at the broader area it operates in and its multiple stakeholders, its ecosystem, even if outside of their main customer, improves investor perception. Hohenberg says, 'There's a collapse in boundaries that's crucial today for achieving organic growth. Companies that are growing today go out and engage with players that are not even somewhat related to their industry.'

By way of example, they cite a car manufacturer who partnered with the digital experts at Google, Apple and Microsoft in pursuit of autonomous driving. Another is a chemical company which partnered with a digital start-up to create a new business model where the company is selling its data, rather than developing chemicals. As Hohenberg explains, 'We always used to tell our students to start by understanding the market. But in these interviews, we found that successful companies do a lot more than that' (Kinonen, 2020).

There are two ways of interpreting this. Firstly, understanding the world around you informs you about what 'society' is thinking; it will allow you to consider not just what customers think of your products, but what the wider world does as well. You need to go beyond conventional thinking and try to see what is happening that may affect your business in unexpected ways. This is critical for informed empathy, which may previously have been seen as irrelevant, but now is an imperative. The reality is that there have been examples where businesses focused purely on customer appreciation. When the customer has been satisfied, the business has considered anything else superfluous, yet in examples we will illustrate elsewhere in this book, by not being aware of other opinions, business and marketing campaigns have been undermined. As such, part of understanding the world might be seen as understanding the widest set of societal stakeholders. The critical addition to this is appreciating that such stakeholders, however broad, do not have a fixed opinion or necessarily a comparative similarity in opinions on any given issue or at any given time.

This is actually part of the conundrum. By way of illustration, your customers might be delighted, sales flow well, and in turn this creates growing market share and so delights your shareholders. That would appear to suggest all is well, but your product might be seen as harmful in some way, perhaps either environmentally, say for example in the extraction sector, or to personal health, say in tobacco or, increasingly, its alternative, vaping. It is not your customers or shareholders who are likely to cause the business issues, but rather lobby groups, citizen activism and policymakers. The pressure, the risk around sustainable success for the business, therefore, can often rest with people well beyond the traditional focus of your communications. This means inevitably that you need to be interpreting trends and wider thinking, equally as much as you pore over customer data or worry about shareholder quarterly figures. You need to be adept at predicting the impact of, in these instances, firstly a growth in environmental activism and secondly public health concerns. Neither were things our predecessors in marcoms were ever concerned about, but if you aren't both concerned and capable of predicting their implications on your business, you aren't now doing your job. As John says, 'Business, quite simply, is now greater than simply its business'. This is borne out by Interbrand's Ricca, who told us:

> Many of the most valuable global brands have a macroeconomic force and influence, far more than institutions and governments – and with that comes a responsibility towards the environment, societies, culture. People increasingly look to these brands for leadership, for a clear stance on the greatest social issues of our times. In much of the developed world, people no longer accept being passive consumers, but are active constituents. We have to be adept at understanding this and scanning the future.

However, and this is important, we ourselves are not, in this book, going to fall into the trap of trying to predict the future or suggest that informed empathy allows you to do so to some magical effect either. The harsh reality is that the level of unexpected occurrences, through which businesses have navigated in recent years, don't necessarily illustrate what will arise in the future.

They simply help us be better equipped in understanding how to cope with unexpected occurrences when they do arise and be more capable of navigating that which has already changed in society as a result. Yes of course there will be trends and you will assess them as all good leaders in business will, so you might consider the implications of flexible working or online retailing or geopolitical factors, but to be effective you need to interpret those things which may appear less directly connected to your business and be sure your leaders can appreciate them as well.

The first of two examples of this was when the Black Lives Matters movement erupted in 2020. John was advising a CEO in the UK communications sector who couldn't understand why he was getting increasing agitation from his workforce around the death of George Floyd, an American, and the demands that he and the company make a public statement. He thought it neither relevant nor right, given he had a very small percentage of BAME staff and 'it' was, in his words, 'a long way away'. Eventually John was able to convince him to act, to issue a carefully reflective position statement because, he explained, the agency's employees felt his silence on something they were concerned about showed a potential lack of concern for them and what was happening in society generally. This is about empathy not just with individuals, but with societal incidents. It requires new thinking, diplomacy, awareness, the informed empathy previously not necessarily required.

The second illustration was when John was advising a UK financial institution at group level. The group chairman brought him in to assist in advising on a new business which, in the wake of the financial crisis, he wanted to launch as the most ethical in its space. A newly appointed CEO made a surprising statement at a board meeting that they had identified how a significant saving to the marketing spend could be made, by creating an offshore vehicle to channel necessary production and media-buying costs. The chairman asked John his opinion, and almost instantly the CEO protested, saying, 'I have checked with the accountants, it's all perfectly legal'. John took his time, but was conscious that at that very time, British newspapers were full of stories about entertainment and sporting celebrities who had been identified as paying minimal tax, via offshore structures. Again, although legal, these were being seen in society generally as something underhanded, not 'paying one's way' for British public services, and shame was being heaped on those identified. Here was a situation where an unrelated issue was in effect likely to make a corporate decision appear equally tainted. The issue was not whether the offshore marketing spend structure was legal, it was whether the action would be seen as ethical or not by a wider public, some likely to be group customers, who might view the business and the wider group's reputation as tarnished. In that instance, the group chairman decided against the proposal and, as it happens, within three months of appointment the new CEO was let go, clearly ill placed to match the ethical expectations of the group. We can see from this how easy it is to potentially be blind to the world and general trends. Afterall, the CEO was meant to be the smartest in the room.

We talk further about risks associated with such requirements in Chapter 3, but these two examples illustrate the need for leaders to be prepared to go beyond what might be thought of as a linear view of the world, from their business to their customer, to one which expands into a multi-dimensional set of awareness, all of which makes for greater under-standing of the bigger picture. Accepting that, then what is the world around us? What is happening on the global Rialto?

Well, the 2020s were already being seen as a massively decisive decade for us all and in particular for businesses, even before the COVID-19 pandemic. There were increasing societal demands on businesses to not only do something, but for us in our roles to be far more effective in saying what we were doing, building reputation and recognition with society on related issues. It became untenable, for example, to suggest that climate change, poverty, diversity and wider SDG issues were irrelevant.

The gradual rejection of Friedman thinking around the purpose of business, covered further in Chapter 3, but essentially focused on profit return to shareholders, had created a strong belief that the 2020s would be the decade where a combination of enlightened self-interest, government legislation and people power, either via protests or purchasing choices, would see dramatic shifts to more sustainable products, reduced emissions, less single-use plastic, greater equity of opportunity and more besides. These would help achieve the aspirations of the 2015 Paris Agreement on carbon reduction and rebalance our global economy and ways of operating, to achieve a more harmonious life for everyone within our planet's natural parameters (Sullivan, 2016).

This is also the decade where many business leaders are now coming together to collectively look at how their businesses will play a part in creating a new set of sustainable business strategies, capable of playing a newly defined role in society. These strategies in turn will help them navigate what was described as a VUCA world (VUCA1.0 as we labelled it in our Introduction) (USAHEC, 2019). Multiple initiatives, collaborations, frameworks and statements of intent have emerged to assist in this endeavour.

These include the United States with the Washington-based business lobby organization Business Roundtable and their redefinition in 2019 of the purpose of business, albeit slightly (although not surprisingly perhaps) via a US-centric 'charter', through to the 'Future of the Corporation' framework, published by the London-based British Academy (2017). As they focused on the larger national and multinational businesses, others have created various networks of ethical and sustainability-focused business groupings, often focusing on smaller, founder-led businesses, with passion to grow in a new purposeful way, including the US-originated B Corps and the UK-based Blueprint for Better Business.

If there is any risk that you think these are irrelevant, then you need to understand you are wrong, because they are being signed up to either by your current boss, if you work for a major business, or by your potential boss, those smaller businesses intent on disrupting the sector. Whether such charters actually affect business leadership and a collective change still remains to be seen, but they are part of your wider understanding of the world and the trends in motivation around business leadership which will require you to think and act differently.

Few will deny that the world is a huge array of complex, interrelated factors which have either undermined previous business thinking or indeed negated the strategies which may have seemed sensible just a year or so ago. They are also so urgent, and yet will affect us in the long term, that they need new approaches to achieve impact quickly as well as relative simplicity of thinking to afford easy adoption. Obviously, our business of marketing and communications cannot solve these problems alone, but we can be the means through which clarity of purpose can be amplified and audiences reached, thereby helping them make informed decisions that will have a positive effect.

Welcome to VUCA2.0

The worlds of business, media and academia have for decades prided themselves on creating labels to help explain the complexity that is happening around us. As we mentioned in our Introduction, VUCA became increasingly popular in business around the mid-2010s, having been coined by the US military in the late 1980s to explain the post-Cold War era of uncertainty and threat. In very quick terms, the four accepted terms can be described as follows.

Volatility is the speed at which things change.

Uncertainty is the way in which things are harder to predict.

Complexity is how much the harder it is to analyse and understand.

Ambiguity is the lack of clarity to allow us to interpret things.

These are, of course, in the definition used, all related; it is the overlapping and multi-dimensional aspect, when these four characteristics are defined, which creates even greater challenges to the business world. However, any suggestion that this is something new needs to be quashed. In our combined half century and more of working with senior business leaders, we have always seen them being assailed by such factors. We can remember the introduction of the internet and emails, mobile phones, environmental legislation, the emergence of China, e-commerce and many other instances where businesses had to reassess how they had done things before. Such is the life of a business leader. But – and this is the big BUT – we have never seen the conflation of four interrelated factors. These can best be labelled as economic health, the planet's health, the health of geopolitics and the health of the individual.

This is why, in our estimation, these times and challenges are unprecedented. In the same way that business strategies of the past have been superseded, these four combined issues have in effect injected steroids into the potential of a VUCA perfect storm, what we call VUCA2.0. In order to appreciate how these can impact your business, you only have to look around you. Unlike, for example, the 2008 financial crisis, which primarily affected our economic health, recent events have reset our understanding of worse case scenarios, where business continuity plans were wanting, where just-in-time supply chains failed, where entire fleets of transport have been made redundant, where people have retreated from what had been their normal lives.

We cannot, in the confines of this book and the constraints of part of a single chapter, focus too heavily on the enormity of these combined challenges, except to set up your appreciation that to successfully apply the approach we outline within this book, you must strive to understand the wider world. This is not, therefore, a book that simply says how to commission a creative response to a brief, run a social media campaign or customer loyalty strategy – it is something much more profound. Put simply, we indicate how your change in thinking, of the world, of human truth, of purpose and your work, will, if embraced fully, offer a much more enlightened and thereby clearer path for your success.

To attempt to navigate the *Purposeful Age* requires your appreciation of the role you personally will play in shaping the way in which decisions are made. That can only happen if you see your role as much bigger than perhaps has been traditionally the case. It means that you must see responsibility in responding to the challenges we now face, how you will use compassion and empathy in your decision making, how longer-term thinking can create greater clarity than short-termism, how your business is *not selling a need to people, but is about solving people's needs.*

From how you recognize the wider world, we want now to bring you insights into the questions and influences that shape the approach necessary to succeed, and which we lay out in greater detail in future chapters. Having understood the need to look out into the world generally, the next influences are those that explain why marketing and communications now need to behave differently. We will drill down into these in future chapters, as authentic truth, purpose, the way businesses need to evolve, where messages will originate from and how they will then reach and be effective with their audiences.

We believe that there is a simple reason why communicators sometimes struggle to act successfully with coherent messaging and credible follow-up actions and this is because of the wider range of stakeholders and influences now coming to bear on business. If you are without clarity of purpose, then how can you have clarity of communications, particularly if you are attempting to address simultaneously the interests of employees, investors, suppliers, your local community, customers and others? Without a singular appreciation of why your business exists and its contribution to the world, it is inevitable that tensions will arise if you are striving to communicate a disparate set of activities and messages. We cover this extensively in Chapters 2 and 3 but let us in anticipation introduce a little background to you and then set you up to ask yourself some critical questions.

Welcome to the world

One of the longest standing, largest and most successful advertising agencies in the world is BBDO, established in the United States in 1897. When we spoke with a head of planning there, Melanie Norris, she drew the very clear significance of what this wider understanding means for them and their work:

> For us, an understanding of your position in the world is absolutely critical; none of us exist in a vacuum and this has never been truer than in 2020 – context is king. We always put our client's business or brand through this lens; it is how we better understand another aspect of their role or another aspect of their value to people, to society and beyond. A solution rooted in this understanding is going to get us to a far more powerful position and result.

She went on to explain that truth as a key component of this understanding is also vital:

> We use truths very intentionally in our process. When we talk about truth we are asking ourselves to really stand by what we are arguing, advocating, or selling, in the context of the wider world.
>
> We live in an unforgiving time; one misstep and you will be called out and you will be held accountable. Consumers have a wealth of choice and a wealth of opinions; they vote with their wallets and they are not afraid to call you out loudly and very publicly. But this shouldn't be the only reason your purpose penetrates every aspect of your business. If it is truly your purpose it will naturally permeate every touchpoint, every detail, every behaviour. Purpose should guide in every sense. I think to some extent purpose has become hygiene in consumers' eyes and rightly so. They want and expect to see your values in every interaction they have with you.

Truth is the basis of how you can measure the authenticity within a business's or brand's purpose and it is how we create the awareness of the human-based focus at the core of successful communications. In conversation, Malcolm Devoy, EMEA Chief Strategy Officer at Omnicom's PHD, cited the controversy surrounding Gillette in 2019. This was the time of the #MeToo campaign and Gillette used their advertising to advocate changes in male behaviour. Criticized for a variety of reasons, one of the glaring illustrations of a disconnect between the proposition of its purpose, its communication and its actual business, was that whilst apparently attempting to address sexism, Gillette actually charged more for its female shaving products than for the same type of product for men. This is an unfortunately common practice of gender-based discrimination. Devoy is of the view that very soon, indicators of truth will start to appear in some form because audiences and customers demand it. Rather like the sugar or salt content on a cereal box, which illustrates the credentials of the product within, the public now demand to see the credentials of the business, particularly when they foray into public campaigns and debates (Tempesta, 2019; Taylor, 2019).

This sphere of public influence is matched by the ability for employees to act as whistle-blowers as well as increased demand to show ethical and sustainable accreditation. It is driving an expectation that is empowered by social media at a point in our history where the general public have grown tired of seemingly detached and immoral corporate behaviour. In Devoy's mind he believes that truthfulness is an upward trend that will require brands to adhere to their stated principles. He says, 'It won't be a straight line – but on a macro level, these will continue to rise'. He also believes there may be dips, due to economic issues where consumers may be adversely affected by other means, but as we show elsewhere, they are not the only sphere of influence; cultural developments and societal expectations all impact on today's business in a way which was previously less significant.

When John's bestselling book *The Power of Purpose* was published in 2017, he was basing his thinking not specifically on experience in marketing, branding or campaigning in a PR sense, but rather on the basis of how businesses impact across society in the round. The great challenge in our sector now has been the misunderstanding that purpose is purely a means of marketing or communicating a message about a business, rather than being the core of why and how a business exists. We deal with this in much greater detail in Chapter 3, but by fusing with David's experience in the communications space, we have combined to address what is an increasing risk for purpose in our sector. This is because there are multiple illustrations of brands that have used purpose as a term in this way, often championing a particular cause, often without any connection to their business or, at worst, with the type of disconnect we saw with Gillette earlier. This runs the risk of becoming a 'purpose wash', where a lack of understanding and thereby poor examples create a cynicism which permeates both the profession and the public.

Devoy went so far to describe Purpose as a *dangerous game*, which we would agree with, but only if those playing the game don't understand it or misappropriate it. Where it is done well, with authenticity and of course a brand truth, businesses can benefit.

Mind the gap

One issue arising out of this risk, however, is a gap between public perception of what business is capable of doing, what it is doing, and the communication which is working or not. An interesting illustrative piece of research was undertaken by Portland Communications as its 'Total Value Index', an assessment by sector (publicly – or for a business, privately) of the gap between the actions of a business and the public perception of the business over a number of indices (Portland, 2020). The means through which this is effected, of course, is the way in which the business communicates and markets itself, either through formal means or simply through its products, services and actions.

This index came about because businesses were being expected to do ever more, in terms of responding to issues and addressing societal questions. Their leaders were and are being increasingly judged against a broader range of such activity and needed assistance in understanding how they (the business) were being perceived. In a period where consumers and others are quick to mobilize and governments respond by being ever keener to intervene, reputational and regulatory risk has never been greater for those who fail to live up to wider expectations. This framework created insights to help businesses identify risks and opportunities and tell their story more effectively. It does so by illustrating the risk of the 'Gap'.

This is the gap that can arise between the business and the world's view of it, in two different ways. The first is where the business is actually doing less, or being poorer on an issue, than the outside world thinks it is. The result is that if the credibility gap between the two is found out, there will be reputation issues. The second is where this is inversed, where the public are not aware of the fact that the business is doing great things and meeting or exceeding their expectations. The resulting risk there is that the business suffers a lack of reputation which can damage market share and affect confidence and performance. Neither are good and yet both are a direct result of communication not truly reflecting reality.

This reality of course is also based on being truthful, authentic and, importantly, being seen as transparent. The rise of all manner of what might be described as 'fake', in terms of news, followers, influencers, and the crossover of ambiguously sourced material, has created a groundswell of 'need' for truth and transparency both within agencies and in businesses.

Interviewing Lindsay Pattison, Chief Client Officer at WPP, she was clear: 'Transparency and truth has to come to life across the entire organization, in media strategy, in every touchpoint across the customer journey, in the internal employee experience.' She explained this was broad:

> Truth has to come to life across the entire organization, not just in advertising.
> Transparency is needed in media strategy, in every touchpoint across the
> customer journey and in the internal employee experience. We have seen

that recently with the Facebook boycott. Audiences, both customers and employees, will hold brands to account if their behaviour doesn't match their communications, and consequently companies were made to re-evaluate their internal practices.

Pattison explained that such trends were being highlighted across many different networks and that many of her clients worked with the Global Alliance for Responsible Media (GARM) (WFA, 2020a) to understand the nuances of truth and transparency in the media ecosystem. Their work bears out our own research and is interesting because although originating in the need for digital safety through bringing media, advertisers, agencies and others together, they have completed some interesting CMO research.

Their 'Marketer of the Future 2020' research (WFA, 2020b) consulted 700 marketeers in 30 countries. Critical and insightful results included what respondents felt would become more important parts of their roles in the next five years:

- **Sustainability** 80 per cent.
- **Data ethics** 74 per cent.
- **Brand purpose** 65 per cent.

Bear in mind this is what you and your peers think. We can conclude from this combined research firstly an acceptance by practitioners that their jobs are changing and in the direction of what we would described as ethically based purpose, and secondly that the gap between reality and perception is going to be one of their great challenges to address.

This gap is also identifiable around perceptions on purpose itself. In a McKinsey survey with more than 1,000 participants from US-based companies, around the specific issue of its importance, 82 per cent recognized the importance of a business purpose, but only 42 per cent said that their own company's stated 'purpose' had any great effect (Gast *et al*, 2020). If there is such limited impact within the business, it will hardly be surprising that it won't have a great effect on its communications or on external audiences, or the world at large. This in turn illustrates another challenge, that regardless of investing in the language of purpose, many purpose statements are generic and are not applied authentically within the business to have a true impact.

PURPOSE AROUND THE WORLD

We should at the outset also acknowledge that by necessity we have drawn our examples and commentary on truth-based, purposeful marketing and communications from the English-speaking markets where we have worked most, but of course the principles and ideas apply far beyond these countries. In fact, one of the compelling features of 'purpose' based on human truths is its universality: people everywhere are drawn to ideas, products and services that fit squarely, and credibly, with their needs and expectations, for themselves, their families and their communities. However, *where* purpose fits amongst people's priorities and *how* it is defined can vary, sometimes widely, based on differences in culture, business history and economic systems. Because in our highly connected global reality so many communicators must work across borders, regulatory jurisdictions and cultural zones, it is essential to consider local or regional interpretations and differences when applying the concepts of this book to purposed-based planning and activation.

A complete inventory of purposeful communications practices around the world would require a whole other book, so we have compiled a short set of 'snapshots' of current thinking on the topic from expert colleagues in different countries to illustrate the kind of difference you may want to examine.

Many markets today place purpose at least as high as, if not higher than on those we have discussed previously. In the Netherlands, for example, home to the headquarters of many multinational corporations and an important domestic market in its own right, consumer research undertaken by Omnicom PR Group in Amsterdam found in 2019 that 84 per cent of the respondents would consider switching to a 'meaningful' organization for goods or services, and nearly half are more likely to talk to friends and family about a company that is pursuing a social goal. Conversely, 80 per cent of the Dutch population claim that having a purpose that is not credible will result in negative consequences. 'Our research shows that the Dutch consumer is well engaged and highly values companies trying to make a positive impact on society,' explained Rosalinde van de Wall, the consultancy's managing director in the Netherlands. 'However – and it's a big however – for the Dutch, actions must speak louder than words,' she said.

Purpose is similarly well established in France, according to Omnicom PR Group's general manager in Paris, Sandrine Cormary. 'We like to think we invented the idea of raison d'être,' she joked, 'and the French have a long history of expecting more from business than profit. But the French consumer is also extremely wary and will respond badly to false pretenses or purpose washing.' One reason French companies are taking purpose so seriously is that it is literally now enshrined into law, she explained, through a bill adopted in 2019 on business growth and transformation, called the PACTE law. Cormary told us:

> This law stipulates that companies must take into consideration the social and environmental issues related to their operations and can put their mission into their by-laws and managerial duties, so it is top-of-mind with executives. It's increasingly important to our clients and their customers, too, and we believe that brands with the most visible values and that put humanity at the centre of their communications are going to be the ones most likely to succeed.

In Germany, Europe's largest economy, businesses lucky enough to have purpose 'built in' have a distinct advantage, said Sabine Hueckmann, chief executive for Ketchum Germany. But, she advised:

> If you are in a business under pressure or even just review by the public, you need to be very careful not to step into the trap of designing an artificial purpose just for the sake of trying to have one while there is none. Ask yourself the question: what would the world look like without you? The answer to this question might be irritating but it will help you make a corporate self-commitment and then draft some nice words for it.

In our experience, purpose is generally taken seriously across Western Europe, with most Europeans similarly disposed, viewing corporate promises with a mix of high expectations and robust scepticism, but in Eastern Europe there is another reality to contend with: the free-market business as we know it is itself a relatively new concept, with modern capitalism only having emerged in the post-Soviet 1990s. As Maxim Behar, CEO and Chairman of M3 Communications Group in Sofia and ex ICCO President, put it:

> For decades, the only purpose in the markets of central and eastern Europe was to supply the shops with basic goods. But today the picture is totally different. Strong competition and very demanding customers, open trade borders and hyperconnected international markets have all made it essential for local producers to define very clearly the purpose of their brands, and to deliver this purpose through their products. And what is more, Central and Eastern European countries these days are big exporters to the Western markets, and they must speak to the Western consumer now, too.

In other markets newer to competition, purpose is emerging as an important differentiator, too, but the focus may be less on connecting with foreign consumers and more on resonating domestically. In China, for example, competitive jostling is fierce and, as Prince Zhang, CEO of Ketchum Greater China, told us:

> Chinese consumers prefer to use the service or buy the products with a clear brand purpose. However, they expect it to be localized and culturally relevant. This brings challenges for international brands around how to define a corporate or brand purpose domestically in order to build new layers of trust and respect with Chinese stakeholders. Local players have an advantage, as shown by the internet giant, Tencent. Their corporate mission, 'Tech for Good', conveys technology as a tool for social benefit and as a conscious consumer choice. During the outbreak of COVID-19 in China, Tencent proactively leveraged the power of their massive tech/data infrastructure to combat the spread in a way that would be almost impossible for foreign companies to even attempt, and this resonates with Chinese people.

In Russia, Catherine Overko, Zhang's colleague and chief operating officer for the Ketchum consultancy in Moscow, told us, 'Brand purpose is not yet a fully established concept…but it's definitely beginning to change how success in business is defined.' In the relatively short history of post-Soviet business, there is 'definitely a growing interest in impact investing, but as a young market economy, short-run profit maximization remains a major motive for Russia's entrepreneurs and business leaders'. Even so, she said, 'a number of companies are listening closely to consumers on the issues they consider important,' citing for example the organic food retailer VkusVill, which has gone from selling dairy products in a local market on Moscow's outskirts to aiming for omnipresence in Europe and the United States as a platform for local producers, or the manufacturer of oral care solutions SPLAT, a family-run business striving for better-for-the-planet packaging.

In markets such as Malaysia and Singapore, business competition has been well established for decades, but purpose as we have described it remains an emerging concept. As Omnicom PR Group's Singapore general manager, Shafaat Hussain, explained, 'Corporate and brand purpose is becoming more mainstream in the current environment. It existed with a niche set of businesses that practised this approach, but now is becoming more widespread across companies of all sizes and across sectors.' Initially, he said, this was driven by a desire to give back and to connect with customers who share similar affinities and was probably closer to cause-related marketing. Now, however, he says it is part of 'a conscious effort on the part of most individuals and corporates after the coronavirus pandemic of 2020 to be more socially responsible and purpose-driven and this seems likely to endure.'

Lee Nugent, Asia/Pacific regional director for the consultancy Archetype, also based in Singapore, agreed and said that elsewhere across the region:

> Issues such as climate change and gender equality can dominate global purpose, but many Asians are more interested in issues that feel closer to home – eradicating poverty, improving healthcare, access to clean water, better education, reducing plastic waste, and economic growth. And that's not to say they don't care about these more 'global' issues, they do. Just not necessarily at the expense of these more immediate challenges.

An added factor, he said, is that:

> while many Asian consumers want brands to stand up for causes, they do also want 'value' in the products they buy – and price sensitivity, especially in emerging markets, remains significant. Supporting purpose cannot come, for most, at the cost of a more expensive product to buy.

And then there is India, a country that Girish Balachandran, founder and chief executive of On Purpose, a consultancy focused on communications to drive social change, believes is at a 'tipping point' as companies and brands compete and for goodwill and trust in marketing, aiming to become $5 trillion-dollar economy within the next few years. As he told us:

> I imagine that brand purpose will take centre stage in boardroom discussions, as India is divided by polarizing views, and the expression and tolerance for dissent and debate. Brands taking a stand on issues that matter will gain further goodwill (and sales) as employees and customers both look for more meaning and purpose in their own lives and align with organizations and institutions that reflect them.

Wherever we looked and whoever we asked, we heard the same refrains. Truth matters as much in Lagos as in Buenos Aires, Paris or Boston and it is to a business's advantage to be clear about its purpose and authentic in its pursuit, no matter where it operates. But people's priorities and values can vary widely and change quickly, as we have shown throughout this book, and there are no shortcuts or substitutes for listening carefully to what those are.

Further insights

At this point, we introduce some quantitative research of our own, undertaken in association with Stickybeak, the specialist online research company. We refer to this research, alongside that of others and our own conversations throughout the book, and so we share with you here who exactly undertook to assist us.

Almost 400 participants joined in, ranging across the breadth of marketing and communications, from across all geographies, and we were specifically broad-ranging in the request to participate. Almost 60 per cent were either agency or in-house specialist communicators and represented all specialisms. Sixteen per cent were senior, mainly c-suite, as were the media and government participants who were invariably senior, that is CEO, MD or board level. A further 18 per cent were a mixed group of academics in this space, business media journalists and ethical business, CSR, sustainability and purpose consultants.

As a start point, we asked two questions relevant to this section. The first was to what extent participants felt that societal expectations of business and purpose had changed in recent months. This was posed at the mid-point of 2020, with COVID-19, Black Lives Matter and an economic downturn acting as significant global issues. Not surprisingly, perhaps, 95 per cent said expectations had to some extent changed, with 82 per cent saying they had changed either to a great extent or very significantly. The days of business ignoring wider social trends are over.

Given all this data, our own research, our interviews, senior contributions and practical client-facing work, it can be almost overwhelming in terms of interpreting such intelligence for your own needs. The fundamental question amongst all of this is quite simply, how do you start to understand the world?

A start point may be something your business is already doing. Either ongoing research or what are known as materiality assessments, particularly if you have been involved in ESG, CSR and sustainability reporting, or auditing and shareholder reporting. For those readers who are new to this, it is worth understanding more. A materiality assessment is the process of identifying, refining, and assessing numerous potential environmental, social and governance issues that could affect your business, and/or your stakeholders, and condensing them into a shortlist of topics that inform company strategy, targets, and reporting. We don't suggest you need to undertake a full materiality assessment but if your business is already doing one, it can be the most obvious place to start in assessing external influences and the wider world. The Global Reporting Initiative (2014) is one such globally recognized independent body, which created the first and most widely adopted principles for this materiality reporting. Ninety-three per cent of the world's 250 largest companies utilize their processes.

The second way of looking at this assessment approach is laid out by the International Accounting Standards Board when looking at general accounting:

> Information is material if omitting, misstating or obscuring it could reasonably be expected to influence the decisions that the primary users of general purpose financial statements make on the basis of those financial statements, which provide financial information about a specific reporting entity (IFRS, 2018).

The key to both these definitions is that they acknowledge that for businesses to be well informed, make good decisions and then communicate successfully, there is a raft of information, often from influences that would not necessarily have been considered previously, which should be viewed carefully as risk or potential risk to either the business or its operations. Through analysing both processes, we can distil a set of areas that can act as a lens to help you to question the world at large and your business within it. So, just to reiterate, if your business is doing materiality assessments, then great, use that as a start point. If not, then you can take an approach guided by the shorthand questions below.

You may wish to consider undertaking more structured and formal exercises where you engage various stakeholders to help you find out how important specific issues are to them. The insights gained can then be used to guide your communication strategies and much more but will inevitably be more resource-intensive and time-consuming. Only you will know whether the time and opportunity for that is right, but whether you undertake it with stakeholders, or do so with yourself or your immediate team, the following can act as a guide to your thinking and understanding. You must of course also bear in mind that you are trying through your own analysis to understand trends: trends in the particular sector, trends in society, trends in legislation, etc. No one said this would be easy, but growing that wider understanding of the world and being able to predict its implications on your marketing and communications will set you ahead of the competition.

Through our experience of working with many clients, assessing the world for our own businesses, as well as supporting the communication of materiality, we have distilled the following three sets of start point questions. The first is of course the more expansive and concentrates on taking you further away from the business specific, whilst the second two allow you to then interpret what factors from the wider world might be influencing both the sector you operate in and your business itself.

Society

- What is society currently concerned about?
- What is government currently concerned about?
- What trends are we seeing in the environmental space?

(These are in effect Environmental, Social and Governmental [ESG] questions, which we explain more about in Chapter 3.)

Marketplace

- What trends are we seeing in our rivals?
- What trends are we seeing in suppliers?
- What trends are we seeing in customers?

(These are essentially standard market assessment questions.)

Business

- What trends are we seeing in our employees?
- What trends are we seeing in our leadership?
- What trends are we seeing in our culture?

(These are essentially standard internal management questions, which we talk more about in Chapters 4 and 5.)

There will of course be many general benefits from this approach to understanding your world but what you should find are the following:

- It presents the chance to analyse risks and opportunities, arising from afar.
- It offers a chance to understand better where the business 'fits' in society.
- It will create increased validity for your recommendations and strategies.
- It will allow you to spot trends and anticipate emerging issues.
- It will allow you to better focus your resources.

Summary

In this chapter we have raised the need to be capable of making a broad assessment of the world and the implications of apparent remote aspects of change on business. We have positioned the need for *informed empathy* as being fundamental to your success in applying what will emerge through the rest of the chapters. We have identified the areas for your consideration of the world and in doing so, hope you will have broadened your thinking for the next chapter where we introduce truth more fully.

Such indicators can of course only go so far, but they are complementary and in a simplified way combine to state a critical viewpoint, namely that society expects business to respond to what it cares about, and when it chooses to purchase it will take these credentials into account. We don't suggest that they act in isolation to other factors such as quality and price, but they do illustrate a significance that even 10 years ago would not have been so prevalent.

As we set you towards Chapters 2 and 3, to understand what part human-based truth and purpose plays in creating and amplifying a winning approach to your marketing, we ask you the following checklist questions:

YOUR CHECKLIST

1 Are you ready to lift your awareness of the world beyond the business?

2 Are you clear on how to be aware of trends?

3 Are you confident that you can interpret such trends to shape your strategies?

References

Bail, C A *et al* (2018) Exposure to opposing views on social media can increase political polarization, Proceedings of the National Academy of Sciences of the United States of America, 9 August, https://www.pnas.org/content/115/37/9216 (archived at https://perma.cc/Q7FH-4V8W)

Business Roundtable (2019) Business roundtable redefines the purpose of a corporation to promote 'An Economy that serves all Americans', Business Roundtable, 19 August, https://www.businessroundtable.org/business-roundtable-redefines-the-purpose-of-a-corporation-to-promote-an-economy-that-serves-all-americans (archived at https://perma.cc/HZ6E-UEMF)

Edelman (2020) 2020 Edelman Trust Barometer, Edelman Intelligence, 19 January, https://www.edelman.com/trustbarometer (archived at https://perma.cc/UG8M-ARVJ)

Gast, A *et al* (2020) Purpose: Shifting from why to how, McKinsey & Company, 22 April, https://www.mckinsey.com/business-functions/organization/our-insights/purpose-shifting-from-why-to-how?cid=eml-web (archived at https://perma.cc/K55J-37S9)

Global Reporting Initiative (2014) Materiality: what topics should organizations include in their reports? https://www.globalreporting.org/reporting-support/reporting-tools/ (archived at https://perma.cc/J2CV-DEY9)

Hohenberg, S, Homburg, C and Theel, M (2020) Marketing Excellence: Nature, measurement, and investor valuations, American Marketing Association, 3 June, https://journals.sagepub.com/doi/abs/10.1177/0022242920925517?journalCode=jmxa (archived at https://perma.cc/KN75-4J5V)

International Financial Reporting Standards (2018) IASB clarifies its definition of 'material', IFRS News and Events, 31 October, https://www.ifrs.org/news-and-events/2018/10/iasb-clarifies-its-definition-of-material/ (archived at https://perma.cc/U5LC-8VHE)

Kinonen, J (2020) A New Playbook for Marketing, *Medium*, 3 June, https://medium.com/texas-mccombs/a-new-playbook-for-marketing-77ede332d7da (archived at https://perma.cc/DR56-RLF4)

Ortiz-Ospina, E and Roser, M (2020) Loneliness and social connections, *Our World in Data*, February, https://ourworldindata.org/social-connections-and-loneliness (archived at https://perma.cc/SQ4B-3LU5)

Portland (2020) Total Value Index, Portland Communications, https://totalvalueindex.portland-communications.com/ (archived at https://perma.cc/2PLU-J4CX)

Sullivan, J (2016) Paris Climate Agreement 101: No Jargon, Just Facts, United Nations Foundation, 7 April, https://unfoundation.org/blog/post/paris-climate-agreement-101-no-jargon-just-facts/?gclid=Cj0KCQjwu8r4BRCzARIsAA21i_B0rgSW-4LqNH6MBg4dXzw0osdXGQxVQF2PZwpUUl5DckvhRy0ZKqcaAug-EALw_wcB (archived at https://perma.cc/W57V-BB7D)

Taylor, C (2019) Why Gillette's new ad campaign is toxic, *Forbes*, 15 January, https://www.forbes.com/sites/charlesrtaylor/2019/01/15/why-gillettes-new-ad-campaign-is-toxic/#ad8bc4a5bc9f (archived at https://perma.cc/6NP2-3J5C)

Tempesta, E (2019) 'Woke' Gillette's 'pinktax' on women: Razor firm slammed for hypocrisy for charging women more for the same products as men – while bashing sexism in controversial ad, *The Daily Mail*, 16 January, https://www.dailymail.co.uk/femail/article-6596095/Gillette-slammed-pink-tax-wake-controversial-ad-campaign.html (archived at https://perma.cc/8PU7-6T3H)

The British Academy (2017) Future of the Corporation, https://www.
    thebritishacademy.ac.uk/programmes/future-of-the-corporation/ (archived at
    https://perma.cc/F25G-MSGP)
USAHEC (2019) Who first originated the term VUCA (Volatility, Uncertainty,
    Complexity and Ambiguity)? US Army Heritage & Education Centre, 7 May,
    https://usawc.libanswers.com/faq/84869 (archived at https://perma.cc/FL32-
    MG5G)
World Economic Forum (2020) Fourth Industrial Revolution, https://www.
    weforum.org/focus/fourth-industrial-revolution (archived at https://perma.cc/
    YR9A-F422)
World Federation of Advertisers (WFA) (2020a) Global Alliance for Responsible
    Media, https://wfanet.org/garm (archived at https://perma.cc/65K7-3UKM)
World Federation of Advertisers (WFA) (2020b) The Marketer of the Future,
    https://wfanet.org/leadership/marketer-of-the-future (archived at https://perma.
    cc/F5JH-FN4F)

02

The truth: what we mean by it

'All hat and no cattle' is one of the harsher criticisms levelled at pretenders in David's native Texas. Dressing for the job is not the same as doing it, and there are no shortcuts when it comes to applying or expressing truth in ways that resonate with everyone your business serves and needs for success. But with the benefit of the wisdom of many others, plus new ways of thinking and the occasional cautionary tale, there's ample reason for optimism – so long as your commitment is genuine.

In this chapter we introduce the sometimes-challenging question around what truth is and how it manifests itself in business. The aim of this chapter is therefore to share, through combining our knowledge and that of the dozens of leaders we have worked with over the years and many who have kindly contributed, the necessary understanding for any practitioner either within a business or a supportive agency, to answer these questions. By the end, you should feel much better able to address the needs of the business in establishing the authentic, truthful rationale that will tell your story well. Why is that important? Well, beyond the fact that this will help you be more successful in your role, what really matters to us and what we hope matters to everyone, is that we want the best, most authentic and purposeful businesses to prosper and they can only do so if people, their customers, hear from them and understand what they hear.

The dilemma facing the business world, and in particular all earnest marketeers, is based on multiple complexities. Our respective experiences allow us to answer this challenge in a unique way. Put simply, the proven methodologies for bringing a new perspective for a new age are what is now recognized as the new VUCA2.0 imperative, namely the need for truth in business via authentic purpose. How these experiences come together, where they conflate, will become apparent as you read this book, but to set you towards the right start point, we need to introduce here the foundation of thinking on business expectations, and most importantly what it means for truth – the key to solving the dilemmas we all are facing.

This need for truth is paramount because we are of (and within) an age when we all demand that our businesses are the best they can be. As parents we want our children to be happy in their educational or work environment, safe from discrimination or abuse; we want products we purchase to be of quality and produced with respect for those who work on them. We want businesses to minimize any harmful impact they have on the environment, or at least to offset and innovate away from the worst they do, and to treat their employees, suppliers and investors with similar respect. We want a society where businesses pay their taxes to support public services and pay their bills on time to support a fair marketplace. All of this is an aspiration for an equitable and just society where such ethical and value-based activities are 'business as usual'.

To get to appreciate what truth is, it is important to understand that it both affects and is affected by almost all of what we see happening in the world around us. Such trends, the nature and likely trajectory of them – some technological, others societal, people orientated and financial – what they will mean to businesses, your areas of expertise, are hugely important in creating a truth-based proposition.

This 'new normal' world is one where we know that the personal and economic impacts have fast-forwarded a rethink of how the world does business, how businesses operate and how as communication and strategy professionals we need to support business in growing out of our current situation. Whilst everyone rushes to meet customer needs, from ethical start-ups to the big audit practices, within this chapter we have fused the proven expertise within purpose-driven strategies with communications to propel you, the reader, into a position to redefine how you do the same for yourself. That is why our 'Why', the purpose of this chapter, is to allow you to reset your own expectations around your role and its understanding.

In our current world, we don't see quite the same numbers of bustling millennials we did 12 months ago – some have moved on, and many others work on new schedules, many more remotely. As individuals, we have experienced what so many have: loss, changed circumstances, new recognition of what we truly value, how our work now manifests itself. Critically, however, and regardless of the enormity of this new age, we know that the changed business behaviours we witnessed when we set out with this book have in fact been accelerated. Like the historic developments of such fields as medicine, motorization, mass production and air travel in times of war, the agenda for a new business imperative and how one communicates it has been vastly sped up.

2020 was already developing the essence of VUCA2.0 but the pandemic fast-forwarded and amplified many factors at a time when globalization, for example, was already under serious scrutiny and many people were already looking for alternative ways of leading, growing and marketing their businesses. There were the challenges of the trade war between the US and China, which was fuelling debate around the future of global free trade generally; similar, smaller-scale uncertainties about Britain's relationship with the European Union and other parts of the global economy fuelled a raging debate about the costs and benefits of global interconnectedness and local self-sustainability.

Similarly, since the mid-2000s, increasing numbers of more enlightened businesses and leaders had been pursuing a post-corporate social responsibility (CSR) agenda, described as the 'Purpose' agenda, which was recognizing a new, human-focused imperative around why businesses exist and how they should be operated. Rather than pushing those pressures aside, the pandemic firstly created a perfect storm to illustrate weaknesses around what were still seen as conventional business wisdoms and then created circumstances where business behaviour, how they treated their people, how they produced their goods and then engaged customers became paramount to their long-term credibility and their licence to operate.

Whereas previous natural disasters and national economic issues had created discomfort in the past, they were generally seen as relatively limited, almost temporary stumbling blocks in the ongoing assumptions around both standard primarily profit-based business models and the benefits of globalization. This time it is different, not least because of the extraordinary sums of money poured into business by various national governments and central banks, and although the dust has truly yet to settle on all the outcomes, fundamental assumptions have been swept aside and businesses and society now have a new, urgent need to reconfigure how they operate.

And of course, for many, the pandemic and subsequent economic difficulties seemed like a mere warm-up for the truly existential crisis looming on the horizon: climate change. Some businesses and brands were adapting their assumptions, practices and messages with a sense of urgency to mitigate rising average temperatures, whilst others saw short-term opportunities to apply a coat of 'greenwash' with statements or programmes to imply a stronger commitment to sustainability than they were willing to embrace in reality.

Various economic factors have forced many businesses to the wall, but have also seen others use incredible agility to switch from consumer clothing goods to medical scrubs, or from domestic appliances to health equipment. In short, our human need at that time shifted massively from what might now be seen as more frivolous needs to more urgent and essential ones. The businesses who could pivot quickly, with production close to home, not only demonstrated their usefulness to society, they showed they had the necessary mindset and willingness to do so. This period across so many areas has meant that the question 'Why', once answered, quickly allowed people to answer the others of 'What' and 'How'.

So, we ask ourselves that most important of questions, 'Why', in many different forms: 'Why is society where it is?', 'Why did business "A" get it wrong?', 'Why did business "B" get it right?', 'Why is that person saying that?', 'Why does the media think that?', 'Why is this a challenge?', 'Why do they not see the opportunity?'. Why, Why, Why – it's a question one should never get bored of asking, but inevitably a question one often needs help answering. That is why these questions aren't only important for us as individuals.

Indeed, these are often the type of questions asked of us by clients in terms of the challenges they come to us to help solve, and equally from our colleagues who ask our advice in delivering solutions. It is these questions, perhaps not in so many words of clarity, that are being asked now every day by all manner of people in every type of business, all around the world. This question of grasping what the world now expects of business, how a business responds and then how it tells the world of its actions, is at the core of all we do. It is the basis of our work and the golden thread of this book.

Business leaders and the supporting communication roles have never been under such intense scrutiny, from shareholders, employees, media, government and more besides. Under such pressures it is not surprising that increased demand on marketing and communications has resulted and consequently, professionals in this space have scrambled towards the inevitable market opportunity. Unfortunately, the practices and processes, understanding and knowledge have been mixed and the results have been proven to be equally so.

The reality of the new business era is that business leaders need to reinvent themselves, not simply in some selfish manner to just survive, but to address the risk of being overtaken by the issues they face, in order to deliver, as leaders for all those dependent upon the business. If they fail in this, they fail not just themselves but the pensioners whose income rests on the share price, the employees paying mortgages, the suppliers dependent on their orders, the local economies, the public purse available for health, education and welfare. Never has the need for such leadership been greater, because however good they were before is now irrelevant; it is how good they – you – can be now.

The emergence of what John helped define as the 'Purposeful Age' is now more relevant than ever and yet is, in effect, a new market opportunity that has attracted all manner of approaches.

What are we talking about here? Well the growth of what is often called 'Brand Purpose' (but is best described as 'Business Purpose', covered in Chapters 4 and 5) is the evolution of a new business rationale, set against a shifting set of societal expectations. These include movements as broad as that of climate change and sustainability demands, to the issues of #MeToo, #BlackLivesMatter, workplace diversity and gender pay. We have seen smart-thinking, creative and innovative people in the marketing and communications world grapple and often struggle with challenging demands from clients, who are in turn responding to varied and multiple audiences. Often, they only have a vague understanding and limited appreciation of what purpose in business actually means and how it can assist them when embraced fully and authentically. The appreciation of where purpose fits in a business and what it can do to drive performance, reputation and long-term sustainable success is often simply lacking. As a result, we saw ill-advised campaigns, misappropriated corporate philanthropy, and at best a minimal impact on key objectives but sometimes at its worst, reputational damage and loss of market share.

Business purpose

The notion of 'purpose' has been very much in vogue in recent years and continues to build itself as a much-championed mantra, in no small part due to the efforts of thinkers like John, who have preached its potential to and for business for years. But with its rising acceptance comes an inevitable temptation to reap its benefits for marketing or reputation activity without the work of using it truthfully.

Truth

As we discussed these issues, and basing a book on truth, we realized that the word in itself had so many connotations and potential definitions in business and marketing that it was worth being clear about what we mean by it, its context and the way in which it needs to be thought of in this book and your work. So although it might seem odd, having to write about the importance of telling the truth, as we all know that it is wrong to lie or cheat, we also know that some people might even suggest that truth in key aspects of business such as marketing, advertising and public relations is an oxymoron. We want to get beyond that and ensure that we and all those working in marketing and communications not only approach doing business in a fundamentally truthful way, but that the actual work we create, in whatever form it takes, embraces the necessary honest and human-centric priorities that form the basis of truth. This is because we know that, without stifling any creativity or opportunity, it is the foundation for establishing customer trust and building the long-term relationships that successful businesses seek in order to be sustainable.

So, let us start the chapter's principal learning by re-emphasizing that this book is about the truth, and importantly how we personally believe that truth is the core essence of what is now required, if marketing and communications is to be successful and support business success in this new VUCA2.0 age. This chapter will build on your understanding of the world by understanding truth so that in turn you can go on to explain what truth is as a core part of your business purpose, why it matters, where it rests in business and how you as communicators and marketers can activate it successfully on behalf of your clients and their customers.

We will tie together the truth behind a business proposition and show how it is reflected through its products and services. We will illustrate why it is the foundation on which a business reputation is built. We do this in the knowledge that by doing so, it will act as a powerful force to inspire all aspects of the business, engaging employees, customers and other stakeholders. By creating such alignment with your communications, you will power up a brand's ability to successfully shift relationships from those of passive consumers or employees into fully engaged supporters of what the business is seeking to achieve.

Sitting having breakfast, if our pancakes or porridge didn't live up to the menu description, we would be disappointed and possibly reserve judgement on dining there again. If we found that the waiter was clearly unhappy, distracted and under pressure, we might think further, and if afterwards we found we had supported unethical sourcing or poor hygiene, the decision will have been made. Trust will have been broken, our belief in the truth of the proposition, its menu and its leadership would have disappeared. Simple isn't it? Well, like all recipes, things are never as simple as they first seem.

Let us be clear about the prime aim of bringing a truth-driven purpose to life. In short, we want to help the very best of businesses achieve long-term sustainable success by illustrating that the business both cares for what its stakeholders care for and is working to help solve problems they consider are important. Meeting this human need is directly meeting a market need. It helps open up opportunities for innovation, growth and success. We know that embodying truth into your messaging, so long as it reflects an authentic set of behaviours, will make the communication much more likely to change the way both customers and employees think. So, to put us on the right path we must explain what we mean by truth in this context.

By coincidence, John's main home is a cottage in a small Shropshire village, where the American novelist Mark Twain twice visited in 1873 and 1879. John has long used one of Twain's most famous quotes on life's purpose: 'The two most important days of your life, are the day you are born and the day you find out why.' We could of course also reflect that one often sees quoted the legend 'Established 1908' (or such date) for a business and one could say that the first important day of a business has often been recognized, but when was the second? It may well be that you are going to be responsible for that, but to come back to truth, Twain has another attributed quote that is worth reflecting on: 'If you tell truth, you don't have to remember anything.'

This is part of the challenge here. In private life, if you don't tell the truth, but fabricate an alternative, the challenge is remembering what you said so you don't get caught out. In what we are concerned about here, if you don't tell the truth in business, it's nigh on impossible to get everyone to 'remember' a falsehood and this becomes your short route to being found out. The basis of this book and our experience, however, goes beyond simply controlling the risk of corporate falsehoods, as sound and honest good sense, to actually pointing out that with the right truth within business, a truth based on a clearly defined and authentically lived purpose, you will have a much greater chance of being successful. Let us be clear, therefore, about what we are defining as truth in this context. Truth, of course, is the application of what is true. If you take a dictionary definition, it will read something like this:

> Adjective: If something is *true*, it is based on facts rather than being invented or imagined and is accurate and reliable.

We are talking about the way in which a business operates and communicates as being true, accurate, honest, and correct. The critical appreciation is that when something is true, it can be believed; rather like a sound bell, it 'rings true', and with business and its messaging, the aim must be the same. True or truth may perhaps be open to individual interpretation (like John's interpretation of Mark Twain's visits – which were not to his house, but rather the village) but fundamentally, it is easily appreciated as the opposite of being false.

Of course, as in life, truth as a concept can be difficult to define, unless as a simple contrast to what is clearly false. In all walks of life, we rely on it as an almost absolute. It is the ultimate factor in making decisions, ranging from whether the menu for our breakfast is 'true', to whether the price we are being quoted will prove 'true' when the bill arrives, to whether the person waiting on us is 'true' with their personal hygiene. Without confidence in answering these questions for ourselves, we can hardly progress with breakfast or indeed life, such is the nature of business. It is as human as we are in its pursuit of what is true; it is the foundation on which all successful interaction is based. This human aspect to truth is undeniable.

During our research and conversations this truthful analysis and belief became clear with a wide range of business leaders. Richard Walker, Managing Director of UK food retailer Iceland was clear on the similarity between people and business. When asked what truth in business meant to him, he said:

> Business, like every other element of society, is a mixed bag. Parts of it are intrinsically dishonest – a world of exaggerated claims and white lies in the name of profit. But we all know that, like an individual who continually bluffs and deflects, no organization can build long-term relationships based on mistruths. Honesty is critical to build trust, and only trust can build sustainable businesses.

Not surprisingly he was clear that this was an intrinsic component of the wider marketplace:

> The simple truth is that if business people are unable to trust each other, business fast becomes impossible. More than that, we are given a licence to operate by society – and that means behaving in an honourable way to customers, suppliers, colleagues, and communities.

Of course, as Farzana Baduel, CEO of the London-based communications consultancy Curzon, reminded us, the forces bending corporate and brand narratives toward the truth have been in motion since well before the pandemic and its subsequent aftershocks:

I have witnessed a rise in authentic truth-based storytelling over the past decade. One of the drivers has been social media; the proliferation of communication channels and the democratization of content creation have meant that the public are able to call out brands and organizations for perceived untruths. This public scrutiny has fuelled conscious storytelling as brands seek to avoid public backlash, so therefore are thinking more carefully about how aligned their storytelling is with reality. Hypocrisy and deceit can kill a brand and therefore truth travels up the corporate ladder to its rightful place.

Human truths

The biggest need in business, in terms of meeting the VUCA2.0 age and specifically the need in marketing and communications, is therefore to find the human truth that is at the core of the business. This might be about our human desire for health, as epitomized by the purpose of Walgreens Boots Alliance to 'Help people live healthier and happier lives'. Or it might be Virgin Atlantic's, to 'embrace the human spirit and let it fly'. As we progress, we will stress the need to keep this human truth in your mind, as ultimately your task will be to understand it and amplify it, so that it can be meaningful for all stakeholders.

In many ways there is nothing new in this. Being able to define how a business and its products engage customers on a human scale is as old as the hills. Adverts of 100 years ago equate a bar of soap with a healthy home life, or new technology such as a vacuum cleaner with freedom of time and the easing of effort, or baby food products with a bonny smiling baby. This is human need, desire at its core, making people feel something aspirational, or connected to the story you are telling about your product or service. This, when it rings true, is a deeply held human belief in an undeniable truth. What is key is that truth needs to be authentic, honest and in today's world also sustainable if it is to power up the business successfully. This is what builds the intrinsic link between truth and purpose.

To make this possible you have to think not of customers, but of people. The messaging of a business, its products and its truth, should not be something you project onto a customer; rather it should be a reflection of what you have been able to identity as a response to their (human) needs. We will consider elsewhere the way in which a purpose-driven business meets a human need and therefore meets a market need. However, to understand your potential audience so that your brand, marketing and messaging are memorable and meet their expectations, they must be based on seeing them not as a homogeneous mass, but rather as individuals, with human needs and desires. We would say, using a verbal analogy on John F Kennedy's famous statement of 1961, 'Ask not what your country can do for you...', 'Ask not what you sell to someone, ask what you solve for someone'.

Being human means being emotional, empathetic; it means uncovering people's needs but also understanding both the rational and emotive influences your messaging will directly address. From a person's perspective, you want to make sure you can illustrate the truth as the business believes it and that such truth, through its products and services, addresses their needs. Try and stand in your audience's shoes and ask yourselves key questions: Does the business brand appear trustworthy? Does the product perform as it says it should? How does the experience of the business and product make me feel?

All these questions come back to the truth in the message, the business and the product. As we are sure you appreciate, this final question is the sum of the previous ones and the positive outcome of which is what you are hoping to achieve for the business, as it is ultimately the most important factor in purchasing decisions and thereby ongoing market success. As the US civil rights activist and poet Maya Angelou said: 'People will forget what you said. They will forget what you did. But they will never forget the way you made them feel' (Gallo, 2014).

Moments of truth

This is as good a place as any to raise your awareness of, if you do not know of it, or to contextualize it if you do, the relatively well-known marketing principle based on a set number, normally three, but sometimes more 'Moments of Truth'. Back in the mid-1980s, the President of Scandinavian Airlines, Jan Carlzon, wrote a book called *Moments of Truth*, where he outlined what he saw as the fact that customers make decisions based on specific moments where they judge your product in contrast to the competition. He basically outlined that to win the war for the customer, you needed to identify such moments and then excel at influencing them. The leading proponent of this, who did the most to make the process famous, was AG Lafley, CEO and Chairman of Procter & Gamble. Twenty years after the book was published, he specifically focused on what he saw as two main moments, the first being the moment when the customer is looking at the aisle trying to decide which product to purchase, and the second being how it performed when used for the first time. He subsequently added a third, the point of feedback and reaction to the performance – effectively when they choose to re-purchase the product. A fourth has been added to suggest the time when people are now browsing the web for items, and a fifth in terms of the delay between online purchase and receipt of goods.

We explain more about this model in Chapter 7, primarily as further context, but here we simply identify the fact that the model is established and valued. We would argue that success at these points of truth, perhaps better simply thought of as points of opinion/decision making, is inevitably going to be influenced significantly by all the factors we relate to in this book. So whichever model of determining your brand positioning in terms of either 'moments of truth' as an assessment criteria or any other model, the facts remain that truth as we determine it here, as the bedrock of purpose, will have a profound effect on your ability to shape the customer experience.

Investing in truth

We all know that businesses invest constantly in research and development for new products and services. It is how they survive in competitive markets, create excitement around their business, and attract new talent. However, so much effort has in the past been focused on building products rather than building the values and business behaviours behind them. This has fundamentally changed, as the values and behaviours are what create the perception of brand and today are incredibly influential in the customer's decision-making process and ongoing relationship. A product is made in a factory or office, whereas a brand is made in the mind, with emotion, character, with authenticity and humanity. To develop as a business in the Purposeful Age, you have to invest as much in creating a true purpose as in creating new products.

FleishmanHillard's 'Authenticity Gap' report (2019) analyses reputation across seven sectors and hundreds of companies worldwide. Its research produces some interesting statistics, most notably that people say only half (51 per cent) of their perceptions and beliefs about a company are shaped by their expectations around the company's products or services. The other half (49 per cent) is shaped by broader information on how the business behaves, its leadership, and how the company is having a wider impact on society. This includes how it treats its staff, its environmental credentials and its role as a concerned corporate citizen. This inevitably has important implications about how and what companies choose to communicate with their audiences, both internally and externally.

If, in the past, the corporate story has tended to focus on simply detailing customer benefits alone, even if focusing on customer care, innovation and value as traditional drivers, for the future, greater emphasis should also be placed on those broader, more purpose-oriented stories of leadership behaviours, the corporate culture, values and wider societal outcomes. Businesses should therefore become broader in the stories they tell and rather than relegate what have been seen as peripheral, CSR type credentials to secondary communications, should maximize the opportunity to share what is critical reputation-building content. It is clear from this report that businesses must move beyond simplified messages about service and product qualities, to a narrative which encompasses the wider qualities of the company as a whole. And as we shall see in Chapter 5, this approach has to be reflected in a co-ordinated way, across marketing, PR and every other area of communication. As Nick Andrews, Senior Vice President and Senior Partner, EMEA Leader, Reputation Management at FleishmanHillard says:

> Since the beginning of human history, we have told stories as a way of passing on knowledge and learning. At some point, the corporate message replaced the story, causing a disconnect with stakeholders. A greater understanding of authenticity, its drivers and value, has seen a renewed focus on the essential role of stories and those who tell them.

It isn't just PR that sees stories to be truth based, although when we asked Jim Moser, Europe Chairman of Advertising giant BBDO, he had an interesting perspective. Citing McCann Erickson's 'tag line', which reads 'truth well told' (McCann, 2020), he said, 'But one person's truth is not always another's truth. It is more and more difficult to make any claims in advertising that cannot be substantiated fairly and honestly.' This reality, he explained, means that 'companies and brands will be found out – then they lose credibility and authenticity in a more significant way than previously.'

Moser went on to explain that, in his view, a broader set of behaviours and actions have become far more important, and as we discuss further in Chapters 4 and 5:

> What's become a bigger trend is 'actions' and not words. A company or brand's actions are far more important today, and far more scrutinized today, than ever before. So, they can say all they want but if it's not backed up by consistent actions, they will lose out commercially.

We know from our own experience that this reality is where words must follow deeds and that the human truth aspect, its rationale, must form the basis not just of the messaging, but of what drives the business and its purpose.

Truth and purpose

Purposeful businesses are based on such human truths. They are also empathetic in understanding how the people they are engaged with, either employees or customers, are affected by their products. The product's positive attributes will be based upon brand qualities, reflective of the business purpose. They will effectively demonstrate the ideals that both the business and others care about, thereby connecting with people in a much more powerful way. This connection aims to be both deeper and higher, if that does not sound contradictory. It is through an emotional connection that customers and employees are left feeling that a business or its products have helped them as humans, in their lives. This creates a higher sense of connection, whilst the resulting loyalty creates a depth of a relationship which goes far beyond a conventional consumer relationship. Such embodiment of a truthful purpose goes well beyond profit as it offers a promise to establish and reinforce the higher-ground connection that customers and employees find emotionally meaningful. By thinking beyond simply the transaction and the profit, you reveal your commitment to connecting with people in truly significant ways.

Truth in business is based not just on thoughts and fine ideas, or even a nicely crafted tag line to simply reflect this human ideal, but more significantly on the identifiable behaviours, ways things are done and solid attributable results. For a business to be believed, it needs to assert its truth through such behaviours, as simply saying something will not necessarily make it true. Simply put, if a business says it cares for its employees, yet demonstrates through its policies and practices it treats them poorly, the business is plainly promoting a falsehood. It is proved to be untrue in its assertion by its very behaviours. It simply is untenable as a truth.

Such a truth will undoubtedly be more likely to be recognized as true if it fits comfortably into a larger, coherent system of beliefs. In this context, the global move towards ethical and sustainable business principles, the wide-scale recognition and adoption of measures such as the Sustainability Development Goals (SDGs), creates the wider, coherent system.

Malcolm Devoy, Chief Strategy Officer at PHD, the communications planning and media buying agency, is very clear on the significance of truth and how it sits within the purpose agenda he is seeing with clients. He explained to us:

Truth becomes an important measure of a company's purpose. Truth is becoming more available and companies are being held accountable. This process has already begun but it is inevitable that there will be further scrutiny of brands that champion purpose.

Widescale adoption of truth agendas and purpose drives a demand for greater transparency.

Of course, if everyone is complicit in creating a giant lie, entirely detached from reality, then it would fail, but in business and in today's society, such widescale fabrication of a market truth is incomprehensible. Individual companies might fake a proposition, but such is the openness of the world's production and markets, as well as citizen journalists and whistle-blowers, all the people cannot be fooled all of the time, or certainly not for long.

Iceland's Walker was optimistic about truth but also had an interesting perspective when it came to the risk around people not telling the truth:

> In my work, I find that most businesses I deal with do tell the truth. They just don't tell the whole truth, because they are protecting their commercial interest, avoiding scrutiny or just plain deflecting blame. Sometimes that can't be helped – we all have to follow HR protocols and stock exchange rules – but on the biggest agendas of the day, like pollution, plastic use and sourcing, we see big companies carefully curating the data they choose to make public, to maximize positive profile, maintain the status quo, and protect profit.

Now this potentially bodes badly for those of us working within or as supporting agencies to those companies who might prefer to maintain the status quo, but Walker goes on:

> But you know what? Our world is in crisis. We now have a moral obligation to work together to tackle the unique set of wicked problems that are impacting both planet and people, and we can only do that by telling the truth about the scale of those challenges and then working together to make things better. We need to insist on the truth, but we also need to increase transparency.

Trust, truth and transparency

Of course, it could be said that in an age that has seen the proliferation of 'fake news' anything is possible, including market manipulation by multiple players, but we know this would be highly improbable. Yes, misinformation could be promulgated, driven by social media and unattributed articles, but that more likely means that businesses are at risk of, for example, malicious attacks, as opposed to being the creators of such fake or untruthful 'news'.

The role of mainstream media in this is important. When business speaks the truth, it is obviously important that journalists are responsible in their actions to reflect this. Equally, however, business must be prepared to accept the truth being spoken to or about it. If a journalist finds out something worrying about either a product or operating procedures, businesses must be ready and open to hearing such truth and respond equally responsibly to address it. Any other action will be self-defeating.

It is also, however, a tremendous opportunity for businesses and their leaders to try to help build greater levels of trust through true and transparent messaging. The 2020 Edelman Trust Barometer, which has been measuring trust across four sectors – government, business, NGOs and the media – for 20 years, showed that although there was generally a strong economy (prior to the COVID-19 pandemic) and full employment, levels of trust across all sectors was at an all-time low. There is a perceived lack of belief in the equity of wealth in the world, a growth in cynicism around business generally and the capitalistic system where people, be they employees or customers, consider they are at risk or are being exploited in some way or another. With challenges around climate change and of course the more recent pandemic, people generally don't have faith in such institutions in building the future.

We believe trust is based on truth and a confidence given by people that they believe what an institution is saying and doing is empowered by transparency. Edelman's survey showed that the perception of businesses was that they were efficient, with the highest level of competence, but there was a 25-point gap when it came to their ethical credentials, in contrast to NGOs, which were thought to be ethical but not so competent. Put simply, there is a perception that much of what business says is not true. Here lies the challenge and the opportunity for businesses, their leaders and us as communicators, to increase the level of messaging around values and behaviours, beyond those standard attributes that promote efficiency and competency. These are essentially telling truthful stories and this will counter fake news, fake truths, and can create higher levels of engagement and of course trust between your customers, communities, and the company and its brand. We cover the storytelling.

An interesting insight into this area was provided to us by Sir Peter Bazalgette, Chairman of ITV, the UK broadcaster. When we asked him about truth and whether truthful stories were becoming more prevalent, he started with a direct reference to us as humans:

As human beings we have a fundamental need to tell and be told stories. This is how we develop our empathy muscles – the nation's social glue. From literally true news and current affairs to essentially true dramas that mine our lives and experiences, this is the gold standard we aspire to. But here's another truth: the anarchic internet world, one of rumour, gossip and paranoia, has created a rise in untruth and currently represents a massive challenge to our civil society.

Such an appreciation is critical in today's media world, where even mainstream channels can occasionally either be tricked or unintentionally mislead by spurious stories. For business, we need to be sure that the truth Sir Peter refers to and our 'empathy muscles' are recognized and strengthened.

As individuals, we also connect with brands because it is one thing we can influence through our choices. We can perhaps feel we can force some degree of accountability from business, simply by choosing where to spend our money and where to repeat that spend – or not. Millennials and Gen Zs in particular, who choose brands they are happy to be associated with, will endorse by their purchase and by extension help identify to others their view of the world. It isn't of course just those generations; we do expect, though, that the brand we choose will have a trustworthy relationship with us. Rather than spreading fake news, we want, through the power of our social media, our followers, our imagery and lifestyle projection, to express a truth in 'our news', which will be recognized by our circle of friends. If achieved, this is a direct contrast to the inundation of the fake into our lives.

Interestingly, Bazalgette has another intriguing observation when it comes to social media and the belief that audiences, who are your customers, have greater expectations around truth, transparency and authenticity. He told us:

> Yes and no. Yes: audiences crave authenticity and disdain falseness and insincerity. No: the racism, the homophobia, the bullying, the anti-vaxxers, the conspiracy theorists, etc etc that we meet online would not gain currency unless there was a demand for it. I cannot reconcile or explain how these sentiments sit side by side.

Equally uncertain as to how one explains this observation, we can draw the conclusion that when it comes to our focus of marketing and communications, there will be ever-growing scrutiny linked with a powerful after-effect should expectations not be met. We talk more about this in Chapter 7.

Undoubtedly, audiences differ from sector to sector but of leaders we spoke with, most were clear that audiences are demanding greater transparency. Iceland's Walker said:

There is no doubt that younger audiences expect business to do better – and are voting with their feet and with their wallets. People from all backgrounds are also more able to fact check and share information than ever before, which means unproven claims are easily exposed.

He is clear, however, that recent events have also increased a fundamental desire for truth:

Part-truths are part of the convention of marketing and we will no doubt continue to see them, but there is a bigger picture as we come through the COVID-19 pandemic, and that is simply about honesty. Consumers may tolerate a superficial story, but they are now much more emotional and vocal in their condemnation of businesses and brands that are seen to be disingenuous. Cancel culture, fuelled by social media as the physical world went into lockdown, is here to stay – and is a stark warning to businesses who don't aim for authenticity.

Leading truth

As we will see in the following chapters, leadership of a purpose-powered business and its communications strategy starts with its truth aligned, capable of explaining why the business exists and how it draws an emotional connection between that core truth, its behaviours, and product credentials, which drive the loyalty of customers and propel the business. This is now much more than a simple development of business strategy. It is about a fundamental repositioning of how business exists within the world, how it responds to unimaginable issues such as climate change, which generally was unappreciated 50 years ago, as well as changes in the expectations of post-baby boom generations who quite simply expect more from their work than simply a pay cheque. The millennials, the largest demographic bubble to join the workforce since the baby boomers, seek meaning in a way which we (the authors) didn't think of when we were that age.

All of this takes a broader appreciation of the role of business leaders in the world and a deeper understanding of what motivates them. Such understanding will allow the business to find its truth which, as it becomes the foundation of its purpose, will become the North Star, serving as the leadership's guiding light, directing behaviours and shaping the corporate culture.

Iqbal Wahhab is a London-based restaurateur, renowned for having founded two of London's most successful restaurants, The Cinnamon Club and Borough Market's Roast. His approach was to get a set of principles around ethics and sustainability in the food business which permeated every aspect of how he operated. His approach is based on a human and truth-based attitude. As he told us:

> Truth in marketing for me is about empathy: how do I fill my next restaurant not just with customers, but with customers who share our values, who buy into our commitment to inclusive employment, sustainability and keeping things local wherever we can? I've applied this across the board of all key stakeholders, including my investor; I wanted one who was aligned with everything we stand for, not just focused on the bottom line, but understood what was behind it.

This thinking is being acknowledged across all manner of businesses, large and small. As Marjorie Benzkofer, Global Managing Director, Reputation Management at FleishmanHillard puts it:

> Today we find a new set of forces converging, ones that force us to reimagine how we craft our brands in ways that speak to the changing demands of our world. In this time of upheaval and discord, truth remains the North Star of our work. How we illuminate and authentically live that truth is the challenge we face today.

Get it wrong, steer off the highway and there will be an inevitable erosion of the truth and a corresponding loss of trust. Just think of the damage done to Volkswagen in the emissions scandal and you have all you need to know.

It is of course worth considering, though, that some industries have formal checks and measures, which demand rigorous truth-based communication at all time. These will relate to environmental issues such as in the VW case, and is of particular importance in the pharmaceutical industry, which is heavily legislated. As Emma Sergeant, President of DAS Group of Companies Europe explained:

> I have been involved in healthcare for many years and truth in healthcare marketing is key, evidence-based and peer reviewed. The requirements in this sector have been greater and more stringent than many, for obvious reasons.

We wondered how this affected the actual marketing activity and when pressed, Sergeant explained:

> In the healthcare space there are checks and balances in place with legal, medical and ethical sign-off. However, sometimes those safety nets can stifle initial creativity and innovation to the detriment of better communications that are appropriate for consumers who are more sophisticated and digitally savvy. There needs to be a safe zone where boundaries can be pushed and explored,

knowing that the checks and balances will ensure that it is supported by evidence and independent review.

This requirement for balance is a key one, as often the desire to create ever more extreme creative thinking around positioning a product or responding to a particular audience perception can become an apparently primary driving force. It is of course necessary, therefore, to have one's own checks and balances, perhaps someone who is not close to the project, who has a particular external role in tempering what might push too far. In this, there should be understanding of how the truths detailed above all combine.

Combined truths

If we take the combined truths identified above, then in Figure 2.1 we can illustrate how they influence each other and indeed could be mapped against 'moments of truth' if that is something you are utilizing. We have:

- Human Truth: what people feel, their need, that which the business will identify with.
- Corporate Truth: your business purpose, why you exist to help people in a set way.
- Practice Truth: the authentic, demonstrable behaviours through which you operate.
- Product Truth: the qualities and characteristics of the product that does a job well.
- Truth Effect: the impact on the lives of the people purchasing and their world.

If you look at it in this visual way, you can see that rather like a pebble in a lake, the start point of a human-centric truth, as crafted into a truthful corporate purpose, is an incredibly powerful mechanism, which, when supported by authentic behaviours and good-quality products and services, has a hugely positive effect on the person you have served. Note we said person and not customer, because again, as we reach the end of this chapter, it is good to be reminded we are talking about people and their lives. Truth is so powerful because it is in effect something which cannot be bought. Unlike a better battery or a higher-quality material for example, truth isn't held in a store with a price label on it, even though in the marketplace it is highly valuable. Ask yourself how much you value truth in others, their messages, products and services, and you have your answer.

FIGURE 2.1 Five interrelated truths

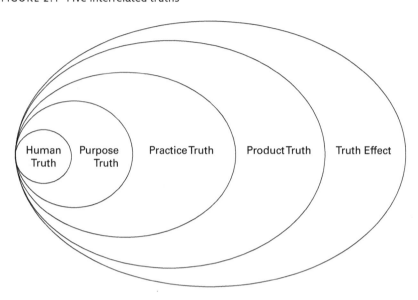

Human Truth | Purpose Truth | Practice Truth | Product Truth | Truth Effect

Taking this perception, this mapping of truth within the context of our agenda, it is interesting to consider what our research revealed as to the existing truthfulness of communications. When asked how true their business or brand's communications were to the reality of publicly stated purpose, commitments and actions, only 27 per cent were able to vouch for them being true. A high proportion, 45 per cent, expressed a non-committal analysis, suggesting a high degree of uncertainty or disconnect surrounding the relevance, whilst 28 per cent stated a level of untruth existed. These findings, when assessed against others we will share through subsequent chapters, illustrate the gap that exists between recognition of the value of truth, a purposeful strategy, and then the communication activity of a business.

Pascal Beucler, French semiotician and seasoned brand strategist, was clear on this when we discussed it. Echoing previous comments of Richard Walker, he said:

> There's no business integrity without truth: how would you trust someone who once lied to you? Which customer, partner or employee would keep working with an organization which is not trustworthy? And what about shareholders: isn't their confidence in the management of the company they choose to invest in the cornerstone of the whole system?

Our answer is of course yes, and this book will allow you to address the distinction between both the gap as identified above and the belief in Beucler's assessment.

Summary

In this chapter we have built on Chapter 1's assessment of the world by focusing on truth, its definition and implications across business. We have positioned truth as core to the application of purpose in business and how it manifests itself across your operating environment. We have categorized five interrelated truths in order to illustrate how they impact upon each other and the implications that would arise should they not be fully appreciated. In doing so, we show that if businesses develop truth, aligned with purpose and transparency in the way they behave and then how they tell their story, this will become the reality. The next chapter explains more fully this inherent connection between truth in business and purpose in business. However, before you move on, set some time aside to think through the following checklist of your understanding of truth.

YOUR CHECKLIST

1   Are you clear on what the human truth is that resonates with you and your proposition?

2   Are you clear on how your business purpose meets that human need?

3   Are you confident in the truth of how you operate?

4   Are you confident in the qualities of your product or service?

5   Envision the effect of you aligning all of the above.

References

Edelman (2020) Edelman Trust Barometer, https://www.edelman.com/ trustbarometer (archived at https://perma.cc/25NB-2XGW)

FleishmanHillard (2019) Authenticity in an Uncertain World, https:// fleishmanhillard.com/products/authenticity-gap/ (archived at https://perma.cc/ E9CE-HVNY)

Gallo, C (2014) The Maya Angelou quote that will radically improve your business, *Forbes*, 31 May, https://www.forbes.com/sites/carminegallo/2014/05/31/the-maya-angelou-quote-that-will-radically-improve-your-business/#7fdf2d72118b (archived at https://perma.cc/ZQ4J-HDBN)

Kennedy, J F (1961) John F Kennedy's Inaugural Address, John F Kennedy Presidential Library, https://www.jfklibrary.org/learn/education/teachers/curricular-resources/elementary-school-curricular-resources/ask-not-what-your-country-can-do-for-you (archived at https://perma.cc/QX3M-MKDF)

McCann (2020) McCann World Group, https://www.mccannworldgroup.de/en/ (archived at https://perma.cc/RE5Q-9F3A)

03

The why: understanding the context of truth and purpose

They say that you don't win the next war by preparing for the last.

In our world, we also need to agree that to tackle today's business challenges, we must not simply apply what was the old way of doing things; we are in effect rejecting what was known as 'business as usual'. What is now required is a new 'as usual', one which does not ignore the valuable lessons from our history, but takes the wisdom learnt and creates new ways to win today. This chapter, therefore, is going to provide you with the context between truth and purpose, why we are where we are, and explain often-confused language and overlapping agendas, in order that you can win the marketing and communications battles ahead. We will provide insight and learnings from recent years because, to put it simply, today's solutions are based on yesterday's lessons. This chapter provides the important context of how truth and purpose have evolved in the world of business, complementing what you now understand about the evolution of societal issues which we discussed in Chapter 1. We will help you in your readiness for winning with your marketing and communications, by taking you back in time, to understand not just where your start point is, but also the start point of business leadership generally and its significance in our society, in order quite simply to fashion the means to envision the future.

We acknowledge therefore that the VUCA2.0 period has seen the global economy disrupted, national resources stretched, personal wealth diminished, and opportunities for many people severely restricted. The combined health and economic situations have disrupted the way we live and conduct business in a way never before experienced. So why would we consider building a chapter around understanding what people may consider is history? Well, put simply, we cannot truly understand where we are heading unless we know where we have been. Leaders and the communicators who have to accelerate their decisions must be prepared to cope with opposing influences as a direct result of the fallout of recent years.

As history repeatedly tells us, leaders need to first anticipate what is coming next, shaping strategy and direction, building the vision, and simultaneously delivering results *today* – all while avoiding the distractions of the immediate and urgent at the expense of the longer term. If they don't get this right, their behaviour and decisions will be governed only by short-term thinking and will never allow for longer-term progress. To take the 'long view' is a recognized virtue, but it is also a mechanism through which a leader can truly assess the current, put situations and difficulties into perspective and then envisage a way forward. The long view looks forward to build foresight for future developments and uses the benefit of hindsight by looking backwards and learning. Good leadership is based on both and allows someone to be better equipped for making the best decisions they can going forward, by learning what worked and what didn't from the past; where influences have merged and with a general appreciation of context. This is where great leadership lies.

Taking historical leaders, we can look back at the actions of Winston Churchill, or Nelson Mandela, or even further back at someone like Abraham Lincoln. We can recognize and then be assured that regardless of the pressing nature of their 'now', they always remained looking beyond that to a vision of a better future, one of aspiration which would be secured once the challenges of the now had been addressed. They knew where they were, where they were going and, equally important, where they had been; and most importantly, in that collective knowledge they were able to take their people with them. This is what is required for our now.

Having a vision, which we will cover later in this chapter, is especially important when one is facing systemic chaos, where the world is behaving in ways that are unprecedented, where one's own experience is thereby at risk of potentially being rendered irrelevant. Of course, proven ability to operate successfully under what was known as normal business conditions is by no means wasted, so long as it does not constrain your thinking and willingness to adapt to the new conditions. Actually, if we take recent experience, we have seen huge shifts in the ability of businesses to adapt themselves, where entire sectors have adopted new ways of operating which otherwise may have taken much longer to evolve so effectively.

We now take for granted online shopping, 'telecommuting' and a variety of teleconferencing and online facilitation software. Many countries are looking at major shifts in their healthcare provision, where they now view much greater risk in 'just in time' procurement and global supply chains. If you stack these and the many other factors against potentially lasting implications of reduced commuting, masses of unemployed, higher personal debt levels, longer working lives and more yet-to-be-determined implications, the simple fact is this: the basis on which your business model was built has already been disrupted beyond anything anyone could ever have envisaged.

As the world drags itself up and forward through the 2020s, it is no good being stuck in the 'now' or the past, but we do need to contend with both if we are able to go forward. This is why this book creates insights based on proven wisdom and experience. It places that wisdom into your hands, to do as you see fit, to determine your future, that of your business and/or the clients you advise in this new reality, and you need to prepare for that reality now.

So, to start, we want you to picture yourself, at a time within the old 'normal', as one of 250 top MBA graduates recruited this year into one of America's most respected and valued businesses. Your boss, who recruited you personally, is a Harvard Business School graduate, a CEO seen as the embodiment of impressive business leadership and acknowledged as having transformed the company with the help of some of the brightest analytical minds around.

This sounds like the aspiration of so many leaders of the last 40 years and of course it was, so quite rightly, by the standards of this imagined but once perfectly achievable scenario, you consider yourself privileged to have been selected. When you received your confirmation, you celebrated with your family, basking in the glow of opportunity with one of the world's most admired employers, on a salary and bonus plan that would be eye-watering to your parents and the envy of your friends. You know the company has been working alongside a top-tier management consultancy, offering further experience, innovative methodologies and extraordinary growth opportunities. You now find a career launching with a business transformed from a lumbering giant of old 'industrial' America into a modern global enterprise based on innovation, agility and data, with the entire world as its market.

At your on-boarding, the mission statement strikes you as novel and inspiring – a new code for a new generation of entrepreneurialism:

> We treat others as we would like to be treated ourselves… we do not tolerate abusive or disrespectful treatment. Ruthlessness, callousness and arrogance don't belong here.

Your 64-page induction booklet on the company ethical code reads like a blueprint for the future, and the list of values in this code are virtues you embrace: Respect, Integrity, Communication, Excellence.

In this, your first year, performance in monetary terms has outstripped any market expectation. Revenue has doubled to $60 billion and resulting profits have risen by 45 per cent to $919 million. You are proud to be associated with such business success and know that by such association your CV will stand out from others and open many doors in the future. Life is good, pay is great, bonuses are generous. Sure, the business is very focused on performance and the hours and demands are long. Yes, perhaps some of your old friends failed to hit the mark and they were moved on pretty quickly, but this is what corporate life is about. Get real – it's the deal. It is what great businesses are meant to be.

But how complete is your view? Behind the scenes, as you and your colleagues go about your work, no doubt adhering to the stated ethics, what if something else, hidden, is happening? Do your CEO and the most senior executives, or even the board, the final defence for the company's ethical governance, truly comply with the same values you have embraced and on which the company promotes itself?

What if they were colluding with their auditors, *colluding*, in its fullest definition, to 'cooperate in a secret, unlawful way in order to deceive or gain an advantage over others'? To create an increasingly complex and ambiguous set of business partnerships and structures, in order to hide financial irregularity, failed projects and massive debts. What if the board might even decide to formally suspend the ethical code you work by, whilst they made decisions on those very partnerships? It sounds ridiculous doesn't it – how could a board suspend its own ethics?

Welcome to Enron in 2000, a golden flagbearer of corporate America and global business. Once the dominoes started falling at Enron, it was impossible to control. The senior leadership and their auditors specifically betrayed not just the trust of their owners and workers but also the trust between business and society more generally. Does this sound like something that could only occur 20 years ago? Of course not. The motivations, selfishness, and opportunity for such excessive unethical behaviour are as prevalent today as they were then; what is different is that we now know it ultimately doesn't work and as a society it isn't acceptable.

It is, however, the basis of such successive corporate scandals of the 2000s onwards, perhaps reaching their height, although not ceasing, with the financial crisis of 2008, which brought the world to the point of demanding something more. It is that demand which we, as business leaders, communicators and marketers, have been attempting to understand and advise clients about in recent years and it is why it is so important that this time we get our part in this right (Thomas, 2002; Segal, 2020; FBI, 2020; Hill, 2011; Skilling, 2006).

Enron, of course, is only one of the many corporate scandals that have wiped out billions of dollars of value, made hundreds of thousands of people unemployed, lost shareholders their investments and pensioners their security in life. Examples of scandals vary as to the cause and not all businesses completely collapse. Enron did and it brought down its auditors Arthur Andersen as well. Between them (although some members of Arthur Andersen then formed Accenture) the combined numbers of Enron and Arthur Andersen employees affected by this was estimated at 100,000, not counting pensioners whose savings were erased, almost overnight (Brown and Jeanne, 2002).

Corporate scandals can vary in the detail but almost all of them are based on greed or undue pressure to perform to deliver shareholder value, which are often indistinguishable. At the root of this is the motivation of leaders and the rationale they invent for their behaviour, and the culture and incentives they create to enable their goals. Let's consider some more recent cases.

CASE STUDIES

Filthy air

The Volkswagen (VW) emissions scandal, more commonly known as 'diesel-gate', blew up in 2015, when the Environmental Protection Agency (EPA) in the United States believed that VW had cheated on results for harmful emissions tests for its engines. Subsequent investigations showed that the company had been creating technical adaptions that were so advanced they included software that could detect when the cars were undergoing tests and as a result amend their functionality to reduce nitrogen emissions. The cars would then appear to be within the parameters necessary to comply with the US's stringent emission standards, even though some were shown to be well over the limits. This discovery led to global investigations and estimates suggest the scandal affected up to 11 million cars. It certainly affected VW, who have paid out $4.3 billion in civil and criminal penalties in the US alone. It is estimated that the total compensation paid out by VW has reached $21 billion, and the reputation and brand value loss will continue to be assessed (Parloff, 2018; Laville, 2019).

Spy ware

But it isn't just heavy industry that has fallen foul. In 2018 Facebook found itself in serious plight when the *Guardian* and *New York Times* reported that data had been harvested from millions of Facebook users without their consent. This was made possible because a previous version of Facebook's privacy policy in 2013 had allowed apps to access data about users' friends, including their name, birthday and location. This had enabled a company called Global Science Research to mine information on over 80 million users. What was so remarkable was that this was possible even though only 30,000 people had used their app. These details in turn were sold to Cambridge Analytica, a data analytics and political consulting business, which infamously used it to create very specific targeted adverts to encourage people to vote for then-presidential candidate Donald Trump in the US and the Brexit campaign in the UK (Confessore, 2018; Zialcita, 2019).

Bad blood

If there is a really specific case study to highlight the issues we face in communications, it must be the story of the 19-year-old Stanford drop out, Elizabeth Holmes, who in 2004 founded a company called Theranos. She was determined to revolutionize the diagnosis of multiple conditions through blood analysis, via a new technological process and equipment. Ten years later the company was valued at $10 billion and she was the world's youngest female paper billionaire, lauded by Silicon Valley and presidents alike as the next Steve Jobs, even purporting to have deepened her voice and wearing black turtlenecks to make the comparison easier. The trouble was, the whole business was a lie, a case of 'faking it until making it'. With her COO lover Ramesh Balwani, she was able to convince the greatest in the land to join her board, part with millions of dollars and even defend her once investigations started to shine a light into this cold, dark business. The resulting collapse in 2018 and the fraud charges against her mean that if found guilty she and her lover could spend decades in jail (Carreyrou, 2018)

Most worrying was that as they grew the business, their false diagnostic processes and results almost certainly had harmful effects on individuals' health. This outwardly 'purpose driven' business was rotten to the core. The governance was non-existent, the staff were hampered by the toughest of US non-disclosure agreements, and it is believed that the actions enforcing them led to the suicide of one ex-employee. This is not a purpose-driven business based on values we recognize. Part of the trouble was that everyone wanted to believe, everyone wanted a female Steve Jobs; Silicon Valley disruptive attitudes gave space for people to think they could ignore or circumvent due diligence and health regulations. Blind ambition, a good story and a touch of glamour made this possible (Burns, 2018).

She had a smart brand, a sophisticated PR campaign, was photogenic, articulate with the media, passionate about her purpose and was part of the digital/tech-enabled world. Marketing and communications gave her both the oxygen and the opportunity to build the most dangerous of deceits. We should all beware.

Dirty money

Of course, we have to leave our final illustrative scandal to the daddy of them all, the 2008 financial crisis. 2008 was the biggest shock to our global financial system in almost a century and it pushed the world's banking system towards the edge of near collapse. As memories fade, it is perhaps not surprising that the specific reasons behind the crash become less prominent, but alongside the trigger, the collapse of the sub-prime mortgage market in the United States, what it exposed was a catalogue of other related and sometimes parallel behaviours by businesses, which were all based on greed and the manipulation of markets in some form or other (The Economist, 2013; Coghlan, McCorkell and Hinkley, 2018).

If you haven't seen the 2015 film *The Big Short*, it's definitely worth doing so. Starring Christian Bale, Brad Pitt and Steve Carell, it gives an unconventional but entertaining explanation of the occurrences that led to the sub-prime collapse and the resulting crisis. You will also find a great quote from Mark Twain on opening credits, which reads:

> *It ain't what you don't know that gets you into trouble.*
>
> *It's what you know for sure that just ain't so.*

(Baldwin, 2019; IMDb, 2015)

So, what happened as a result of the collapse of the sub-prime mortgage products? Well, within just a few weeks in September 2008, Lehman Brothers, one of the world's biggest financial institutions, was the first to go bankrupt, with the result of £90 billion wiped off the value of Britain's biggest companies alone in one single day. This money matters. It is the pension pots of millions of people and the ongoing failure of banks which was triggered, on such an impending scale, could, if not for state intervention, have reduced society to poverty. Lehman Brothers had been borrowing significant capital to provide loans to those looking to buy real estate.

As a result, it faced a situation where its outstanding loans exceeded its liquid capital many, many times over. This meant it would risk collapse if the housing market faced a downturn and so to hide this, they used to repurchase agreements to disguise their own 'at risk' assets. Perhaps not easily appreciated by us non-bankers, but the key is the word 'disguise'. It was a deceit to mask greedy market behaviour and as the sub-prime mortgage crisis took effect, Lehman Brothers found itself unable to repay its debt as clients defaulted on their loans. In the UK and US, such effects went on to hit many other mighty and global financial institutions, many of whom may well have been – or are again now – your clients. In the US alone, $5 trillion dollars in pension money, savings, bonds and real estate value simply ceased to exist. It disappeared – forever. Eight million people lost their jobs, six million people lost their homes. The implications of this around the world were enormous (Chu, 2018).

A purpose defined

Rather than risk an entire chapter on the countless companies who have added to the list of scandals in the last 20 years, we now need to put this into context in order to set the scene and explain why the much-lauded concept of Purpose has emerged as the solution, and to do that we need to take you even further back in time.

It is 1962, a year which proved one of the most dangerous in the Cold War, when the Cuban missile crisis dominated the summer and then later, as the world caught its breath, the Beatles made their chart debut in the autumn with 'Love Me Do'. By coincidence it is the year John was born, but more importantly, also emerging into this world of seismic events was the single most significant proposition about business purpose in the 20th century. It was this year that the renowned economist Milton Friedman published his book *Capitalism and Freedom*. Within it he declared that 'There is one and only one social responsibility of business – to use its resources and engage in activities designed to increase its profits' (Friedman and Snowden, 2002).

Maximizing shareholder value became the definitive statement that would shape business teaching and business leadership behaviour for the next 40 years. It inspired huge motivation in the creation of financial value and ultimately led to the promotion of activity which culminated in the demise of society's trust in business and the 2008 crisis.

This ethos, promoted firstly at his own affiliated institution, the Chicago School of Economics, and soon taken up by other business schools and management institutions in the United States, became the predominant thinking and teaching on business leadership and management research. It did so because up until this date, business and management education had been somewhat woolly, with vague notions around people, leadership, cash-flow, and production cycles, amongst others.

The Friedman philosophy, built on as the foundation for strategic business thinking, created a compelling mantra which afforded a teachable approach to business management education. It also created a relatively standardized approach to business leadership teaching. This filled firstly US boardrooms with singularity of thinking, a 'group think' perhaps, and then spread around the globe as it was adopted by institutions and businesses worldwide. For those subsequent 40 years, a generation of business leaders graduated into businesses based on what is now seen by some as a flawed concept. As a result of the corporate scandals we have touched on above, even some of the most ardent proponents of the philosophy subsequently came to appreciate that simply creating financial return was not and should never be a purpose for business.

The late Jack Welch was the world-famous CEO of General Electric from 1981 to 2001, and from a financial performance and reputation perspective was seen as the exemplar of business leaders focused on maximizing shareholder value. However, in 2009, as part of the post-financial crisis awakening within global leaders, he stated in an interview that shareholder value was:

> The dumbest idea in the world. Shareholder value is a result, not a strategy... Your main constituencies are your employees, your customers and your products. Managers and investors should not set share price increases as their overarching goal... short-term profits should be allied with an increase in the long-term value of a company (Guerrera, 2009).

That reaction was echoed by different comments and actions from different perspectives. Paul Polman, one of the world's equally famous proponents of purpose in business, arrived at Unilever in 2009 and started to change behavioural expectations, not just inside the business, but with investors and customers. What is different about the approach is it takes leadership as being about more than the bottom line; it emboldens people in a positive way that doesn't happen purely by returning shareholder value.

As he told the *Guardian* in 2013:

> I know we all have our jobs, but that has to come from a deeper sense of purpose. You have to be driven by something. Leadership is not just about giving energy; its unleashing other people's energy, which comes from buying into that sense of purpose (Confino, 2013).

The final insight at this point has to be from Lord Browne, former CEO of BP. In 2015, he was discussing the role of corporate social responsibility (CSR) in business behaviour and was explicit in saying 'CSR is dead' (King, 2015). He talked about the purpose of business being a positive contributor for the many, not an extraction of wealth for the few, or a set of offsetting initiatives, but something much more fundamental, as a contract between business and society. His views were perhaps forged in part from the aftermath of the BP 'Deepwater Horizon' oil spill disaster a few years earlier in the Gulf of Mexico.

Unfortunately, despite such denunciations of the old way and advocacy for the new, the concept of shareholder value still lingered on in the minds of many, not just up to but also through the COVID-19 pandemic, with some businesses still maximizing the concept of profit over people, to dire effects. The reality is that unfortunately, because it has been 'business as usual' for so long, shareholder value thinking is still ingrained in many who are now graduating into the senior roles in business. As a philosophy, linked with personal greed, it still influences business behaviours over a wide range of topics, from how a business is measured by investors to executive compensation and workplace culture.

Thankfully, however, we had already entered a new purpose-driven business era because new voices, not least some powerful investors and ever more consumers, are demanding much greater emphasis on determining why a business exists and the values and ethics through which the business is led. The assessment of whether a business is a good business to work for, invest in or purchase from is now as much determined by its impact on society and the environment, as a return of value for all stakeholders, rather than shareholders alone.

For many in the marketing and communications sector, those developing brands, creative partnerships with NGOs, and cause-related marketing and campaigns, purpose has been embraced and/or seen as a natural development of their particular specialism. This is too narrow minded but also potentially dangerous if, for example, a brand specialist simply looks at it through the filter of the brand, or a PR professional through the lens of publicity and campaigns. One of the reasons why so-called purposeful initiatives by businesses have backfired is that they have not been seen as an authentic, comprehensive component of a business's behaviour. This risk we will address elsewhere, but it is important for readers to appreciate the wider picture and the evolution of purpose as a development primarily of business strategy thinking, not marketing and communication behaviours.

Of course, some might argue that this is just the latest in a long history of 'fads', a temporary addition to what we describe below as the evolution of purpose. Jim Moser of BBDO doesn't think so:

> No it is definitely not a fad. The issue is that some companies have treated purpose as purely statements as such, without fully understanding the significance or the meaning. These companies have denigrated the significance and importance of purpose and many develop statements of purpose that could be applied to any industry, any company. I fundamentally believe that purpose is only going to increase in importance as people look for greater meaning, greater understanding, and greater clarity on the company they work for, the companies they engage with, and the brands and services that they use.

As we show within these pages, there is the increasing acknowledgement that purpose defines both the leadership of the business and its course, rather than simply messaging. Moser summarizes, 'More and more, purpose is going to fundamentally guide a company's direction, priorities, investments, and activities'.

As we have established that purpose is much larger than simply the messaging and have enlarged the picture in terms of why purpose has emerged, let us then just round this section up with the long view, the evolutionary cycle as seen in Figure 3.1 as the way such purposeful thinking can be seen to have developed, looking back at least 100 years.

Starting at the beginning of the 20th century (and even before) we had wealthy Victorian-era industrialists making money and acting as philanthropists. Such activity varied, from creating good social housing for their workers to funding education facilities or civic establishments like libraries. In the UK and US, names such as Cadbury, Boots, Rockefeller and Carnegie were examples of individuals or families with a corporate philanthropy attitude, a philosophy based on *I make a lot of money over here and give a bit of it away over there*, or in some, although not all instances, a shift toward 'enlightened' employment in an age of hard labour and a small societal safety net.

FIGURE 3.1 Evolution of purpose

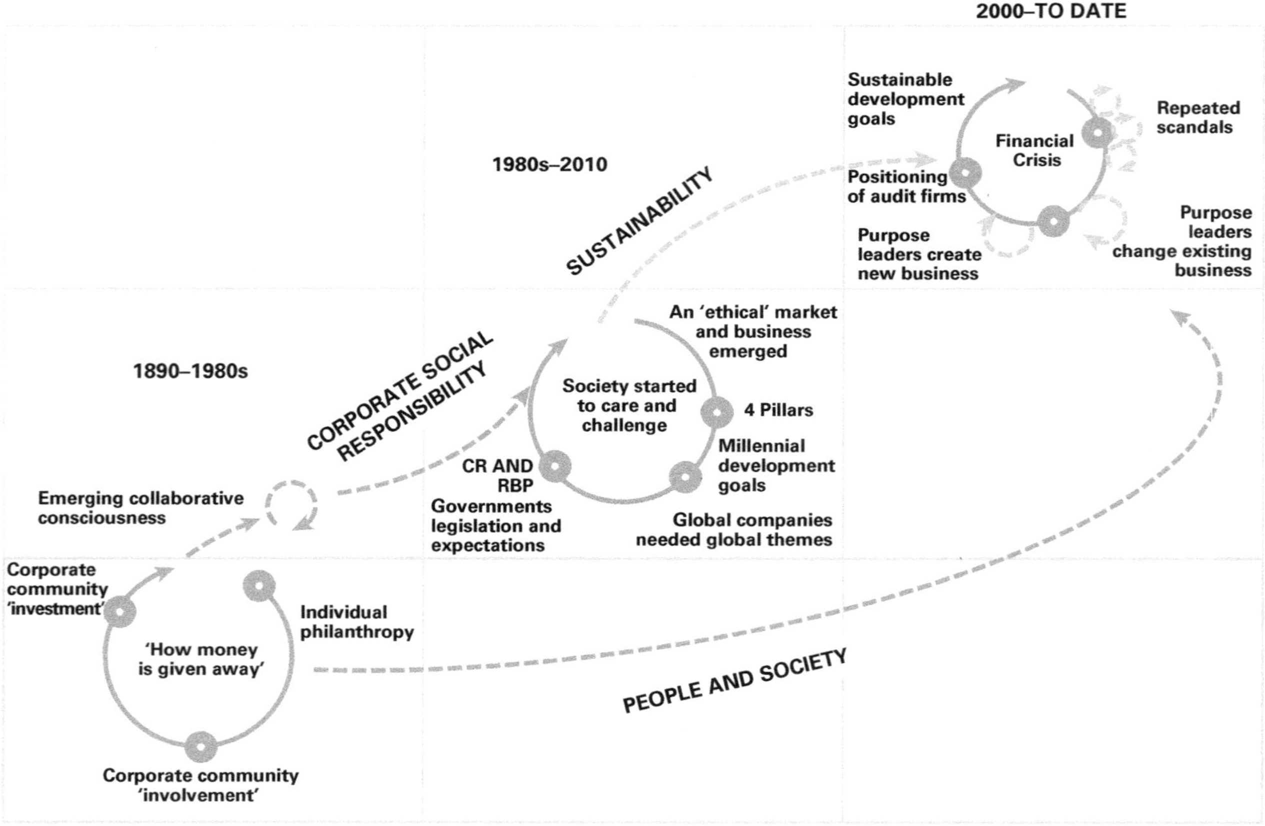

1890–1980s

CORPORATE SOCIAL RESPONSIBILITY

1980s–2010

SUSTAINABILITY

2000–TO DATE

Corporate community 'investment'

Emerging collaborative consciousness

Individual philanthropy

'How money is given away'

Corporate community 'involvement'

Governments legislation and expectations

CR AND RBP

Society started to care and challenge

An 'ethical' market and business emerged

4 Pillars

Millennial development goals

Global companies needed global themes

Sustainable development goals

Positioning of audit firms

Purpose leaders create new business

Financial Crisis

Repeated scandals

Purpose leaders change existing business

PEOPLE AND SOCIETY

The Great Depression

The big test of the 20th century for business and the world generally, was the period between the 'roaring twenties' and post-World War II, before the 1950s. Over this period of the Depression and the War, we saw businesses in the 'western world' either adapt or die in the first, or survive and in many cases thrive in the second. Although we don't need to dwell too greatly in this period, it is worth just reflecting on some of the businesses that weathered these extreme conditions. In the UK consider Cadbury, Lever Brothers (now Unilever) and Rolls-Royce, and in the US Disney, Ford, HP and GE. These were all businesses that were either started in the period of the Depression, or weathered it and the War well, adapting themselves through what were considered the toughest times in corporate and economic history. What is interesting is that it was smart businesses with smart leaders who adapted and grew their dominance in markets during these periods, often going against the perceived wisdom of the time, who built the foundations of the businesses we know today. They perhaps invested in marketing when no one was seen to be buying or pivoted into different products to meet a purpose-driven demand.

After the 1940s and through the Milton Friedman period of the 1960s, not much changed until the early 1980s, when in the UK a set of civil unrest issues impressed upon some of the old established, often still family-owned businesses, the need to invest in their local communities. The emergence of what was described as corporate community investment and corporate community involvement (CCI) had activities ranging from employees being given time to volunteer locally, to specific interventions on supporting enterprise, small businesses or NGO development. This was an important development for two specific reasons. The first was that it encouraged businesses to collaborate on such community activities, rather than singular company-specific programmes. The second significance was that it saw the recognition that there were a number of other stakeholder groups, local to businesses, who were affected and could affect a business, beyond the traditional owners. It also led to a number of brokering organizations, often set up by businesses themselves, to translate business contributions into local groups, most significantly the longstanding business membership organization, Business in the Community, one of HRH The Prince of Wales's personal charities.

Corporate social responsibility

CSR emerged out of CCI in the early 1990s, where a variety of societal influences, such as the demise of traditional industries, growing concerns around the environment, diversity in the workplace and educational attainment levels, made business look harder at its wider stakeholders and impact. CSR became the globally recognized terminology and what can now be seen as an 'add on' component to the requirement to demonstrate corporate citizenship. In some countries such developments were forced by legislative requirements in key areas such as employee welfare and the environment, whilst in others it required businesses to recognize the business case for certain changes in behaviour and then do so voluntarily, often then forcing others in the sector to adopt similar practices, as expectations rose. It also saw the emergence of a useful and widely adopted framework for illustrating impact over four key areas.

This model, called 'Winning with Integrity' and developed by Business in the Community, saw four key areas impacted by a business. These were 'workplace' (how they treated their employees), 'community' (how they behaved where they were based), the 'marketplace' (how they treated suppliers and others) and finally the 'environment' and their impact on that. Still in use both as a terminology and framework, it remains useful, but the challenge was that it was often peripheral to the leadership approach, and secondary to the key purpose philosophy of shareholder value and the cultures that drove overall performance (Baker, 2006).

Sustainability

Sustainability was the next critical development in this agenda. Although one can trace the concept of sustainability back well over a century, if not further, into ancient Greek philosophy, the concept as a corporate agenda item really only moved into the mainstream in the late 1990s. At a high level this is the recognition that in order for businesses to develop and maintain production, access to resources must be sustained well into the future, and these resources are often directly or indirectly related to the natural environment. The agenda, therefore, is to find ways in which the business can operate in harmony with nature in order to support present and future generations.

This is a very broad definition around a concept which supports a multitude of measures, focus areas, initiatives and agendas. What was an interesting catalyst for corporate adoption, though, was the emergence of what might be described as the 'Green Economy'. This was where consumers started to look at everything from organic food and beauty, to alternative fuels and recycled products. This saw the creation of pioneering movements and businesses, probably the most famous being The Body Shop, founded by British entrepreneur Anita Roddick. Roddick was well ahead of her time, setting up the business in a small way in the late 1970s, but the gradual recognition of pioneers like her not only led to consumers thinking differently about products, their ethics and credentials, but also forced other mainstream businesses to change their own ways in order to meet that interest. The emergence of this was part of the wider corporate appreciation of sustainability and its adoption of various initiatives. This led naturally to businesses recognizing the UN Sustainable Development Goals (SDGs) as directly relevant to their operations and the expectation that they, as a major driver of resource and economic activity, had a direct responsibility to see alignment with this most ambitious statement of global intent.

It would be appropriate to see the SDGs and the business sustainability agenda generally as part of the evolutionary process as it supports another way to improve and assess the old profit maximization model. Sustainability is best seen as an approach that recognizes wider societal and environmental goals and impacts and in turn helps a purpose-driven business to appreciate its place in the world and manage its investments and decisions accordingly. But it isn't, on its own, 'purpose'.

Socially responsible investing

SRI is increasingly significant as investors are of course crucially important to most modern business enterprises, giving them a leading role in shaping corporate behaviour and practices. Generally, investment strategies focus on the money and are shaped around the level of risk and rate of return expected by investors, but over the last decade or so a more conscientious approach combining financial as well as societal/environmental goals has become popular within some investment circles.

Also referred to as sustainable investing or ethical investing, SRI has a long history, dating back at least to John Wesley, 18th-century founder of the Methodist Church, whose tenets of social investment included not harming neighbours with business practices and avoiding investment in industries that harmed workers. In the last century, similar investment philosophies played important roles in coaxing business to re-examine its role in the wider social and often volatile social issues of the times, including the civil rights movement in the United States and apartheid in South Africa, among others (The Ethical Partnership, 2020).

Over the past few decades, sustainable investment became more closely associated with climate change mitigation, but it is also a force in other areas including diversity, gender equity and human rights, as well as other concerns labelled under the heading ESG – environment, social justice and corporate governance. One of the better-known and most successful ESG firms, Generation Investment Management, founded in 2004 by former US Vice President Al Gore and his business partner David Blood, has raised the profile of sustainable investment with the language that matters most on Wall Street and in the City: strong results.

'If you do this the right way, you don't have to trade values for value. Indeed, with some good fortune and skill, you can get enhanced returns,' Gore said in an interview with *Institutional Investor* in 2015. The success of Generation and similar firms, with their longer-term focus and values-based preferences, has helped usher in a new way of thinking about business and investment that goes beyond the 'do-good' ESG community, too (Smith, 2015).

According to Steffan Williams, Partner and Head of Financial Communications at Portland, an international strategic communications advisory firm headquartered in London:

> There's a lot of evidence to suggest that buy-side investors and analysts are looking to what's called extra-financial information – disclosures of corporate performance against different social, environment and governance objectives – in just about all of their decisions, regardless of the nature of the business they're evaluating. This isn't about altruism on their part – assessing how a business sees and manages its place in the world is a way to predict risk, resilience and relevance.

People and society

It has to be recognized that much of what business has done, how CCI, CSR and Sustainability have evolved, has not happened in isolation. Indeed, much has been shaped by shifts in societal mores. This is directly relevant to us as communicators, as we base our insights, our work with clients, on understanding audiences, their market and the world at large. If we take a very simple illustration, one can see the sharp difference in the way society now operates, compared to that in which our predecessors operated. What we expect to see, what society accepts and how we portray a client's products is entirely different to the adverts of the 1960s, or even the '70s and '80s. Sexual stereotypes, the use of animals, risqué jokes and suggestions – all now inappropriate as a result of societal change. If we have seen this level of change in our lifetime, what are the new generations expecting?

The next generation is ready. Are you?

Generational research has limits, but a person's age is one of the most useful predictors for attitudes and behaviour across a wide range of areas. Individuals think and act differently, of course, and a host of factors like gender, wealth, location and education influence their views, but age offers two important perspectives: where they are in their life cycle, and what experiences they have in common with others born around the same time. This gives researchers a way to look at groups over time and assess changes in their thinking and behaviour as they experience growing up and beyond, and how formative events like 9/11, or the introduction of the iPhone, or a pandemic impact their outlook and actions.

Generations are defined as those born within a 15–20-year range, and one of the more widely studied is the 'Millennials' – those born between roughly 1980 and 2000. This varies slightly, depending on who's doing the research, and in some places this cohort is referred to as Gen Y, following the Gen X of 1965–1980. We have chosen Millennials, as it seems more commonly used (and searched on Google), and because they're important. The global accountancy firm KPMG estimates them to comprise half of the UK workforce right now, quickly rising to 75 per cent in a few years, so it's hard to overstate their significance as employees, customers, investors or consumers (Kurian, 2017).

Incidentally, Millennials are known differently in other countries, reflecting cultural, historical and social differences. In Norway, it's Generation Serious, in Poland they're Generation John Paul II, and in China, *ken lao zu*, or 'the generation that eats the old', as Kate Lyons wrote in the *Guardian* in 2016. Whatever they're called, and wherever they are, they're one of the first generations to grow up in a truly globalized, highly networked world (Lyons, 2016).

Millennials, now in their early twenties to late thirties, approach their increasing prominence in business and society with a mixed bag of formative experiences, marked by security concerns including 9/11 and the subsequent wars, terrorist incidents and heightened safety protocols; economic uncertainty – many were entering the workforce at the start of the 2007–2008 'Great Recession'; and of course the explosion of the internet and social media.

A number of ideas, not necessarily unique to Millennials, went 'mainstream' or became established as they came of age – expectations of gender/ethnic/LGBT+ inclusion, rejection of privilege, the rise of China as an economic superpower, and intense political polarization, especially in the US and the UK. Given all that, it's not surprising that older generations and popular media have found traits to mock (lazy, entitled) or admire (creative, collaborative and digitally savvy – how we see them, for what it's worth).

FleishmanHillard, the global communications consultancy, studies Millennials and their attitudes toward business and brands, and according to Claire Barry, Youth and Culture Lead in the Brand team for the firm in London:

> They're not passive, and they're not cynical – they're angry and frustrated. They want positive change. Think about it – this is the first generation to be less well-off than their parents, but they're living longer than ever. At the same time, they have immediate access to information on any company, any brand, and the power to share their views in real time and worldwide. So, they have a 'get-right-to-the-point' attitude and a low tolerance for nonsense.

Not surprisingly, these attitudes inform Millennials' views on who they want to work for and what they expect of the products and services they purchase, and FleishmanHillard's data reflects this. From their 2019 report, 'Understanding the Millennial Manifesto for Business', a survey of Millennials found that:

- 68 per cent say creating change is a personal goal;
- 93 per cent want to buy brands that have a 'purpose beyond product';
- 87 per cent believe the success of a business should be measured in terms of more than just its financial performance;
- 75 per cent would take a pay cut to work for a socially responsible company;
- 76 per cent consider a company's social and environmental commitments before deciding where to work (Afshar, 2019).

Millennials are serious about purpose, but what's following may be a freight train. Generation Z were born after 2000, also called We Generation or Generation Change. They grew up in a time of ubiquitous technology, hyperconnectivity, when everything, everywhere, was always on. Diversity, inclusion, and tolerance are their default settings, and they may be the first generation to put purpose over money. They're well aware of online frauds, doctored photos and fake news, making authenticity mandatory. Virtually all media they consume – news, entertainment, personal – is on a mobile device, and this is a generation that won't hesitate to report bad corporate behaviour online.

FleishmanHillard has looked at Gen Z, too in their report titled 'Project Z', and while they share some traits with Millennials with regard to purpose, new patterns may be emerging unique to their always-on cohorts. The most important of these, according to FleishmanHillard's Barry, may be authenticity and culture. 'Our research shows that while they value entities with purpose – one in four rank this as a top priority – interactions need to feel genuine and culturally relevant, rather than an obvious commercial ploy or an attempt to connect,' she said. The need for being real may outweigh the expectation that brands have value, she added: 'Six in ten agree the general population has the most responsibility for social change. For them, it's better to say nothing and be real, than to fill space with half-hearted attempts' (FleishmanHillard, 2019).

As data for this generation emerges in terms of consumption, employment and political preferences, a few traits seem bankable: they shun labels, seek dialogue to resolve differences, organize for causes, and make decisions analytically – all, according to research from McKinsey, anchored in the generation's search for truth, making them the 'True Gen'.

In the management consultancy's report 'True Gen: Generation Z and its implications for companies', this cohort is seen as the one likely to *really* shake things up:

> Companies should be attuned to three implications for this generation: consumption as access rather than possession, consumption as an expression of individual identity, and consumption as a matter of ethical concern. Coupled with technological advances, this generational shift is transforming the consumer landscape in a way that cuts across all socioeconomic brackets and extends beyond Gen Z, permeating the whole demographic pyramid (Francis and Hoefel, 2018).

Millennials and Gen Z, not to mention the rest of the world, have also experienced a formative event unlike any seen in a century with the COVID-19 pandemic and economic impact. Little data is yet available to analyse the real impact on attitudes and behaviour, but similar transformative events in the past have served as crucibles, accelerating and then amplifying trends already underway. With Millennials and Gen Z bending toward purpose and truth before this crisis, it's a good bet they will be even more important in the future.

We should also share a key finding from our own research. Understanding how purpose is currently viewed in our space is important and the following figures provide some indication from fellow professionals. When asked how they viewed the significance of purpose as a business or brand having a role beyond profit or narrow commercial objectives, 88 per cent rated it either essential or highly, with only 3 per cent rating it either of little significance or distracting. Although we have already accepted that the c400 respondents may be self-selective, in comparison with other such surveys, this is a significant baseline and majority opinion. We take it as positive illustration of the well-established direction of travel.

People and purpose

Now we understand where purpose has evolved from, we need to move onto the second part – understanding what will equip you to be better able to navigate the current environment. A great degree of confusion has arisen within this space because of the proliferation of language across various aspects of the overall agenda, often used interchangeably and wrongly. If you are to master the ability to represent truth in purpose marketing and communications, then you must master the language as well, otherwise you are affecting your ability to both understand and to then successfully deliver. You must quite simply be clear in terms of what you mean when talking about it.

The issues that have surrounded such misunderstanding in the marketing and communications world are pretty evident. Malcolm Devoy, Chief Strategy Officer at PHD, finds 'purpose' problematic because, as he told us, 'There are many brands championing a certain cause that we might refer to as a purpose, but some of these brands appear to champion the cause purely as a marketing effort.' This is absolutely aligned with the issue we address in this book, because truth-based 'purpose' is not a marketing campaign, even if marketing is used at times to express it. As Devoy continues:

> Those that wish to harness the power of emotive communications in a space
> that seems meaningful to large audiences, but do not adhere to their own
> principles in the boardroom, in the workplace, or in the real world are at risk of
> being exposed, criticized and denounced as hypocritical, and run a grave risk to
> consumer perceptions of their brand.

Clarifying corporate purpose

We see misuse and misunderstanding in the language of business purpose so often that it is right to ensure its definition is universally understood. What we mean by '*Purpose*' needs setting out with clear terminology. When we say 'We', we don't just mean us, but we state what is universally accepted by leading proponents as the evolved definition of the word – let us call it the 'gold standard' of understanding and an aspirational definition for business. This requires such clarification because one of the great issues we have today is that it is often misunderstood by many in our profession who want to support its adoption as well as many clients who seek such help. So, with no apologies – let's get down to basics.

Defining purpose

This new purpose paradigm in business makes for simple understanding by appreciating that it is a concept based on fusing together two definitions. Let us start quite obviously with our definition of purpose, one which we think will be generally understood as follows:

> **Purpose:** Why something exists, is created or done.

Most of us would have this basic appreciation, but in the new context there is something missing in its application. The reason for this is that such a definition alone is insufficient to define business behaviour and thinking, in a way which counters the influences that created the scandals detailed earlier. For 'Purpose' to mean something in business in a way which goes beyond previous activity, the definition above only becomes fit for its own purpose when it incorporates a second important definition, namely that of *values*. To ensure we all know what we mean, our definition of values is:

> The standards of behaviour or principles which form your judgement of what is correct and key in life, the moral principles and ethics on which you base decisions.

Therefore, the accepted definition of 'purpose' in business, as a basis on which the business purpose must exist, must be built on a foundation of ethical principles.

Stakeholders and shareholders

A business must understand the basis of the principle on which a 'Why' must now be based, going beyond simply making money, to a purpose that creates value in a broader sense, for all *stakeholders*. But by way of slight diversion, let us also just take time to be clear we understand what we mean by stakeholders.

Firstly, all *shareholders* are *stakeholders*, but not all *stakeholders* are *shareholders*. It is pretty simple to understand that if you invest financially then you will have a stake in the business. If you work for the business or supply it or even just live next door to it and benefit from economic spin-off, you will have a natural stake in the ongoing success and the way it operates, but you won't have a share in it. Ironic, but again an important appreciation is that in this day and age, particularly in public companies, money can flow quickly and decisions are made sometimes on market performance rather than individual business performance. This means that shareholders can often have a much shorter-term interest in the business than the stakeholders who may work in some capacity for much longer. It is an extraordinary irony that our system and the obvious Friedman philosophy were geared around those stakeholders who often had the shortest interest, namely the owners.

A critical concept balancing these two interested parties is that to do the morally or ethically right thing, the business leaders must be prepared to make decisions which may, although benefiting other stakeholders, affect shareholder value negatively. As stakeholders measure value in a longer-term manner, for the obvious long-term sustainability of a business overall, activities cannot always be focused around short-term investment-led returns.

We have seen the emergence of organizations where wider stakeholder value is being acknowledged more openly. The B Corps movement (a network of ethically minded and purpose-led businesses) is integrating this requirement into its governance and leadership procedures. This manifests itself in different ways, such as paying employees a higher than normal wage, perhaps incurring short-term extra costs, but thereby building great loyalty and performance in the longer term. Others may choose to provide employees with extra welfare, or make non-regulated investments in green alternatives for energy, transportation or the like. Companies of this kind are investing in activities and resources that might under conventional thinking provide a shorter-term shareholder return, but are in effect using what might have been profit to secure much longer-term sustainability.

BluePrint for Better Business is a UK-based non-profit, created by business in the light of the 2008 financial crisis to help guide and inspire companies with a purpose that benefits society. It does so by challenging core assumptions about the purpose of business and what motivates people. Its CEO, Charles Wookey, has a particular view on how marketing should be perceived within the agenda he and his colleagues are attempting to affect:

We say a purpose-led organization contributes to and meets the needs of society through producing and selling goods that are truly good and services that truly serve. We would define good purpose-led marketing as seeing everyone it seeks to reach as 'someone', and to genuinely serve, rather than exploit them. As we advocate, this puts human-centric thinking, an essential 'human truth', at the core of an approach to marketing.

As Wookey goes on, 'For us, truth in marketing means honesty and fair dealing – are we selling goods and services that truly serve, and marketing them in a clear and responsible way?' Wookey is, perhaps not surprisingly, absolutely aligned with our own thinking and experience. He continues, 'The key is to keep looking through the human lens. Businesses are just people. The desire to build strong relationships of respect and care is deeply human.'

By appreciating such thinking and using the above principles, a 'gold standard' purpose is one defined as being an authentic behaviour-defining statement that sets out how a business helps people and or the planet in the broadest sense. It needs to be demonstrable and directly relatable to the business's activities. The best statements are simple and clear with examples such as:

- Philips: 'Improving people's lives through meaningful innovation.'
- Microsoft: 'To enable people and businesses throughout the world to realize their full potential.'
- Google: 'To organize the world's information and make it universally accessible and useful.'
- Sony: 'To fill the world with emotion, though the power of creativity and technology.'
- Kickstarter: 'To help bring creative projects to life.'
- LinkedIn: 'To connect the world's professionals to make them more productive and successful.'
- BBC: 'To enrich people's lives with programmes and services that inform, educate and entertain.'

Of course, these are just a small selection of the many well-crafted statements that put people at the forefront and are succinct, to the point and memorable. But however challenging it might be creatively to come up with such a statement, the real challenge is making it real. This is where language is so important and where it not only reduces the risk of confusion but can actually, through greater clarity, provide far more effective communication opportunities.

Purpose, vision and mission

In any market there is often confusion around terminology, and *Purpose* and how it is used is no exception. Such language is sometimes used inter-changeably with that of Vision and Mission, which is wrong and can be very confusing. This was perhaps understandable earlier on, as the language reflected an emerging set of thinking and new business ethos, but this should no longer be the case. The interpretation and inter-relation between these three definitions is now accepted, although many clients will not yet fully appreciate it. For clarity, the meaning, definition and inter-relationship of each is described below:

- Purpose: WHY the business exists, contributing something positive to people, and/or the planet. This should be short, memorable and aspirational.

- Vision: WHERE the business is heading, with a view of the world envisaged as being created by being successful in its purpose. This can be both a vision of the world and a vision of where the business is within that world.

- Mission: WHAT the business will do to achieve its purpose over a specified period of time. This can be seen as the specific strategy, the actions and operations which the business will conduct over a set period of time.

A business should look carefully at how it describes itself and how the publication of the vision and mission adds to the general understanding of the business by stakeholders. It may not be necessary or advisable to utilize all three within certain communication.

Time for a cup of tea?

John prides himself on bringing simplicity to complexity, and in regard to the relationship stated above he has a very simple analogy, which, as a Brit, almost inevitably has to be related to tea.

He will explain that if you imagine the *purpose of a tea bag* is to make a British person feel refreshed and contented, its *vision* will be to imagine its changed state after it has been immersed, perhaps complemented with milk, lemon or sugar, and served in a fine bone china cup, and the look of satisfaction on the face of the drinker. Its *mission*, somewhat different to what most of us envisage as a good thing, is to get itself into hot water (we hope there is a slight smile on your face at this point, as when John tells this analogy in various stages, it doesn't always get much more than a groan). So, if we know what it is...

What purpose isn't

Given that our specialisms are a combination of business strategy and communication, it is important to raise a growing concern we all need to address, namely that purpose doesn't fall into purely becoming a communication exercise. We have a collective responsibility not to create a 'purpose wash' cynicism, as related to the 'greenwash' activities of 20 years ago. It is in no one's interest to move in this direction and so there are a number of things that are best identified as being clearly what 'purpose' isn't.

The purpose advisory market

The emergence of purpose as the most significant shift in corporate thinking and its resultant demand for support in the form of strategic thinking, consultancy and communications, has inevitably created a marketplace where many advisory businesses and agencies are creating new purpose propositions. As in any new market, such propositions, however well intended, sometimes fall foul of confusions over language and appreciation of how the situation has evolved and what actually defines the full spectrum of purpose-driven need. Equally and inevitably, agencies approach the new subject area from their existing position and experience, hence a PR agency will have a strong bias around its experience of perhaps publicizing CSR activities, whilst a brand agency will view it from their brand purpose thinking. All such experience is relevant and provides strong credentials for agency propositions, but purpose, as defined in its new form, is broader than a single specialism or channel.

In these days of social media, transparency demands and empowered employees, if there is not authentic engagement with stakeholders, the business will quickly come unstuck. You appreciate that purpose is not just a combination of CSR and PR, it is much more profound and brings a combined value set, behaviours and clarity of leadership for a core unified ethos.

This means that once defined then yes, everything that is a communications channel or output, from a short tweet to a major advertising campaign, will support the activation of that, but alone they do not constitute purpose in itself. To be clear, then, purpose may include, empower or utilize some of the below, but:

1 **It isn't a PR campaign.** PR will play a role in telling the story but if an inauthentic PR story or campaign is created without the reality of it being embedded in the business, the campaign will fail and the business will suffer. It is not solely owned by a communications team.

2 **It isn't simply an employee tool.** Attracting and retaining the best people is a key benefit from a purposeful business. But creating the appearance of purpose purely for this reason is insufficient to build a purpose-powered business. Purpose should not be owned solely by the HR team.

3 **It isn't a strapline.** Creative thinking will go into creating a memorable purpose statement. But it must be authentic, related to the business activity and easily understood and owned.

4 **It isn't a 'retro fit'.** Not everything will necessarily fit into a forward-looking purpose. If so, clients will need to be transparent and develop a strategy that addresses any anomalies.

5 **It isn't a charitable cause.** A business may care about social issues as a citizen does, supporting them charitably if they wish. However, a purposeful business is designed to be positive and impactful, without becoming or adopting an unrelated charitable cause.

One of the challenges we have seen in recent years is when activity of the above kind, particularly when apparently created to simply respond to a popular wave or an issue, has been executed either with poor logic, little credible association with the business product, or where creativity has run away with the ambition, without realizing that the end result, however potentially creative, comes over as either opportunistic or inauthentic. We will be covering how to create successful purposeful communications in the next chapter, but it is worth recognizing just some examples of where previous efforts have gone wrong.

The wrong stuff

These examples, by being so off target, have helped create cynicism around marketing from consumers and other stakeholders alike. They need to stand as warning signs for us all because as such campaigns have become a regular part of every brand strategy, expectations have been fuelled that companies should demonstrate that they care. That isn't the issue; however, the execution is. As we noted above, Millennials and Generation Z will only continue to be associated with brands, either as employees or customers, if they are seen to stand for something they can believe in, or at least show a wider corporate citizenship aspect to their operations.

There have in recent years been some really spectacular own goals and illustrations of 'purpose wash' or 'woke wash', where brands have completely misunderstood either an issue, or the temperament of the audience and wider societal trends. Such mistakes are actually part of the reason this book exists, because to believe in the truth agenda, as it manifests itself in this purposeful age, requires us all to try and help others understand where they are going wrong, both for them individually and of course for the companies or clients they work for. Let's just have a look at some so-called purpose-driven disasters.

Pepsi clearly thought they were on to a winner when they attempted to align their soft drink to the civil demonstrations and outcry around the Black Lives Matter campaign and Women's March. They engaged the celebrity Kendall Jenner in an advertisement which showed her approaching a non-specific demonstration, illustrating her allegiance and then approaching a police officer in a line of apparent riot police. She hands him her can of Pepsi and rather than him being standoffish, he takes a drink, smiles and then the crowd of protestors cheer.

This ad had particular resonance with what was going on at the time and in particular the photograph of Leisha Evans, who was a protestor arrested at the 'Taking a Stand' demonstration in Baton Rouge in the United States. That photo quickly became an iconic expression of the Black Lives Matters campaign and as such it potentially illustrates an even worse illustration of cause appropriation.

The company was forced to halt the campaign and apologize with a statement:

> Pepsi was trying to project a global message of unity, peace and understanding. Clearly, we missed the mark and apologize. We did not intend to make light of any serious issue. We are pulling the content and halting any further rollout (PepsiCo, 2017).

The apology led to even more of a backlash, illustrating just how out of touch the whole thinking was. Put simply, neither Jenner or Pepsi had any credentials as advocates for unity, peace or understanding and as such there was no authenticity – no *truth* behind the message, the campaign or those involved in creating it. The 'short film' was pulled back, but not before significant and lingering damage was done to the brand, leaving months of online criticism in its wake. How such a concept could survive multiple testing reviews is a mystery, but the incident did launch an introspective discussion within the ad industry about the importance of diversity within the creative and executive ranks (Batchelor and Hooton, 2017; Quenqua, 2020).

In 2018, Mastercard ran a similarly misplaced campaign as part of the FIFA World Cup. The concept was to link the number of goals scored by players Lionel Messi and Neymar da Silva Santos Júnior to hunger in the developing world. They stated in their adverts that they would donate 10,000 meals for every goal scored by the two stars, which was immediately lambasted on social media, where critics suggested that FIFA, a multibillion-dollar enterprise, might make the pledge regardless of who scored goals. Mastercard agreed and changed course, but any positive brand goodwill they had been hoping to achieve was well gone by that stage (Lepitak, 2018; and ESPN, 2018).

Many of us will recall the sculpture 'Fearless Girl', commissioned by State Street Global Advisors to 'face down' the Charging Bull on Wall Street. It was a highly creative idea to highlight the fact that they had an index fund that had a higher than normal percentage of female leadership. However, although initially the photograph attracted a great deal of media coverage and positive commentary, it was almost inevitable that State Street would then be shown up as having consistently underpaid more than 300 top female staff in comparison to their male equivalents in the same roles (Stewart, 2019; Stevens, 2017; Hinchliffe, 2019; Holman, 2017).

That was quickly followed by an allegation that they had also discriminated against 15 black vice presidents, paying them less than white staff in the same positions.

Although denying wrongdoing they agreed to pay $4.5 million in back pay and about $500,000 in interest into a settlement fund for affected employees (De Dios, 2017).

They had presented an external image which didn't reflect the *truth* of internal behaviours.

Even organizations with a history of getting purpose right can make mistakes. One such example was Dove, part of Unilever, one of the world's most recognized purpose-led businesses, striving to make sustainable living commonplace, and which under former CEO Paul Polman had transformed much of its business to integrating such thinking within their brand and values sets. They did, however, make a serious mistake when they attempted to represent women of colour in an advertising campaign which actually ended up linking them to accusations of racism. In a Facebook advertising campaign, they showed a series of pictures where a black woman pulled her sweater up to reveal a white redhead emerging. This went so hard and so fast with complaints that the ad was down within hours.

The advert was meant to convey that Dove was for every woman and to be a celebration of diversity. If anyone got beyond the first 'reveal', the white redhead actually peeled back to reveal an Asian woman, but the problem was that no one even recognized that.

At the very least this was an ill-structured campaign, but if you consider that in previous generations, black people had been shown in adverts being washed with soap and coming out white, it was spectacularly misplaced (Slawson, 2017; Astor, 2017).

As one final illustration, we look to a trendy craft brewery, BrewDog, famous for its punk-style branding and desire to be seen as a disruptive, younger, on-trend brand. They wanted to use their beer to highlight the gender pay gap issue. Firstly, we have to ask ourselves why exactly they thought there was a link between why they are in business and this, but let us just give them the benefit of the doubt that this was about them responding to a serious societal issue as a corporate citizen who cares.

What did they do?

They released a range of beer called Pink IPA. The reason one knew it was a female beer was because they branded it pink. The packaging actually re-enforced gender stereotypes and was sold under the tag line 'One for the girls'. It would be sold only to women, at 20 per cent cheaper (to reflect the gender pay gap). Not only was this over-simplistic and sexist in its colour association, they were actually sued for sexual discrimination for refusing to sell it to men.

BrewDog's problem was not that they wanted to address a social issue, but that they forced the issue into their business and product where it clearly didn't fit. For a company that wants to develop a strong sense of citizenship, connection with customers and tackle issues, it should build an authentic *true* purpose aligned to what it does and why it exists. Then it can use its brands to drive change in a much more powerful and impactful manner (Sweney, 2018; McCarthy, 2018; Trendell, 2018).

Now, to be fair to all the businesses cited above, we suspect that for many there was a genuine desire to have a positive effect on key issues and agendas. Unfortunately, they misfired, not necessarily because of a general lack of sentiment, but because of the uneasy line between a concern for a cause and a desire to sell product. This is where we aim to help bring a perspective that will help you avoid such pitfalls yourself.

Summary

In this chapter we have explained where purpose as a concept has originated from and in particular the way in which history has played a part in shaping behaviours and the appreciation of how business and society interact. This period, of greater uncertainty than ever before, requires clarity in understanding and commitment to be the agent of change.

To help bring clarity, we have explained that in this context purpose is defined by fusing two dictionary definitions: firstly why something exists and secondly the values and ethics on which it stands. We have explained how stakeholders now outgun shareholders in the long-term influence of success in business, and how understanding them and maintaining great relationships with them is a key task for all communicators. We looked at some scandals that have driven shifts in societal demands and at the same time the evolution of business thinking from early corporate philanthropy to today's sustainable development goals and the relevance of them both to still shape the activation of purpose. We have looked at some general examples of what purpose isn't and specific examples of companies getting it wrong.

In the next chapter we will start to show where you find the human truth and purpose within your particular business. This will assist you in building both awareness and a strategy that can avoid the sorts of issues highlighted above. The goal over the next few chapters will be to understand enough about your business to create the underlying *truth* that will create the basis for a purpose that aligns with your business and your stakeholders. However, before you move on, set some time aside to think through the following checklist of your understanding of Purpose.

YOUR CHECKLIST

1 Have you reviewed and defined existing activities as CSR, Philanthropy, Sustainability?

2 Can you put into perspective the evolution of these activities in your own business?

3 Are you clear on the distinction between your Vision, Mission and Purpose?

4 Have you an ability to define or refine any existing language used in the above?

5 Are you confident that others in your team or business understand the above distinction?

6 Start to think about the clarity such understanding could bring to your people.

References

Afshar, P (2019) The Millennial Manifesto for Businesses, *Fleishman Hillard Fishburn*, 18 April, https://fhflondon.co.uk/2019/04/the-millennial-manifesto-for-businesses/ (archived at https://perma.cc/RX5V-UJYN)

Astor, M (2017) Dove drops an ad accused of racism, *New York Times*, 8 October, https://www.nytimes.com/2017/10/08/business/dove-ad-racist.html (archived at https://perma.cc/AGC5-3R2S)

Baker, M (2006) BITC sets the standard for principled money-making, *Briefing Corporate Citizenship*, 25 September, https://ccbriefing.corporate-citizenship.com/2006/09/25/bitc-sets-the-standard-for-principled-money-making/ (archived at https://perma.cc/2J44-9BXG)

Baldwin, J G (2019) 'The Big Short' explained, *Investopedia*, 15 February, https://www.investopedia.com/articles/investing/020115/big-short-explained.asp (archived at https://perma.cc/YQD2-XGTR)

Batchelor, T and Hooton, C (2017) Pepsi advert with Kendall Jenner pulled after huge backlash, *Independent*, 5 April, https://www.independent.co.uk/arts-entertainment/tv/news/pepsi-advert-pulled-kendall-jenner-protest-video-cancelled-removed-a7668986.html (archived at https://perma.cc/77EX-VNYT)

BBC (2020) Our Values, *BBC Careers,* https://www.bbc.co.uk/careers/why-join-us/values#:~:text=Our%20aim%20is%20simple%20%2D%20to,care%20how%20we%20do%20it. (archived at https://perma.cc/V3VD-TK8N)

Brown, K and Jeanne, I (2002) Arthur Andersen's fall from grace is a sad tale of greed and miscues, *Wall Street Journal*, 7 June, https://www.wsj.com/articles/SB1023409436545200 (archived at https://perma.cc/83HJ-B6VG)

Burns, J (2018) WSJ reporter tells downfall of troubled Theranos, *Dark Intelligence Group,* 29 May, https://www.darkintelligencegroup.com/the-dark-report/laboratory-management/wsj-reporter-tells-downfall-troubled-theranos (archived at https://perma.cc/D3US-BU5Y)

Carreyrou, J (2018) *Bad Blood: Secrets and lies in a silicon valley startup*, Alfred A. Knopf, New York

Chu, B (2018) Financial crisis 2008: How Lehman Brothers helped cause 'the worst financial crisis in history', *Independent,* 12 September, https://www.independent.co.uk/news/business/analysis-and-features/financial-crisis-2008-why-lehman-brothers-what-happened-10-years-anniversary-a8531581.html (archived at https://perma.cc/5E8Z-XN29)

Coghlan, E, McCorkell, L and Hinkley, S (2018) What really caused the great recession? *Berkeley University Institute for Research on Labour and Employment,* 19 September, https://irle.berkeley.edu/what-really-caused-the-great-recession/ (archived at https://perma.cc/57J7-Z2MK)

Confessore, N (2018) Cambridge Analytica and Facebook: the scandal and the fallout so far, *New York Times*, April 4, https://www.nytimes.com/2018/04/04/us/politics/cambridge-analytica-scandal-fallout.html (archived at https://perma.cc/ABM7-V582)

Confino, J (2013) Interview: Unilever's Paul Polman on diversity, purpose and profits, *Guardian*, 2 October, https://www.theguardian.com/sustainable-business/unilver-ceo-paul-polman-purpose-profits (archived at https://perma.cc/RGP9-BHE2)

De Dios, N (2017) State Street to cough up $5M in back pay over discrimination claims, *S&P Global*, https://www.spglobal.com/marketintelligence/en/news-insights/trending/e8eox1pf_tozc-hpiwofsw2 (archived at https://perma.cc/JMX6-AQN4)

Economist (2013) Crash Course: The origins of the financial crisis, *The Economist,* 7 September, https://www.economist.com/schools-brief/2013/09/07/crash-course (archived at https://perma.cc/F2GS-KVDJ)

ESPN (2018) Mastercard ends campaign to donate meals for every Lionel Messi, Neymar goal at World Cup, *ESPN UK – Football*, 4 June, https://www.espn.co.uk/soccer/fifa-world-cup/story/3517847/mastercard-ends-campaign-to-donate-meals-for-every-lionel-messi-and-neymar-goal-at-world-cup (archived at https://perma.cc/X7RM-YQ6K)

Federal Bureau of Investigation (FBI) (2020), Enron, *FBI: Famous Cases & Criminals*, https://www.fbi.gov/history/famous-cases/enron (archived at https://perma.cc/678P-FB9H)

FleishmanHillard (2019) Project Z: Understanding Gen Z, *Fleishman Hillard Fishburn,* 1 August, https://fhflondon.co.uk/2019/08/project-z-understanding-gen-z/ (archived at https://perma.cc/M57Q-67SF)

Francis, T and Hoefel, F (2018) 'True Gen': Generation Z and its implications for companies, *McKinsey & Company*, 12 November, https://www.mckinsey.com/industries/consumer-packaged-goods/our-insights/true-gen-generation-z-and-its-implications-for-companies# (archived at https://perma.cc/3BXC-FJ8E)

Friedman, M and Snowden, P N (2002) *Capitalism and Freedom*, Chicago University Press, Chicago

Google (2020) Our approach to Search, https://www.google.com/intl/en_uk/search/howsearchworks/mission/ (archived at https://perma.cc/65LP-VC2E)

Guerrera, F (2009) Welch condemns share price focus, *Financial Times*, 12 March, https://www.ft.com/content/294ff1f2-0f27-11de-ba10-0000779fd2ac (archived at https://perma.cc/BB22-9QZN)

Hill, A (2011) Enron: Ten years on, Enron remains an open sore, *Financial Times,* 17 October, https://www.ft.com/content/9d57f8da-f66d-11e0-86dc-00144feab49a (archived at https://perma.cc/L86U-EUL8)

Hinchliffe, E (2019) The firm behind 'Fearless girl' has a dubious record of backing gender diversity as a shareholder, *Fortune,* 1 April, https://fortune.com/2019/04/01/state-street-fearless-girl-shareholder-resolutions/ (archived at https://perma.cc/4TMW-4NLK)

Holman, J. (2017) Bank behind Fearless Girl statue settles gender pay dispute, *Bloomberg News,* 5 October, https://www.bloomberg.com/news/articles/2017-10-05/bank-behind-fearless-girl-statue-settles-u-s-gender-pay-dispute (archived at https://perma.cc/LTK2-YEL2)

IMDb (2015) The Big Short, *IMDb,* https://www.imdb.com/title/tt1596363/ (archived at https://perma.cc/PKS8-FUWU)

Kickstarter (2020) Our mission is to help bring creative projects to life, *Kickstarter,* https://www.kickstarter.com/about#:~:text=Our%20mission.-,Our%20mission%20is%20to%20help%20bring%20creative%20projects%20to%20life,to%20create%20it%20requires%20protection (archived at https://perma.cc/QHE9-L92V)

King, I (2015) Corporate social responsibility is dead, *The Sunday Times,* 14 September, https://www.thetimes.co.uk/article/corporate-social-responsibility-is-dead-so-what-happens-now-hqdvfcd5xmm (archived at https://perma.cc/PG7E-ZCM4)

Kurian, S (2017) Meet the Millennials, *KPMG,* 1 February, https://home.kpmg/content/dam/kpmg/uk/pdf/2017/04/Meet-the-Millennials-Secured.pdf?utm_source=twitter&utm_medium=social&utm_campaign=itsherfuture&hootPostID=980a3c6a76bcd323bd134d41a090fbf6 (archived at https://perma.cc/ESX2-UMJG)

Laville, S. (2019) Volkswagen emissions scandal: class action begins in UK, *Guardian,* 1 December, https://www.theguardian.com/business/2019/dec/01/volkswagen-emissions-scandal-class-action-begins-in-uk (archived at https://perma.cc/7BGL-VMMD)

Lepitak, S. (2018) 'The worst marketing I've ever seen' – Mastercard's World Cup children's meals campaign stirs debate, *The Drum,* 2 June, https://www.thedrum.com/news/2018/06/02/the-worst-marketing-ive-ever-seen-mastercards-world-cup-childrens-meals-campaign (archived at https://perma.cc/SS6R-WZUW)

LinkedIn (2020) LinkedIn Mission and Vision Statement Analysis, *Mission Statement Academy,* https://mission-statement.com/linkedin/#:~:text=LinkedIn%20mission%20statement%20is%20to,that%20runs%20the%20entire%20company (archived at https://perma.cc/8U7K-4U5T)

Lyons, K (2016) Generation Y, curling or maybe: what the world calls millennials, *Guardian,* 8 March, https://www.theguardian.com/world/2016/mar/08/generation-y-curling-or-maybe-what-the-world-calls-millennials (archived at https://perma.cc/P9VW-2V42)

McCarthy, J (2018) Drinks watchdog says BrewDog's pink 'Beer for Girls' did actually appeal to someone – kids, *The Drum*, 10 July, https://www.thedrum.com/news/2018/07/10/drinks-watchdog-says-brewdog-s-pink-beer-girls-did-actually-appeal-someone-kids (archived at https://perma.cc/T8F6-YTKN)

Microsoft (2013) Annual Report 2013, https://www.microsoft.com/investor/reports/ar13/financial-review/business-description/index.html#:~:text=Our%20mission%20is%20to%20enable,work%2C%20play%2C%20and%20communicate.&text=We%20do%20business%20worldwide%20and%20have%20offices%20in%20more%20than%20100%20countries (archived at https://perma.cc/K86L-54FS)

Parloff, R (2018) How VW paid $25 billion for 'Dieselgate' – and got off easy, *Fortune*, 6 February, https://fortune.com/2018/02/06/volkswagen-vw-emissions-scandal-penalties/ (archived at https://perma.cc/9NH5-VKH4)

PepsiCo (2017) Pepsi Statement Re: Pepsi Moments Content, *Pepsico*, 4 May, https://www.pepsico.com/news/press-release/pepsi-statement-re–pepsi-moments-content04052017 (archived at https://perma.cc/6BQF-ASAQ)

PTC (2020) Philips: Improving lives through meaningful innovation with PLM implementation strategy, *Philips Case Studies on PTC.com*, https://www.ptc.com/en/case-studies/philips#:~:text=Philips'%20mission%20is%20to%20improve%20people's%20lives%20through%20meaningful%20innovation.&text=Through%20the%20use%20of%20a,Sales%2C%20Service%2C%20or%20Marketing (archived at https://perma.cc/33D4-XA9N)

Quenqua, D (2020) Pepsi says 'sorry' and removes Kendall Jenner ad from the web, *PR Weekly*, 5 April, https://www.prweek.com/article/1429761/pepsi-says-sorry-removes-kendall-jenner-ad-web (archived at https://perma.cc/F7J9-JJP2)

Segal, T (2020) Enron scandal: The fall of a Wall Street darling, *Investopedia*, 4 May, https://www.investopedia.com/updates/enron-scandal-summary/ (archived at https://perma.cc/9HXX-K3NB)

Skilling, J (2006) Enron: The fraud that changed everything, *Independent*, 9 April, https://www.independent.co.uk/news/business/analysis-and-features/enron-the-fraud-that-changed-everything-6104114.html (archived at https://perma.cc/L73T-WA2Y)

Slawson, N (2017) Dove apologizes for ad showing black woman turning into white one, *Guardian*, 8 October, https://www.theguardian.com/world/2017/oct/08/dove-apologises-for-ad-showing-black-woman-turning-into-white-one (archived at https://perma.cc/3HE8-HWML)

Smith, I R (2015) David Blood and Al Gore want to reach the next generation, *Institutional Investor*, 8 September, https://www.institutionalinvestor.com/article/b14z9wt9vk3ycy/david-blood-and-al-gore-want-to-reach-the-next-generation (archived at https://perma.cc/ED4A-29E6)

Sony (2020) Sony's Purpose and Values, Sony Global, n.d. Available from: www.sony.net/SonyInfo/CorporateInfo/purpose_and_values (archived at https://perma.cc/C3P3-FKLA)

Stevens, M (2017) Firm behind 'Fearless Girl' statue underpaid women, US says, *New York Times*, 6 October, https://www.nytimes.com/2017/10/06/business/fearless-girl-settlement.html (archived at https://perma.cc/7B7S-GK2A)

Stewart, E (2019) The firm behind Wall Street's Fearless Girl statue isn't as pro-woman as it could be, *Vox Business & Finance*, 3 April, https://www.vox.com/business-and-finance/2019/4/3/18293611/fearless-girl-state-street-etf-she-nyse (archived at https://perma.cc/BN4E-3LYL)

Sweney, M (2018) Brewdog's pink 'beer for girls' criticised as marketing stunt, *Guardian*, 6 March, https://www.theguardian.com/business/2018/mar/06/brewdog-pink-beer-for-girls-punk-ipa (archived at https://perma.cc/MUM4-MQ5G)

The Ethical Partnership (2020) The history of socially responsible and ethical investment, http://www.the-ethical-partnership.co.uk/HistoryofEthical Investment.htm (archived at https://perma.cc/QR2X-MKNH)

Thomas, C W (2002) The Rise & Fall of Enron, *The Journal of Accountancy*, 1 April, https://www.journalofaccountancy.com/issues/2002/apr/theriseand fallofenron.html (archived at https://perma.cc/8XF9-26CE)

Trendell, A (2018) 'This is not a 'beer for girls'' – Brewdog's new 'Pink IPA' has upset a lot of people, *NME*, 6 March, https://www.nme.com/news/not-beer-girls-brewdogs-new-pink-ipa-upset-lot-people-2255774 (archived at https://perma.cc/R2RE-7K86)

Zialcita, P (2019) Facebook pays $643,000 fine for role in Cambridge Analytica scandal, *NPR*, 30 October, https://www.npr.org/2019/10/30/774749376/facebook-pays-643-000-fine-for-role-in-cambridge-analytica-scandal?t=1594639533463 (archived at https://perma.cc/ZP7J-TQLE)

04

The where: finding truthful purpose in business

Having established truth as the foundation of purpose, and what this demands in this volatile world, in this chapter we will show where the credentials of truth actually rest within your business. This will put you on the path to understanding how your knowledge of telling the truth and purpose will ensure you are a successful marketeer and communicator. This chapter gives you an overview of how to understand where purpose and related stories manifest themselves across all aspects of a business. It ties together and explains concepts and definitions including ESG, CSR, Sustainability, Corporate Philanthropy and Corporate Citizenship. It will allow you to go on a journey of discovery across areas which may be less familiar for the professional marketeer, or are often ignored, yet offer great credentials and stories.

So, what do we mean when we say this learning will allow you to be successful? Definitions of marketing have changed somewhat over the years, but they usually mention a set of activities, processes and outputs that help promote or sell products or services. We like one put forward by the 2000 book, *The Cluetrain Manifesto*: 'Markets are conversations' – and by extension, anything tied to marketing is tied to human conversations. The book includes 95 such 'theses' and they collectively speak to the iterative, human nature of conversation, and the need to reconcile the conversations happening inside a business with those happening outside (Weinberger, 2000). This makes a lot of sense to us and resonates with our own core thesis: at the heart of these conversations is a purpose built on human truth.

The last 40 years of the 20th century may have distorted this idea of human-to-human conversation. Massive brands were built on mass communications, first in print and later on radio or television, usually through one-way advertising campaigns that were broadcast (a term that comes from the throwing of seeds widely to plant larger areas of land) to reach the largest number of people possible. Famous adverts and the jingles behind them resonate with us still and have left a lasting impression of how marketing works.

But it works this way no longer. Or at least much of it works differently now, for a simple reason: the internet. Digital technologies have fundamentally changed the way information is exchanged and shared about products, services, brands, charitable causes, political ideologies and, well, you get the idea – everything; because markets are now conversations, not one-to-many broadcasts, but many-to-many relationships.

Ironically, it's the internet that has returned us at least partially back to human conversation. People expect now to be heard, and they have the means to do so, regardless of whether we want to hear them or would prefer to stay on the messages we have carefully designed to sell or persuade. In some ways we're back to where we were before the age of mass media, with marketing built on human-to-human interaction. However, in other ways we are in something far different, because those humans are increasingly networked, highly capable of creating their own content, and not necessarily compelled to even include us in their conversations in the first place.

By the way, we occasionally use the terms 'marketing' and 'communications' interchangeably, but we recognize the differences between the two. Without going down a terminology rabbit hole, communications generally involve interaction at the organizational level between the company or institution and its many external and internal stakeholders, whilst marketing is generally associated more specifically with sales and promotion. These functions overlap a great deal, obviously enough to govern them with the same principles of truth and purpose, and to assert the same fundamental qualities required for success. They are:

1 Know your client (or your customer).

2 Know what they want to achieve.

3 Know what you can do to assist them.

4 Know how to tell their story.

So even though the world in which we operate has changed, the four key personal skills still ring true. What does this have to do with purpose, we hear you ask? Well we contend it is directly correlated as follows:

1 Know your client – you must understand 'why' they exist, their truth, their purpose.

2 Know what they want to achieve – understand the desired impact on their purpose.

3 Know what you can do to assist them – how you fit within their team and strategy.

4 Know how to tell their story – an authentic, credible story that embodies purpose.

Having the capacity to fully appreciate the purpose of a business and bring a perspective to help them achieve it, is how you will positively act on behalf of the business. Successful marketing is no longer just about producing great creative ideas, it is much more about understanding what is true for a business and then creating appropriate strategies to deliver that truth to the desired audiences. This is where creativity is still important, as the means through which to tell the story. Companies and their brands need to be capable of being inspiring, accessible and relatable, through human stories. This is why understanding the business and the purpose story is key, as it will shape your approach to meeting the brief.

However, equally important is understanding where purpose can create a rich seam of credentials, capable either of supporting an advertising campaign at one end or helping resolve reputational issues at the other. The better you are at understanding where *purpose* manifests itself within the business, the better you will be able to represent your clients, create new and exciting opportunities, and be better prepared if external factors such as societal issues or campaigns require responses.

Ethical restaurateur Iqbal Wahhab had a particular approach to representing his sustainable and community-based thinking across all aspects of the business, from its sourcing of ingredients to employing disadvantaged staff. This had a surprising effect, as he explained: 'People increasingly seek validation that they have made the right consumer choice. So, if they find we source responsibly and ethically for both our ingredients and our people, they get that sense of affirmation even before they eat or drink anything.' This manifested itself after the *Evening Standard* newspaper ran an article on his restaurant's recruitment practices, Wahhab continues: 'The response was game-changing for us. People sent us messages saying largely the same thing: I've never been to your restaurant but now I know you do things like that, I'll start coming.' The critical thing was that the message that got out in the media was true, verifiable and arose out of all aspects of the business. Wahhab is also clear that it had a profound impact upon how he viewed his own contribution to business and society.

It is pretty clear that the secret to doing better work is being better at feeling what the client feels. If you take one of John's mantras, the statement that we are creating 'external value for the values held internally', it is only through clarity on how purpose manifests itself within the client's business that you can be confident of success. We would argue therefore that within your client management, you should have at the forefront of your mind *all* aspects of how they talk about themselves. You should envelop yourself in their culture, their values, their sense of purpose. So, answer this: when you accept or win a piece of work, how often do you then go beyond the brief to truly understand the client? Do you visit the factory, do you have their values posted up on your wall? Do you consume the item and gain a personal sense of the experience? It is surprising how often the answer is 'no'.

One of the challenges we have seen within the rise of purpose-driven marketing activities is not only the misunderstanding about what purpose is, but also where it rests within the business. This is important because reputational risk exists in areas which marketers may not be normally familiar with, but which equally offer great potential in terms of stories and opportunities that could work very well for the business.

In leading businesses, purpose will sit at the core and permeate all aspects of operations. As such it has a huge significance as a truly embedded strategy, and alongside behaviour-setting, guiding leadership, will build culture and shape its reputation. It transcends functions, affecting manufacturing, production and service provision; it is central to how the people of the business are recruited, retained and incentivized; it is key to shaping the messaging and communications activities and ultimately is the foundation for the financial management, reporting and associated governance. Truth-based purpose, when fully integrated, is actually where stories originate and can be the raw material for all marketeers and communicators, from investor relations and public affairs teams to advertising, public relations and channel marketing.

Findings from our quantitative research clearly illustrate that rather than being thought of solely as an externally beneficial campaign or association, purpose manifests itself in the overarching value of the business. We believe this illustrates an increasing awareness that purpose is both applicable and, where correctly integrated, vital to whole business thinking and development.

When asked what effect they thought an authentic purpose-driven strategy had upon the overarching value and growth of the business, a straight 80 per cent of respondents believed it had a positive influence, whilst 14 per cent were ambivalent and only 6 per cent had a contrary, negative view – overwhelmingly positive results. This indicates the overarching belief in its importance we have explained in this chapter.

When our respondents were asked whether they would describe their current organization as being 'purpose driven', 61 per cent stated it was to some degree, 23 per cent expressed an average appreciation, whilst 15 per cent stated little or no sense of purpose. Therefore, in assessing the above, we can conclude that although a significant proportion felt they did not currently work in a business greatly influenced by purpose, many more believed businesses can be influenced for the better if they are. This strikes a chord with wider assessments where people express a desire to work for and engage in more purposeful businesses, yet see much more progress still to be made. Senior leaders we discussed this with are pretty clear on the expectations that now exist around truth and its purpose application.

Sir Peter Bazalgette for one explained very clearly the breadth of significance he believes it has within the company he chairs. He told us:

> In my business, at ITV, this has multiple meanings. First, the truth of our news programmes which contribute to our democracy... it can't function without a properly informed citizenry. Second, it relates to an honest definition of what our company's public purpose is – culturally, socially, democratically and economically with our support of SME's, regional business ecologies and the talent base of the creative industries. Third, it defines straight dealing in business, which promotes mutual benefit between partners.

This gives a clear insight that across production, leadership, societal commitments, financial probity and people, truth and purpose are key defining factors of the business.

To help people understand this and also to be aware of where negative issues may emerge, we share Figure 4.1. This illustrates the four universally accepted standard segments of any business, along with specific identified areas of influence and activity under each quadrant and of course the central functions of leadership, values, strategy and culture.

FIGURE 4.1 Purpose in business

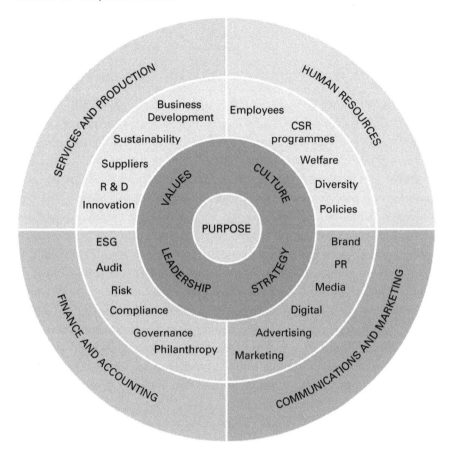

This model is one which defines a business into the well-accepted four key segments of marketing communications, HR, finance and accounting, and production/services. In addition, at the centre sits leadership, the company strategy, values and culture. At the core in the purposeful business sits the defining and unifying rationale for why the business exists.

It should be noted that for clarity's sake, certain labelled activity has been placed within set quadrants, even if their activity may straddle more than one functional area. In this model we have for diagrammatic reasons placed CSR policies within HR, as they often, although not exclusively, engage employees in various activities. On the same basis we have sustainability within production and services, as certainly the environmental impacts rest predominantly there, whilst corporate philanthropy, the granting of donations, we have placed in finance for obvious reasons. This diagram is not, therefore, a structural one, but rather a theoretical illustration of key relationships. Let us look at each segment.

Marketing and communications (marcoms)

This is of course the area of speciality most readers will be fully familiar with. It embraces all aspects of the communications and marketing of a business and in effect is the amplifier of the ambition of the business, the voice of its leadership and how it reflects to customers and clients the products and services, manages the channels to each stakeholder and audience and tells the story, as well as from time to time managing matters which create reputational risk. One risk we have alluded to is that sometimes we see a client ask for a creative marcoms message, around either a cause or societal issue, which has little connectivity to their business. Then, unless it is appreciated that such stories, however they manifest themselves, must be rooted in the truth of the business, the creative response can actually create a reputational risk in itself. How ironic is that? If a business has an authentic, truthful purpose culture, marcoms should flow naturally from its behaviours, culture, products and people. The moment you have to force connectivity between a message and the business is the moment you should know you are potentially creating a risk. You are in effect moving away from the truth.

It is worthwhile at this point to bear in mind that as professionals in marketing and communications, we live by a set of ethical values which dictate how we work and what we expect of those we work with. This is something which we are sure all readers will consider important, not least because experience shows that when people stray from such a path, they may achieve short-term success but they will ultimately fail. False product claims, doctoring of images, hiding negative facts or distorting statistics, really shouldn't be options anyone in marketing would consider appropriate. This isn't to stifle creativity in any way, but it is essential to be uncompromising with your own professionalism and reputation. This is your truth, which should in turn make you attractive to the best of clients. Where businesses have suffered – and indeed some of us will know entire agencies that have collapsed (no names, no pack drill) – this has occurred because of either poor governance around financial diligence, inappropriate behaviours in the workplace, or unethical activity in the marketplace. These are the pitfalls you need to be alert to and which of course allow you to then consider how those looking to employ you also behave.

Let us just look at a very simple issue. A brief comes to you and you are thrilled to win it – a major advertising campaign for a new drink range, with a big budget and no shortage of creative licence. The client provides you with certain key aspects it wants promoted. They include that the drink is not only nutritious but that in *proven trials,* people's *mental health* was seen to improve over a period, with a *happiness* quotient higher than those who didn't have it as part of their *daily diet.* Of course, you can read between the lines that none of these words actually mean anything unless there is external accountable and credible testimony from another trusted source. The question for you, however, is what do you do?

Now although the client may not consider it, we as marketeers actually should feel obliged to answer such questions, not just to the client but also their customer. We have a moral and ethical obligation to not knowingly falsely sell or be complicit in spreading misinformation which may influence people to make life-changing decisions. Fundamentally, of course, if you have to act as the client's conscience, even at the potential cost to your business, you should. Ultimately it won't pay to try to deceive the customer and if you think your client is at risk of doing so, and it may be purely inadvertently, then speak up. You will be saving your own reputation as well as sleepless nights, saving the reputation of your client and who knows, you may be even saving the lives of the general public. There is nothing frivolous or lightweight in the work we do; we act on behalf of... you guessed it, *truth.*

It is helpful, as a communicator, someone hoping to tell the truth to the public, if you consider some of the following when faced with any sort of dilemma between what a client claims and what you may think is true:

- Embody ethical purpose within your own role and business that goes beyond just making money and allows you to focus on people and the societal implications of your work.

- Ensure your business has a set of ethics-based values which help guide decision making, particularly when client demands may seem ambiguous.

- Consider a trusted coach or advisor or friend with whom you can share a dilemma and see how they react to any ambiguous proposals.

- Nurture an organizational culture that puts integrity at its core and celebrates such behaviour, even if it loses you work.

- Build your own reputation as an honest, trusted ethical leader in your field. Why wouldn't you? Build this not by what you just say, but how you behave.

Given that most readers will understand marcoms functions and their particular role within this space, we are not going to dwell too long in this chapter on how the various functional areas must complement each other. This will be explored further in Chapter 5. The important understanding, what we want to emphasize here, comes from appreciating the other functional areas of the business and how purpose manifests itself within them. This is where opportunities will arise to tell the *truth*, build reputation and support the wider recognition of a good business.

The opportunity for purposeful expression rests through this functional set of activities and it is through much of this that you will build the brand reputation. The whole reason for this book (and you reading it) is that we can acknowledge that in this age where reputation is critical to the ongoing success of a business, the integrity of the brand and how it is communicated is crucial. A brand can of course activate a fantastic all-encompassing marketing plan, which presents its purpose, illustrates its collective commitment around a particular set of complementary agendas etc, but if the brand experience doesn't match the communication, people simply won't believe it.

It is critical then that when you are developing the communications, you fully understand what the brand promise is, how the business will deliver it and have transparency in expressing this, as well as the creative input to make it stand out. The way in which you build such purpose-driven trust is relatively simple, at least in theory, but like so many things it is worked hard for but easily lost. It is of course all about trust, and trust is based on truths. Such truths are based in turn on some very simple principles, which for us are critical in shaping how we can build brand success through our marketing strategies. These are:

- **Products and services must be fit for purpose.** Having the most wonderful, ethical and sustainable purpose won't mean a jot unless what you are actually selling can do the job. It needs to do it well and at a price the customer thinks is fair. If it doesn't, then it will fail and the best of us marketeers will be unable to do anything about it.

- **Messaging must be consistent.** When defining the purpose position and messaging be sure to be consistent. Consistency ensures that your brand message is reflected in the same desired way, regardless of channel or audience. Such qualities are the way to ensure recognition and such consistency creates trust and confidence.

- **Creative must align to values.** We would be appalled now to see 1950s sexual stereotypes in adverts or the use of animals in demeaning situations to sell products. But more subtly, mismatched thinking can make some creative interpretation out of kilter with the brand values. So, if a company has strong sustainability credentials and cares about the environment, it would be a mistake to make an advert that showed activity that was about excessive consumption and at odds with that. It sounds obvious, but often, when seduced by the excitement of highly creative ideas, the link with such values can be lost.

- **Have a human voice.** If you accept that purpose-led businesses exist to solve a problem for people, then be sure to put people at the core of your marketing. Make your creative focus on the human, make this emotional, as this becomes much more believable and relatable. Customers will find it easier to believe that you are aligned to their own beliefs if the brand can speak with a human voice.

- **Be responsible and open.** A purposeful brand takes responsibility for all aspects of the customer experience and that includes when things go wrong. Be truthful and if necessary be ready to apologize when there are issues. Transparency and responsibility will build stronger relationships with your customers.

- **Tell stories truthfully.** Indeed, when planning a campaign, think about how great, truthful stories can speak on the behalf of your brand and can create a much more authentic experience than any contrived voice. Real stories from the people in the business or customers establish authentic credentials.

Let us move on to a quadrant that in many regards is often not particularly a focus for marcoms activity, that is Finance and Accounting.

Finance and accounting

Figure 4.1 summarizes many of the key functions that rest within this quadrant. To appreciate the significance in this space, one has to understand that one of the biggest trends, complementing that of CSR and sustainability, has been the emergence of ESG reporting (environmental, social and governance). This is most often a function that is led out of the governance, auditing and accounting space, but attempts to place the CSR and sustainability activities, alongside aspects of governance, within a measurable and reportable set of data. We will give more insight into this below.

FIGURE 4.2 Negative and positive behaviours

| NEGATIVE | REPUTATION/EFFECT | POSITIVE |

Negative	Positive
We take a long time to pay suppliers: People get frustrated by our policies	**We pay our suppliers on time:** People see us as great to work with
We lack transparency in our accounting: Investors worry about our probity	**We have strong, visible audit practices:** Investors are confident
We have a passive board who easily sign off our policies and practices: Stakeholders have little confidence in governance	**We have a diverse board who question policies and practices:** Stakeholders have confidence in governance

Other aspects of the running of a business that fall into this space can either be an opportunity, illustrating a positive story and reflection of a purpose-driven business, or a negative if behaviours and practices are different.

These simple examples of how policies or behaviours in this space can either be a positive illustration of how the business operates or a negative, are shown in Figure 4.2.

Good and bad: one can easily see how the negative behaviours on seemingly routine, behind the scenes activities can create reputational risk for a business. This could be illustrated by a host of case studies of where untold damage and in some cases a business collapse has occurred. However, if one takes the positive illustrations, these can be enormously powerful in communications to key audiences such as investors, public contractors, governments etc, who are looking for good finance and governance when making decisions about contracting, finance or even legislation. They offer opportunities for the business to tell a true and good story, bolstering reputation and potentially creating a positive effect in the marketplace.

ESG is a key component of this space that is worth referencing in more detail because it is the process through which much activity is assessed but also because it is where, increasingly, public relations and public affairs key interests, particularly those of investors, require good communication of the results.

ESG is made up of non-financial indicators, such as carbon reduction, governance and pay policies etc, which are, by today's societal expectation, necessary to give assuredness that a business is alive to issues which could, if not handled intelligently, jeopardize the long-term success of the business. Given the significance of this and the rising importance now given to it by the investor community, we communicators should be thinking about how best to take this information and actively promote it to the key audiences in much more creative ways than simply printing it in the back of an annual set of accounts. It may not appear at first glance as exciting as the latest online influencer campaign or TV advertisement, but it's arguably much more important in making sure the business has a long-term future.

ESG is therefore accepted by many as the more tangible basis through which an assessment can be made of how a business that purports to be acting responsibly, actually measures its activities. A simple way to think of this is that if one sees CSR-type initiatives illustrating some of the practical ways in which a business is behaving, and positively influencing key stakeholders (employees, local community, market suppliers, environmentalists), then ESG measuring, management and reporting is critical, as it can share its efforts with wider stakeholders, normally on an annual basis. It is an effort, developed mostly over the last 20 years in particular, to present an accurate and auditable assessment of how the business is treating its employees, responds to environmental issues, manages its engagement with supply chains, and its general trust issues.

Although sustainability and CSR activities (of which we talk more later) have been part of many companies' reporting for some years, the challenge has been that such activities have more often been disconnected from the core strategy of the business and the subsequent influence. Many companies took a somewhat sporadic approach launching various ad-hoc programmes to either enhance their credentials in this space as a result of societal expectations, or to comply with new legislation. Such activities reflected an attitude of something external being applied to the business as an add-on, rather than treating the overall agenda as something with a direct impact on the business. As communicators, we have been complicit by effect of not recognizing the value of such activities to building value with audiences. To be effective we need to be able to advise businesses of where they have assets worthy of telling their story.

ESG is used increasingly by investment markets to assess the overarching management of a business and good corporate governance, as the means to inform the likely future financial performance and their own investment decisions.

So, let's just get some further insight here. BlackRock CEO Larry Fink is now famous for his annual letters; in his last three he has made significant statements concerning the need for purpose beyond simply money and believes that climate change now requires a new paradigm between business and finance and their operational sustainability. He is quoted as saying we are at 'the edge of a fundamental reshaping of finance' and that he and BlackRock have committed to placing sustainability at the centre of their investment policies (Meredith, 2020). This has had a knock-on effect with other previous (let's call them) *conventional investors* now looking carefully at ESG indicators, not least because they in turn are finding their own clients, pension funds etc are demanding a more 'ethical' approach. As Fink also says, 'Without a sense of purpose, no company, either public or private, can achieve its full potential. It will ultimately lose the licence to operate from key stakeholders' (Pederson, 2018).

Put simply, the message now is that if you don't demonstrate a purpose, practical and ethical, you are at risk of losing your investors.

This shift has meant that increasingly we are seeing companies having to force these functional areas together, to join up communication and thinking in a way which hasn't been necessary or indeed easy in the past. Specifically, this is where investor relations are now having to be built on both finance and sustainability reporting, fused in a way which gives a unified and convincing illustration of overall corporate intent, as well as operational reporting of the present.

John has been known, when talking publicly, to stand on a stage and lambast his audience. He likes to think he does so in a way that is not too hurtful (normally he survives) but one such statement he makes when asked to speak at conferences goes as follows.

To an audience of sustainability directors:

> The problem with you sustainability directors is that you go to sustainability conferences to talk about sustainability to other sustainability directors – instead, go to a marketing conference to talk to marketeers about sustainability – you both might learn something.

You guessed it, when at marketing conferences he says:

> The problem with you marketing directors is that you go to marketing conferences to talk about marketing to other marketing directors – instead, go to a sustainability conference to talk to sustainability directors about marketing – you both might learn something.

So, the critical thing here is to help people in the silos of corporates to break out and see each other's worth. We, the communicators, have the ability to create the connection, see the value in the credentials and then craft the

FIGURE 4.3 Internal and external values

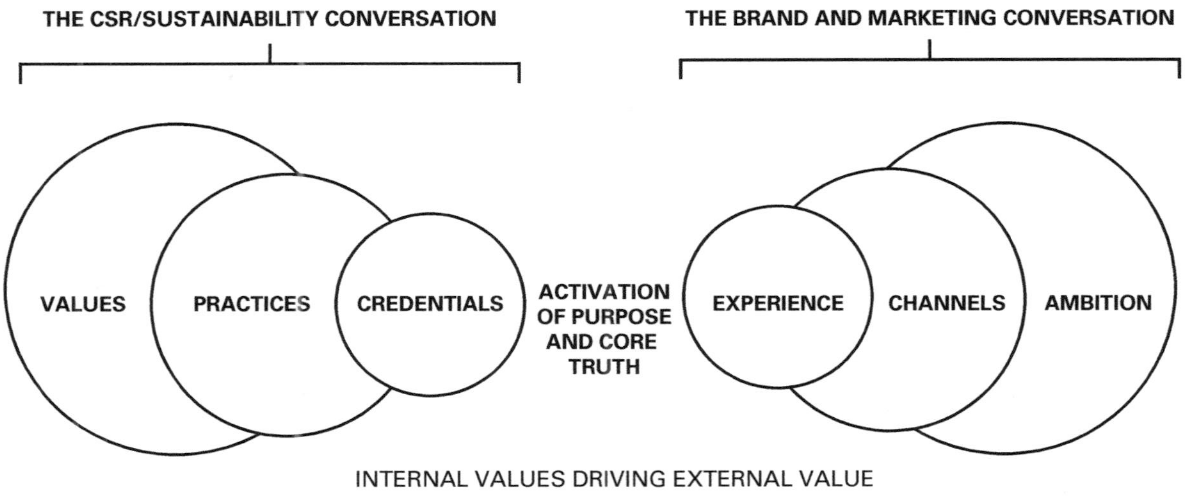

THE CSR/SUSTAINABILITY CONVERSATION

THE BRAND AND MARKETING CONVERSATION

VALUES

PRACTICES

CREDENTIALS

ACTIVATION
OF PURPOSE
AND CORE
TRUTH

EXPERIENCE

CHANNELS

AMBITION

INTERNAL VALUES DRIVING EXTERNAL VALUE

story. When we do, then for goodness' sake, let's apply the same degree of creativity to the ESG credentials as we do to the latest product advert. We know of agencies that exist almost entirely on churning out, year after year, sustainability and CSR reports that may be worthy but are incredibly dull. Put aside for a moment whether half of them would actually stand up to scrutiny in respect of real, scalable impact; they are so uninspiring that many simply will never get read other than by other 'sustainability directors'.

In our view they therefore fail on so many counts from a communications perspective that we should be collectively ashamed, simply because they don't reach the audiences who should be interested in them. But if we accept Fink's analysis as being correct, that capital investments will now be seeking demonstrable evidence of sustainable business activity, then investors will need new information to appreciate the implications of ESG-type activity and this means that businesses will need much better ways of communicating this to them. Equally, such reporting can be useful and quantifiable information to support communications across all stakeholders.

When talking with clients we often use Figure 4.3. It illustrates what each 'side' of the conversation brings to the table and how bringing them together can activate *purpose*.

The diagram shows that the CSR/sustainability side is where values are created and demonstrated, where they turn themselves into behaviours and practices which in turn form the truthful credentials of the business. On the other hand, marketing holds the ambition of the business, understands the channels and audiences through which this ambition will be recognized, and creates and reflects the customer experience. By fusing these together, you create the spark for successful activation.

Of course, much of the impact being measured through ESG is at the core of how products are produced, or services delivered. This will bring us nicely on to our next quadrant, but before we do, it's worthwhile just talking about *Corporate Philanthropy*.

It's good to give, but is it Purpose? We have placed this in this quadrant for the clear reason that it is most often seen in the form of straightforward financial donations. Of course, it can also manifest itself in gifts in kind, such as products being given to local charities, or pro-bono professional advice. Often, we see what is in essence philanthropy being described as purpose. This is wrong. Philanthropy can be part and parcel of how a business illustrates its purpose, how it supports its positive impact and interaction in the world, but by way of example, making a donation to a mental health charity is not the purpose of a car manufacturer. There is nothing wrong with this as an act, worthy as it is, but it is simply the misunderstanding of how it supports a company's purpose.

Many businesses will feel they wish to support causes and issues in society that are part of responding to wider societal need or the expectation of being a good citizen. They may or may not wish to take a high brand position, or indeed see particular gain coming back in coverage etc, over and above the belief that it is the 'right thing to do'. Equally, some businesses may wish to become very closely involved with a cause, perhaps encouraging employees to also embrace it, but others may simply wish to write a cheque. We always advocate, where possible, that philanthropic giving is aligned to corporate purpose as part of an integrated strategy, but emergency appeals etc may mean this is not always the case. So long as stakeholders appreciate why this is happening and it doesn't appear to be a cynical jumping on a bandwagon, it shouldn't negatively affect the business or brand. There is no reason why it should not happen, but communicators must understand why it is done and how it fits.

The critical thing to bear in mind, therefore, is that in this quadrant there are two types of activities that are relevant to communicating and marketing the organization. The first is that if there are practices in this space which don't conform to legislative expectations around governance, accounting, due diligence etc, or don't comply with societal/stakeholder expectations on ethics, transparency etc, this could potentially be where reputational issues emerge. Then your job will be all the harder.

The second aspect is somewhat like the Positive/Negative diagram shown in Figure 4.2, because on the other hand, if activities here are very purposeful, perhaps exceeding legislative expectations and illustrative of the values and qualities held across the business, then they can be market-defining positive news stories. They can help illustrate good management and a great corporate culture. Why would you not therefore find appropriate channels to highlight such 'good news' and build further positive reputational collateral? It will also show those who work in this section of the business that their efforts are just as appreciated, helping them recognize the type of behaviours that are the type to be celebrated as being 'on purpose'.

Production and services

You don't have a business unless you either produce something or provide a service. You probably won't have a business for the longer term unless your products and services evolve. Often, of course, such evolution in what you produce is shaped by external forces, either legislation on ingredients, market factors demanding a new type of service delivery, a technological development, or cultural activity. These forces have sparked innovation in business which manifests itself in everything from the growth of vegan ready meals to entire business sectors such as renewables or phone apps.

It should therefore be no surprise that purpose, in the form of either changing consumer demands or indeed sustainability-driven issues, can be seen to create uncertainty around products and services, yet at the same time drive extraordinary innovation. Such innovation will not only allow business to be ahead of the curve in meeting customer demands, it can create new markets or grow market share. We know that today's conscious consumers are motivated to purchase more purposeful products. Equally, in the business-to-business market, clients seek products and services which bring innovation to them and or meet their own ethical credentials in a way which strengthens their own supply chain, customer offer or reputation. These will be the very products and services you might be called upon to promote, so understanding that and delivering campaigns and messaging that reflects that understanding is critical, if we as marketeers are going to do our job well and our clients proud.

Across this whole section, the way in which products are created and then communicated creates the most powerful expression of the corporate truth. The production values, as well as where components are sourced, how research and development is invested in and why, are critical parts of the company credentials that should fuel marketing opportunities.

Interbrand's Manfredi Ricca was clear when it came to how the expression of a corporate truth, via its brand, needed to be reimagined. He told us:

> While traditionally brand strategy was meant to create differentiation around an existing business model and structure, today's fastest-growing companies show that business models and structures are built to make brands constantly relevant. That relevance must be around a brand truth – they no longer create a promise around capabilities, but build capabilities around an overarching promise. This means that in an increasing number of cases the brand acts as a central organizational principle – the 'truth' that brings everything together.

Let us imagine then, a couple of scenarios that could illustrate this. What if you were a major soap manufacturer who was aware that in sub-Saharan Africa, your bars of soap are used for traditional clothes cleaning, almost always by women and often where water has to be carried some distance either by them or their children. As a business driven by a sustainability-oriented purpose, you start to consider how you might alleviate the burden of carrying water, etc by reducing the amount of water needed to use the soap efficiently.

This would not only reduce the labour required to fetch water, but would use less water, better in all regards. The only slight issue is that the traditional way in which women consider that the clothes are getting clean is by the amount of soap suds that are created. So, what is required and what leads to product innovation, is a new formula of soap, which creates the same amount of soap suds but uses less water to do so. This of course proves popular because women quickly see that the effort of carrying water, etc is reduced but that the soap does the same job, thereby being more efficient. Of course, the added bonus to the business is that it becomes the soap of choice over the rivals because of that efficiency. This is a great example where firstly, the company looks at knowing and understanding the circumstances that surround their products and the people using them, but then sees how their sustainable perspective, their core purpose, can create a win-win situation. Not surprisingly perhaps, that company is Unilever, whose purpose is to 'make sustainable living commonplace' (Unilever, 2020). Innovation around purpose can of course drive an entire business in its formation or development.

We have placed sustainability in this quadrant as it is most often where innovation as well as traditional environmental impacts are of greatest influence. In the knowledge that many of us talk of sustainability but may not necessarily understand what it means, it is worth getting it clear in your mind. Sustainability is meeting the needs of the present without compromising the ability of future generations to meet their own needs. Its application is across three key areas, namely, economic, environmental, and social, linking what are often known as the three 'P's: Profitability, Planet and People.

Businesses with sustainability as a key influencer, rather than a peripheral initiative, frame their decisions in the longer term. They will set themselves goals, perhaps around such things as emissions, or alternative energy, waste reduction, people retention and diversity, all of which they will publish progress against and consider as important as reporting their financial performance.

Ultimately, sustainability thinking is not only a way of maintaining the innovation and evolution of products, it is a way of positioning the business for the longer term, as it is anticipating the demands of its audiences and customers in an ever-changing world, whilst at the same time helping educate people as to the best solutions for those needs. This therefore reiterates the fact that the least likely channel for that to be effective will be the traditional annual sustainability report. Rather than a sustainability director commissioning a report, it should be the marketing and communications professionals recognizing the opportunities afforded by such content and then using new creative ways of getting the credentials out. The days of the sustainability report being the only place where a business's sustainability message is presented have gone; such messaging should be up front and central across all platforms.

Human resources

Marcoms and HR may seem some distance apart, but not only are we increasingly engaged on internal employee communication and engagements strategies, we find an increasing appreciation of the significance of the HR function to affect external brand reputation.

Let us take this back to basics. Having a purpose-centric corporate culture is no longer a matter of choice. Today's people and the generation fast coming into employability consider the nature of an organization's purpose credentials as much as they consider salary or other benefits. It is now an expectation that if they are going to spend their time working for a business, that business will be a brand that stands for something they will feel is aligned to what they care about and in turn cares about them.

Purpose-driven companies most often make a very conscious effort to build a strong awareness in their staff of their purpose. It is often why people are attracted to work for them. As was found in the 2016 LinkedIn 'Purpose at Work' global report, 74 per cent were satisfied with their jobs if they felt their work was meaningful to themselves, the company and the community.

Such effort builds strong cultures and creates unique brands that are embodied by the way employees feel. Such companies experience significant benefits, from attracting the best talent, having well-motivated employees willing to go that little bit extra, through to creating a network of former employees who speak well and can even create new market opportunities. Part of being able to do this is a strong purpose story that creates a unified understanding of why they do what they do, but most importantly it's the contribution of each employee to achieving this.

Now, regardless of what you may think about Facebook, there was an interesting illustration of this that formed part of a speech by its founder

Mark Zuckerberg. He was delivering the commencement address at Harvard University in 2017, invoking the words of President John F Kennedy, who recalled a visit to NASA in the 1960s. It is said that Kennedy saw a janitor carrying a broom and asked him what he was doing. The janitor responded immediately by saying, 'Mr. President, I'm helping put a man on the moon'. Zuckerberg went on to say, as clearly as we possibly could, so we might as well quote him: 'Purpose is that sense that we are part of something bigger than ourselves, that we are needed, that we have something better ahead to work for' (Zuckerberg, 2017).

In this story, you can sense the fact that although this janitor might have featured as low on the organizational chart as anyone could possibly have, his pride was no less than that of the person at the top. Quite rightly. As an aside, part of the challenge we now face with outsourced, night-time office cleaning, is that we never really realize that there are people behind our daily workplaces, who we never see but without whom our jobs would be severely affected. Unfortunately, in such a model it's unlikely there is any great sense of pride or association with the businesses they are looking after.

So yes, of course, pride and satisfaction in our work is something we all want. It wasn't always the case of course, as in previous times, work was mainly regarded simply as a means to earn money with which to be free from poverty, to achieve a certain quality of lifestyle. However, nowadays in the West, we have both a higher standard of living and welfare which reduces that interdependency, and a much more widely held view that work should be a positive part of life's fulfilment, not just the means to support fulfilment elsewhere.

When people are considering an organization, the corporate purpose, if truly active, will manifest itself in its HR policies, its diversity, its CSR-related activities in this space, and will reflect a human approach. When you are looking to support a business in promoting itself, a key audience is therefore all its employees.

Firstly, they are a critical litmus test for whether true purpose is embedded within the business. Everyone can appreciate that in theory, every employee is a potential whistle-blower and through the power of a mobile phone and social media has access and capability to post either anonymously, or perhaps as an attributable source. Many major corporate scandals have emerged through employees shining a light on hypocritical practices or sharing personal experiences. It is this type of activity which, rather like in finance and accounting, can either be a weak spot for an inauthentic business, or incredibly powerful if employees are passionate advocates for their business and in effect ambassadors for the brand.

The mistake some companies make is that they focus all their communications and marketing activities on external strategies, often involving expensive advertising campaigns, or advocacy with key stakeholders such as legislators or investors. What can often be relegated is effort into quality internal communications that make employees feel connected to the corporate messaging and understand their role in turning the purposeful aspiration into a market-defining reality. Let's face it, if a company is not inspiring its people to be passionate advocates for the business and its products or services, it is definitely missing a trick. What is fascinating is that the research indicates that customers trust employees to speak more truthfully than a company's adverts and messaging, senior representatives (CEO) or PR department (Arruda, 2013). So, people trust what employees of an Amazon warehouse say about their workplace far more than if Jeff Bezos was to say it. Perhaps that is why Amazon TV adverts do exactly that, but it is equally important in face-to-face customer and employee interaction.

This means that rather than paid influencers and expensive TV actors, the most effective brand ambassadors are more likely to be 'normal' employees, but they do need to be individuals who are thoroughly engaged, have the necessary facts and understanding of what the key messages are, and are sufficiently enthusiastic for the business. Given that this makes good sense, how do you as the communications expert help businesses invest in this employee-oriented brand representation?

- **Think human** (again). It's personal: employees are individuals, just like your customers. So, think of them as such. Let them explain things in their own words. Don't give them a corporate script to recite, simply give them the facts and qualities and let them tell their own story about it.

- **Think purpose.** Can you imagine walking into a shop where the person serving was genuinely focused on making you feel happy rather than simply trying to sell you something? As we state elsewhere, empower employees to understand how their role is the active amplification of the human business purpose.

- **Forget hierarchy.** Even if the employees are not technically in a leadership role, they have an important role to play in the way the customer feels about the business. Their voice may for a variety of reasons seem more authentic than your own or that of their 'boss'. Don't let 'rank' get in the way of good communication.

- **Equip and empower.** Simply ensure they have the necessary facts and information to know their message and then let them go.

We will talk about corporate culture further on, but as a marketing communications professional, what do you need to be familiar with in this quadrant as other sources of good stories?

Firstly, we have obvious practices in this space that are critical indicators as to whether the business is aligned with societal expectations. The type of issues that rest here include diversity generally, gender-related management and pay issues, welfare policies, and CSR programmes that engage employees in activities as part of a collective employer-led initiative.

As we help companies communicate the positive aspects of their workplace, we should also be alert to the fact that some may try to falsely create what might be a purpose proposition, for either employees internally or prospects through a recruitment positioning, which simply doesn't stand up to scrutiny. Like any other 'product' or message from a client, we need to be sure for ourselves that we are creating messaging that is authentic and true.

The pressure that may emerge here is that few business leaders would argue employees' workplace experience doesn't matter to their success. We live in a world where companies, like everything else, can be judged and ranked on no end of different websites or forums or indeed formal indices where employees get the chance to 'judge' their workplace. Take a look at just one of the most well-known rankings for employers, *Fortune*'s '100 Best Companies to Work For', which assesses input from over 230,000 anonymous employee surveys every year, in order to compile lists of companies that provide the best working experience. If you feature highly on these then it directly affects your ability to attract the next wave of new talent. If you are managing employee engagement communications for a business, you'd better be fully appreciative of the significance of how employee opinions are inherently linked to the experience and in turn an experience led by a sense or otherwise of the company purpose.

It is not the point of this book to go into great detail about how you build purposeful workplaces, but the insights that are part of this are what effective marketeers should be looking for. These include:

- Does the company provide purposeful work for all, which is fairly remunerated and complies with what would be the standards expected of stakeholders? If the workforce is going to be an example of the business's core purpose, then their working conditions and levels of satisfaction are extremely important. We all know of major companies that have promoted one set of values through their communications but then have been found out for not having such values applied to all their employees.

This is why, as marketeers, it is worth looking behind the brief, exploring the essence of what it is like to work for the client. If you are going to have a good assessment of risk for a client, then look at their policies and see if they ring true. For example, it's one thing for a company to say they value diversity, but if whenever you go to a meeting, everyone you meet in the business is a middle-aged white male, you have to question how far such a statement is effective in their recruitment policies.

(We must state here that we are not picking on middle-aged white males – obviously we fall into that category. In fact, we also feel that diversity is not always about the most obvious aspects of visual identity but should embrace aspects of upbringing and other experiences, cognitive diversity etc; the above was utilized purely to illustrate the point.)

- Consistent communications are what we would expect as part of our work, so is the business conforming to this internally? In the purposeful age, business leaders must be confident and assured as effective communicators internally, in order to ensure their employees are clear on the purpose and values of a business. This is as important for employee communications as it is for external communications. We have already identified that everyone with a mobile phone is now a potential whistleblower, so if the messages internally don't match those externally you will be found out very quickly.

- Finally, in the same way we have placed Philanthropy and ESG in Finance and Accounting, and Sustainability in Production and Services, we put CSR in HR for purely representative reasons. We have also explained its part in the evolutionary path towards Purpose in Chapter 3, so here we are simply alerting you, the marketeer, that as an asset of initiatives, many will rest here, as they either affect employees or utilize employee engagement to affect external stakeholders such as local communities.

This can be important for understanding the stories behind a client, as CSR can happen on a number of different levels and of course can be both local and global. Effectively there is a CSR footprint which should reflect the size, scale and reach of the business. CSR programmes remain an important area for providing practical illustrations of how a purpose is lived, so find out what is going on and see if the stories, hopefully good ones, are getting out to their audiences.

At this point we have another term it will be helpful to understand in the context of all the others with which it is often used, exchanged with and abused, and that is corporate citizenship. It will be appreciated that the invention of corporations made such an impact because in a legal sense they became an accountable body, can own property and assets, and can be held accountable legally if they do something wrong, in the same way as a person is. Corporations can and in many ways should be viewed as living entities with 'rights'. With such rights, therefore, come responsibilities; a sense that corporations have obligations to society as a whole, not just to investors, but also to employees and customers, as we have discussed elsewhere.

However, the inter-relationship of these various terms is probably best understood as an overarching sense of responsibility, whilst a company's activities, be they employee practices, CSR initiatives, philanthropic donations or sustainability efforts, are how they deliver that responsibility. It is the equivalent of an individual demonstrating their desire to be a good citizen by volunteering, making charitable donations, recycling and treating their neighbours with respect.

When we asked Jim Moser of BBDO his view on how businesses he worked with saw the significance of CSR, ethics and sustainability, he was pretty clear: 'I think it fundamentally comes down to a commercial imperative. If ethical behaviour and sustainable behaviour can result in a better commercial outcome, most companies will embrace it.' This in isolation perhaps doesn't reflect the significance placed by external stakeholders on such activity, as part of the general societal 'licence to operate', but we take Moser's final comment to really focus on the critical point here:

> The great thing is that a company's or brand's behaviour is increasingly under the microscope – customers and consumers are watching how a company behaves. If their behaviour is consistent with their own values, they will do business with them. If not, they will choose another company. And as corporate and brand behaviour is more and more transparent, ethical and sustainable behaviour starts to become more important for a better commercial outcome. This in turn can be used in marketing and communications to secure an existing customer/consumer base and appeal to new customers/consumers.

Summary

'More than you can shake a stick at' is how David's grandmother would have described the information in this chapter, being almost a book unto itself but hopefully is information that is useful. We are covering a lot of ground here without omitting important details because it's crucial to understand where purpose fits in a company or a brand if any communications or marketing activity is to fully succeed.

Let us recap. Marketing (and communications more broadly) is no longer a one-way street, with organizations shouting through a megaphone at a crowd of random people; it is a conversation among people, which can be powerful, even transformative but requires new ways of thinking and acting. Fundamentally, the way you talk inside an organization about your purpose needs to match the way to speak on the outside, too.

Purpose sits at the very centre of the organization, not as a campaign or strapline that shifts with sales cycles or seasons. Our handy diagram (Figure 4.1) shows it literally at the heart of the company's culture, strategy, values and leadership, driving all activity across the four general functional areas of any business: finance/accounting, human resources, services/production, and of course communications and marketing. We mapped the connection of purpose with typical activities ranging from audit and risk management, to supplier relations and employee safety, underscoring the fact that it informs *all* activity, not just that associated with marketing and communications. And we have taken time to define a few terms that are frequently confused with purpose, such as corporate social responsibility, philanthropy and ESG, but which can be the sources of the stories we use to communicate and activate the purpose of the business, internally and externally.

We examined seven principles for building trust – essential for any purpose-driven business – including quality, messaging, values, humanity, responsibility and truth. Similarly, we advocated the power of putting employees at the centre of communications, or at least giving them as much consideration as paid influencers or celebrity endorsers, when it comes to marketing activity.

And finally, we warned against the temptation to create a purpose proposition that simply can't hold up to scrutiny by any of your stakeholders – investors, suppliers, regulators, customers and employees. It's far better to work towards authentic purpose and acknowledge any gaps to cover than try to fake or fudge it. And as a final plea to ensure that purpose is credible, authentic and will survive, it must not fail as CSR did.

John is adamant that purpose must never be owned by a specialist team, or be seen as the responsibility of any individual role. In his words, 'It must never become an occupation of the few; it must always be the preoccupation of the many.'

Our next chapter delves into that part of our business map which covers leadership, culture, values and strategy; it is the 'way' of purposeful business and where you as an individual have the greatest opportunity to influence. However, before you move on, set some time aside to think through the following checklist of your understanding of where your truth and purpose rest within the business. This is a short list but a time-consuming one.

YOUR CHECKLIST

1 Review the four business segments and draw up a list of demonstrable purpose practices.
2 Consider any negative behaviours that can affect your reputation and plan to alter them.
3 Identify people from different specialisms who can support the agenda with their expertise

---

References

Arruda, W (2013) Three steps for transforming employees into brand ambassadors, *Forbes Magazine*, 8 October, https://www.forbes.com/sites/williamarruda/2013/10/08/three-steps-for-transforming-employees-into-brand-ambassadors/ (archived at https://perma.cc/A4X4-SPU7)

LinkedIn (2016) Purpose at Work: The largest global study on the role of purpose in the workforce, https://business.linkedin.com/content/dam/me/business/en-us/talent-solutions/resources/pdfs/purpose-at-work-global-report.pdf (archived at https://perma.cc/YWU3-K9ZG)

Meredith, S (2020) BlackRock CEO says the climate crisis is about to trigger 'a fundamental reshaping of finance', *CNBC: Markets*, 14 January, https://www.cnbc.com/2020/01/14/blackrock-ceo-larry-fink-says-climate-change-will-soon-reshape-markets.html (archived at https://perma.cc/6Z6M-6F72)

Pederson, R S (2018) BlackRock CEO Larry Fink letter: words or action? *Sustainia World* 08: Market Strategy, 24 September, https://sustainiaworld.com/blackrock-ceo-larry-fink-letter-to-ceos-words-or-action/ (archived at https://perma.cc/9SSA-UA3C)

Unilever (2020) Sustainable Living, https://www.unilever.co.uk/sustainable-living/ (archived at https://perma.cc/V3KC-FAL4)

Weinberger, D (2000) *The Cluetrain Manifesto*, New York: Basic Books

Zuckerberg, M (2017) Harvard Commencement Address, 27 May, Harvard University

05

The way: how your culture is key

In the previous chapter, we saw that in addition to the main quadrants of any business, there sit at the heart four core attributes that are highly influential in how it is perceived, inside and out. They hold such an important position because they reflect the way in which the business is operated and how a human, truthful purpose manifests itself tangibly and empowers an authentic story to be told. These factors are values, behaviours, leadership and strategy, and in both our experience and as core components within the human truth model, they are the collective principles that constitute the 'way' a business operates. For ease of reminder see Figure 5.1.

This is how human truth lives in the business, how together they form a dynamic, unified engine, crucial for sustaining consistent success in a purposeful business. In this chapter we are going to explain how important this is, how these values constitute the *culture* of a business, the realization of the desired truth and how you can utilize the *way* in which it operates to power up your marketing and communications efforts. This chapter therefore takes you into the heart of the business, where the very beat, the pace, the life of the business and its human truth, should manifest itself and energize marketing, via authentic, verifiable truthful stories.

When we think of a business or brand, what do we really think of?

The answer to this will probably depend on the extent of our personal engagement with the brand, but we may think of a particular, definitive product, as we might with Apple and the iPhone. Or we might think of the ethos it evokes, as we do with Nike, or perhaps the person behind the brand, as we might with Richard Branson and Virgin. Or it might primarily be the

FIGURE 5.1 Corporate culture at the heart of the business

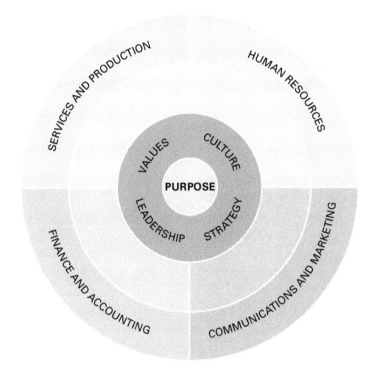

values set, such as with Patagonia. Often, what we think are embodiments of a brand in this way are actually the core aspects of the business that distinguish it from its competitors and as communicators are what we must nurture and protect. At the root of all this is that such aspects are driven by people and their representation of the brand. The critical awareness required here is that businesses are communities of people and people in a business are most affected by the four aspects we have placed in the centre of our model. These are the core elements which, when communicating human-based truth in business, inevitably affect both the message and its impact, for better or worse.

Whether you are part of a business or serving one as an agency advisor, just imagine how you yourself think of the business you are working with. As humans, we almost always judge an organization by how the people in it behave and how they in turn make us feel. We will assess the qualities displayed to us by its leaders, we will recognize what we like about our interaction with the colleagues there. We will appreciate what we see being celebrated in the business and what is frowned upon. As a result, we form an opinion of what it is like to work for that business. These factors combine to create that most critical of business components: its culture. The renowned business guru Peter Drucker is often quoted as saying, 'Culture eats strategy for breakfast'. John often adds, 'Yes, but culture gets its appetite from purpose'.

Drucker's statement is a universally recognized truth that you can have the best plan, the most ambitious and inspiring strategy, but if the organizational culture isn't willing to embrace it, it will fail. John's witty addition also begs a question: what exactly is meant by 'appetite'? In John's mind what builds the cultural appetite to behave in a set way is how a clearly defined purpose, based on a human truth, shapes the values, behaviours, leadership and strategy to meld into the character of the business, namely the culture. This has a direct effect on how we market and communicate for the business.

But why are you bothering with this, you ask? Well, bluntly, the path of campaigns, marketing, PR, product launches, sponsorship and charity partnerships and social media is strewn with the corpses of well-intended, highly creative work, which has failed as a result of not fitting a corporate culture or being undermined by it.

The significance of the overarching culture, however positive or negative, must not be underestimated when it comes to being best equipped to market a business and its projects. As we analyse what corporate culture means in this new age, we will suggest the type of story and cultural collateral you should be looking for. Equally, should these core factors fail to meet the expected standards, you will be involved in either having to navigate the potential negativity or mitigate the resulting reputational damage as it almost certainly arises.

Corporate culture

There are of course entire books on corporate culture, how to build it and the principles by which leaders can focus their energy on creating, maintaining or repairing it. We do not intend to try to emulate those in range or detail here, because we are primarily involved in identifying what collateral and stories emerge from within corporate culture, as opposed to guiding you in crafting it. What we can do is define a generally accepted understanding of what we mean by it and provide the necessary pointers for communication needs. We consider how you can understand the future demands on corporate culture, whilst also quickly setting the context from its evolution as a recognized component of successful business.

In our definition of the words 'corporate culture' we hope you will recognize your own understanding, namely, 'The way in which a business manifests its beliefs and ideas and which affects how it does business and how its people behave'. You may find slightly amended or lengthier versions elsewhere, but this is a succinct and clear definition which in our minds illustrates key aspects.

1 **Beliefs and ideas**: what the people involved in the business generally think. This is a collective sense, the values and the ethics on which they are based.

2 **The way**: how it does business, How the leaders serve the business through their strategy and how its employees behave internally and externally.

We believe corporate culture can be illustrated through the combination of the four factors at the core of Figure 5.1. The first two are values and behaviours, which define how employees engage with others, either internally or externally. The second two, leadership and strategy, are how the business and its employees are directed, led, and in what direction and tone. This combination, when harmonious and based around an authentic human truth and purpose, will be reflected throughout all that a business does. It will be seen in its language, its dress code, the design of its offices and its systems, the 'style' of its material, its decisions on recruitment, response times, staff welfare, shareholder communications and community interests. This is why it creates an inner strength that can outshine any strategy that is contrary to its way of doing things.

This is the type of description that relates to those often-intangible things we know to be true but often seem hard to grasp, mainly because at the root of corporate culture are individual human behaviours. These, like all things human, are open to emotional and sometimes illogical influences. This doesn't of course make it a bad thing. It simply makes it far from formulaic or always predictable. In managing the communication and external presentation of the business, it is important to appreciate that the culture is never entirely fixed as one thing. For the reasons we cite above, the elements that foster the culture are inevitably in constant flux. They will evolve as the business experiences events, as people change, and as a direct result of the communication activity you yourself manage. This means that you not only need to understand the culture, you need to understand the way in which it is affected.

Like so many things in business management, the root of corporate culture as a recognized 'thing' starts in the 1960s and '70s, when the emergence of business degrees and courses at universities and colleges meant that there was a requirement to better define and if possible package up such an understanding of business, in order to teach it. It took 20 years, until the early 1980s, for the term to catch on and then the next decade for it to become the means through which people chose to assess and describe what they felt was the character of the company. So, people would describe a business as having an 'entrepreneurial culture', or as being 'money focused', or 'innovation obsessed', or even 'ruthless'. These were designed to encapsulate the complexity of businesses within short, convenient labels, often from which their leaders, CEOs, boards and others would shape their behaviours to fit the perceived expected character traits of that particular business.

This inevitably meant that storytellers, communicators like us, would end up championing the particular characteristics, building up stories, reflecting the character into or onto their CEOs, to feed media expectations and analyst reports. This in turn started to influence design, branding, marketing and partnership activities. This wasn't always good for the businesses or the individuals within them, particularly where such 'character traits' might have been deemed contrary to employee welfare, but this was a period where neither corporate nor societal expectations were near what they are today.

By the 1990s and 2000s we were seeing much greater influence on corporate culture coming from younger generations of employees and shifts in society generally, with changed expectations on how business should behave, including expectations for greater work–life balance from Gen X and strengthened by Millennials. Corporate culture is now no longer simply shaped by the founder or leadership. Of course, at the start of a business, they are still inevitably the most influential force, because they are recruiting employees and establishing practices and rituals that shape expectations. However, for longer-established businesses, culture is often held more by the many, rather than the few. Often it is the transient 'caretaker' CEO who must comply to an established culture embedded and guarded by people who have long worked at the business and will work there long after the CEO has moved on.

Corporate culture is now greatly influenced by the societies within which the business operates, national and international characteristics, geo-economic trends, technology, sector norms, legislation and much more besides. For globally operating multinationals, there are a multitude of influences that need appreciating, particularly if you are charged with communicating across cultures. Will the same visuals be successful in India, Saudi Arabia, the United States and Nigeria? Clearly that's unlikely, but beyond what an advert might look like, more importantly, if you have offices in each country, can you maintain a consistent set of values and behaviours that makes the business not only 'feel' as one, but also maintains the best employee and community care across all territories? This is a challenge that internal communications and human resources need to manage, and which is critical in ensuring the culture, the character which is portrayed in one region, is the same as that elsewhere.

Of course, culture has always been the result of a complex set of relationships, and as communicators it is our business to understand such relationships, so finding the insight to understand a corporate culture is key to our ability to express and communicate on behalf of the business successfully. Probably the most enlightening learning point at this stage is to understand that if culture eats strategy so completely, then you must see culture as a strategy in itself. Your approach to how you understand the culture, how to advise on its weaknesses and amplify its strengths, is a strategic imperative. If you understand that, then it's best to have greater understanding of its component parts and their relationship with your success in doing your job.

Not surprisingly, our research showed strong views on the significance of purpose within the workplace and on its culture. We focused on two aspects: the personal – asking respondents how important purpose was to their motivation and sense of commitment within the business – and secondly how from an organizational perspective they felt it affected productivity and engagement within the culture.

On the first question, we saw 82 per cent rate this highly, a clear indication and reflective of other research elsewhere which signifies how individuals feel more engaged when working within an organizational culture with strong purpose activity.

When asked what effect they thought an authentic purpose had on productivity, the overarching value and growth of the business, the results were also overwhelmingly in the positive. A very high 88 per cent of respondents believed it positively affected employee productivity and engagement within the culture of the business. Given the acceptance that it is the behaviours of employees that is the most powerful factor within internal culture and external perceptions, it is not at all surprising that with such high indicators, authentic aligned purpose is now seen as an imperative to achieve long-term success.

Such thinking was borne out across many of our individual conversations. One very active proponent of the significance of human-based truth and purpose in defining corporate culture is Paul Lindley, founder of the highly successful Ella's Kitchen in the UK, which makes organic baby and toddler food, and is sold in supermarkets internationally. Lindley's ethos was critical in his building the business:

> I believe that a company's culture is THE most vital part of delivering its business plan. It's vital to success, but it can't be imposed or directed, it needs to evolve with the people in the company because they want it to evolve; it sets the way the team do things to get the main thing done. And that's the key, they need to know what the main thing is. Not the main thing of their individual jobs, but the main thing of the company; the reason why they are all together in the first place.

Such clarity is a clarity of purpose which is integral within the way the business is led. As Lindley explains:

> Articulating, embedding and living the 'why this company exists' is critical to the right culture evolving, which is vital to success. Purpose is this 'why'. Purpose is why the company exists at all and, articulated in its mission statement is the thing that defines success for itself.

Lindley is a highly successful but also very passionate leader who embodies the sense that as a founder, it was his own sense of personal purpose which constituted that of the culture within the business. He is clear why the business exists:

> Ella's Kitchen's purpose has always been to improve kids' lives by developing healthy relationships with food. That purpose, clear to all, embedded in the recruitment process, development, goals, feedback, evaluation, promotion and rewards processes, means that Ella's Kitchen employs people with the mindsets, passions, beliefs and skills to deliver the mission.

As we saw in the previous chapter, this approach means that purpose not only permeates every part of the business, but it also acts as a common thread, running through the motivation, thinking and team spirit within the business. As Lindley explains:

> It means that they all know what it is, how they contribute to it and how they need to collaborate to deliver the mission. From that the unique, mission-led, 'feel right at home' culture that has propelled Ella's success was allowed to evolve and be embedded as a living consequence of a well-understood company purpose.

Values

Values are not just a list of finely polished statements, although sadly they have often become just that in some businesses. For values to mean anything, they need to be an authentic part of the business, capable of describing the culture in a much deeper way than some of the examples suggested above. Although it is important that serious thought goes into articulating the values, they only mean something if they manifest themselves as behaviours, which are the inherent balance required here. Values are often the 'talk', behaviours are the 'walk'. Both create for the communicator either solid foundations of great stories, or monumental risks, so your mastery of understanding them and what they represent is key.

In our experience, companies often approach creating a values set as a one-off requirement, where heavy investment is made, often with external advisors, who will undertake a cross-organizational consultation, develop a reporting matrix for assessment and then formulate an elegant set of words to encapsulate sensible, hopefully inspiring and undoubtedly worthy lists. BUT – and this is a big **BUT** – the sad reality is that often, once achieved, the attention then moves on, leaving the words to be stuck up on a poster or screensaver, squeezed onto a deeply hidden website and, to be frank, incapable of being remembered by individuals unless prompted. This can undermine and negate the very effort put in originally and become an illustration of the lack of authenticity that can often emerge behind such words. This, in turn, can create cynicism, a potentially corrosive element in any business.

Many years ago, David was presenting his agency's credentials to a group of prospective client executives in New York, pausing on the slide listing the values he had proudly helped to create a few months before. He got to the third item on the list – let's say, 'creativity' – when he was stopped cold by the brand director. 'You can move on,' she said, 'we've heard this from the other two agencies before you.' Point taken. Even if you do take values seriously, you can undermine their ability to actually resonate if they lack any individuality or simply reflect what every other company 'says' about itself. Fundamentally of course, regardless of what the actual words are, if they don't get reflected in behaviours, then they are meaningless.

Creating and living by strong values is not always easy; it can be hard work with hard choices, often at the expense of profit or sometimes involving increased costs. A business needs to appreciate this, as do suppliers, investors, owners, employees, all those involved. Sometimes of course a newly defined set of values can alienate as well as embrace, so they require careful management as they start to influence the next key factor, behaviours. It is through a company embedding its values into its behaviours that the bedrock of corporate culture is established.

Of course, for those who are working in businesses from a founder or family establishment, it will be clear that the values and culture they create are those of the leaders and owners. Although this may be more challenging within other types of business, leaders have successfully applied such thinking in their own corporate culture approach and it can be useful to understand how such founders think about their businesses, which in turn can act as indicators for your own activity. Lindley at Ella's Kitchen has a particular sense of what a business is in the first instance, which very much reflects what we believe is critical for success going forward. As Lindley explains:

> I believe that a business is nothing more than the sum of the people involved, be they investors, founders, team, suppliers or customers. Each relationship in the tangled web of carrying out any business is ultimately between people deciding upon what to do for the interests of the other people in their business.

The acknowledgement of this inter-relation within corporate behaviour is of course also applicable to external suppliers, investors or whoever, and Lindley has an interesting perspective on what the basis of a business should be seen as, as well as the role of the CEO:

> The etymology of the word 'company' is from the same genesis as 'companion', and my leadership philosophy is centred on understanding people and getting their motivations, behaviours and relationships right to deliver a vision of a purpose and make profits to sustain the delivery of that mission. I see that a CEO's leadership, therefore, is central to this web of relationships between people. It's key. I saw my leadership as founder and CEO of Ella's Kitchen, and more recently as Chair of numerous organizations, to be that of convenor of people with a stake in the business: the inspirer, listener, facilitator, thanker and the defender of the purpose, mission and values of the business(es).

Lindley's approach is not unusual in founders and is increasingly being sought as inspiration by those who find themselves suddenly in positions of leadership in listed businesses, devoid of either owner-based values or a strong ethical culture. It places a human truth at the core of why business exists and how it is lived. As Lindley continues:

> I have always sought to make the organizations within which I have had a leadership position be human-centred and people-focused, beginning with

my own humanity: my truths, strengths, communication skills, vulnerability, mistakes and beliefs. Hence I have always sought to bring my whole 'me' to my work, for without it human truth is not real, and therefore leadership is not authentic and so I believe the business itself will be less impactful. Business needs a human face, now more than ever.

So, if you believe as we do that such human truth-based values are important, then you have to guard against this potential cynicism, both internally and externally, by ensuring that whatever process you utilize to define the words, you have sufficient perspective to work on the words from both the point at where the business is now and where it aspires to be. If you think you are good or can be good at working in partnership, for example, then as the words are refined, you should be ensuring that such a collaborative ethos exists everywhere in the business. Or if you are going to champion equity of opportunity, then you'd better make sure there is no gender pay gap, or unconscious bias in your recruitment. If such problems are highlighted then you have no alternative than to put as much effort into a plan to rectify that difference, before the rhetoric outpaces the reality.

The critical step to bridge values and behaviours is that the values have to be believed by the people through whom they will be demonstrable as behaviours. We therefore come back to that unifying principle at the heart of this book, namely that for employees and the business leaders to behave in a way that reflects the values, they have to believe in them so they ring true in the business.

Behaviours

Our definition of behaviour is: 'The way that a person behaves in any particular situation or when influenced by events and circumstances.'

Behaviour makes values tangible. You can see them, measure them and in our approach, it is where we as communicators find rich examples of potential content which can highlight the corporate truth and purpose. When values manifest themselves as natural behaviours, authentically adopted, they become the 'way' of doing things, the rituals and expectations people have of the business. This is where the little things really can add up to something much larger and where reputation is built. Behaviours are critical of course because in today's world everything is exposed. One cannot say one thing and then behave in a different way, as you will be found out.

Alex Mahon is Chief Executive of the UK's unique TV broadcaster Channel 4. Her experience in TV and film production, with its close association with the advertising world, makes this very clear for her. In talking with us she explained that this was all about authenticity:

> I have seen a rise in the authenticity that consumers expect from content and from brands and that staff expect from employers. There has been since the rise in social media less and less space for a gap between perception and reality. Woe betide companies that seek to represent themselves in one way and actually comport themselves in another. The pandemic has accelerated the demand from consumers for truth, for transparency and for representation. Young people also want equitable power. Brands who can truly represent their consumer and are seen as aspirational will succeed in this environment.

At the core was the recognition of corporate behaviour as the basis of a company's reputation and how they present themselves. She added:

> For me, brands must represent themselves in a way that is utterly in line with their actual corporate behaviour – how they treat customers, staff, suppliers. Their values as a company must be in line with the ones they espouse in their advertising.

This sense of significance is something which needs both understanding and value being associated with it. Perhaps one doesn't need to go far beyond quoting Warren Buffett, the financial sage of Omaha who once wrote, 'We can afford to lose money, even a lot of money, but we can't afford to lose reputation, even a shred of reputation' (Holm and Das, 2014).

This illustrates how someone world famous for being able to assess value in businesses and investments valued reputation higher than money, and so should we all. It is of course an interesting, almost nebulous thing. It is entirely different to what a lot of us concentrate on, which is the building of the brand.

One truth we can all acknowledge is that judgement and decisions by individuals internally can either destroy corporate reputations or boost them beyond what might have been expected. Social media can jump onto the slightest of stories and amplify them across audience boundaries and geographies, to either bad or good effect. Equally, every employee, supplier or customer is the equivalent of a 'whistle-blower', who by the use of their phone can reward those businesses getting it right, or shame those who aren't.

That is where we, the marketing, ad and PR people, tend to create something that we broadcast out across various means in order to gain awareness and market advantage. Although obviously intrinsically linked, the best way to think of reputation is that rather than being created internally, it is actually created outside of the business, by the way in which people, our stakeholders and the general public and media, feel about the business. That feeling can perhaps be manipulated in the short term by some of the brand-building techniques some use as stock in trade, but reputation is only sustainable in the longer term if those outside the business experience the authentic behaviours which our communications suggest are the *way* of doing business. This is where we need more show than tell, more walk than talk.

This is where leadership plays a key role, as there can be no disconnect between the values of the leader and their behaviour, if a strong culture is to emerge. When we think of leaders and those who show leadership within the business, we tend perhaps to concentrate on those whose job titles reflect a hierarchy, but this of course is too narrow a perspective. So, what are we suggesting leadership entails here?

Leadership

In the first instance we define this very simply as 'the action of leading a set of people or an organization as a whole'.

But that is where the simplicity ends, particularly when we talk of how leaders affect the ability to communicate and of course what one is communicating. We shall come onto who, beyond the hierarchy, will be valuable leadership exemplars for you shortly, but first let us concentrate on the traditional start point.

Between us we have a couple of quips that illustrate aspects of our thinking on leadership, as well perhaps as our national morning drinks. Covering John's first, it very much reflects the hierarchical perspective of a leader who sits at the top table: 'Leaders are like teabags; you only know how strong they are when they find themselves in hot water.'

This often puts a smile on the face of an audience, not least because it is so self-explanatory, but within our context and in the light of so many societal expectations on businesses and their leaders, it becomes a critical component of your need to manage and help your leaders. When some sort of business challenge, corporate problem or societal issue emerges to dominate the agenda, ask yourselves, are your leaders capable of presenting themselves and the business in a coherent, confident and thought-out manner, reflective of the values and desired behaviours within the business? If you cannot answer YES instantly, then you have your work cut out, because as so often happens, and has done in the last 12 months on a variety of issues, external and internal audiences look to the hierarchy to respond and respond well.

It doesn't even need to be something that specifically affects the day-to-day operating of the business. Take for example the Black Lives Matter movement in 2020, which ignited passions, public outcry and a global expectation that every institution should be both accountable and engaged. Various CEOs stepped forward, mostly one hopes with sincere intent, and pledged their commitment to fairness and equity of rights. Several, however, were found to appear to be leading all-white leadership teams, had made political donations to those who blocked equal rights legislation, and had poor internal practices (more on this in the next chapter).

This absolutely undermined their ability to communicate from a strong moral foundation. Even if they could, their personal qualities came under severe scrutiny if they did not appear capable of speaking with authentic honesty, empathy and an expression of the values and human truth in a way which ensured credible acceptance rather than cynical rejection. This should be a major question for you. Managing all forms of representative communication, can they cope with uncertainty and or contrasting demands across such potential agendas? Because this is the key point here; whether they like it or not, be it the Chair, CEO, CMO or other leader in the business, part of their job is being strong in what might appear to be hot water, not just for themselves but for those around them. That is where your ability to understand the external factors that require addressing can be supplemented by a keen understanding and knowledge of demonstrable behaviours that can support the leader's position on whatever the case may be.

Of course, we cite above the example of an external national and international concern which demanded a reaction to something that in many cases one would hope the business was not knowingly or specifically condoning. Most challenges of this kind are more likely to be where something in the business has failed to meet expectations, so it may be the exposure of a poor service record, inappropriate behaviour or another internal 'scandal'. The demand is the same. How the leaders respond should not only reflect the aspirational culture but will inevitably set the tone. The counterpoint to the emphasis on the hierarchical leader is David's national drink quip…

David will say that there are two types of leadership influences on corporate culture, rather like making his coffee: 'There is the cafetière, where leaders push down from high to force certain behaviours, and the alternative is the percolator approach, where leadership behaviours bubble up from the mass below to create the culture.'

We believe the stronger cup of coffee is usually created by percolation and this rings true with encouraging a stronger culture. So, in respect of this, positive behaviours which represent desired values need to be recognized and rewarded, replicated and encouraged, talked about and reported. These are where the story of the store manager who goes the extra mile in response to a local need, strengthens the external reputation, often in a way that a CEO simply cannot do. Highlighting such great effort, from wherever it emerges in the business, needs to be encouraged to percolate. Such leadership is not hierarchical, but it is where you may get great illustrative stories, better able to illustrate your values and culture than possibly those coming from on high.

Strategy

This means quite simply that in your desire, indeed professional need, to better understand culture, you need to know how to manage and mine the necessary means through which you can best reflect it. This is your cultural strategy.

If you are to successfully deploy a communications strategy with culture at its core, then it is vital that you assess how your *truth* and *purpose* directly relate to each of your key stakeholder groups. If you are clear on this and are successful in the means through which you communicate it, then people will take it upon themselves to value the relationship they have with the business. It will attract people with a like-minded value set, build loyalty and encourage people involved in the business – employees, suppliers, investors – to feel a part of something much bigger.

Imagine yourself in each of the stakeholder groups. How does the way in which you are communicating feel? Does it give people the belief that they are working with a culture where values are real, not just words, where behaviours are illustrative of the truth behind the business, and leaders are as committed themselves as those they are talking to? You as the communicators are at the forefront of the culture as your activities both bolster and encourage, amplify and express. This is where your leadership is personally of vital importance as well.

Hierarchical leaders clearly have the power and influence to make things happen. They can create policies, craft an overarching business strategy, hold the necessary meetings and consultations, set targets and organize their teams in order to drive the business forward. However, these do not necessarily either create the human-centric culture or inspire others within that culture. This is where, as communicators, you need to be able to identify how exactly the leadership of the business is moving the organization in its performance against the values and desired behaviours. Working with other senior colleagues, across functions such as HR and finance, due simply to the significant influence of these on the people and business policies generally, you will need to have your own strategy to assess what is influencing such internal audiences.

So, what sort of strategy are we contemplating here? Firstly, the approach we showed you in the previous chapter illustrates 'strategy' as meaning the overall business strategy. It goes almost without saying that for a truth-based marketing and communications plan to succeed, it has to be representing and telling the story of a truthful business. Otherwise, quite obviously, it isn't true. All the corporate scandals we have listed, or the mildly less destructive wrong-footed and embarrassing campaigns, have failed because in essence they don't reflect the reality of the strategy or the way in which the business is operating. However, as we have laboured elsewhere, the use of strategy in this chapter is to reflect upon the communications strategy and how that both influences and reflects the business and what it wants to communicate, and how leadership, values and behaviour are intrinsically linked to its success.

Once upon a time, our role as marketeers and communications professionals could best be described as either creating a myth or a desire or countering a negative truth or reality. We would set a course either to show that our business had the best way to fulfil that desire, or that our business was doing the best anyone could to mitigate a negative reality. Our problem with that is that even by just writing or reading it, it seems almost to suggest something manipulative, something false, even perhaps deceitful. That isn't the *way* the world wants to see businesses operating now. One needs to appreciate at all times that even if you are marketing across an entire customer base, or even society at large, you are talking to every single person individually, you are engaging them as human beings, and each of those individuals deserves the respect we would afford ourselves – truthful information with which to make informed decisions.

Therefore, what we are actually seeking, as justification of us believing in the value of what we do, is to use our very best skills, creativity and understanding to share a human truth. This will undoubtedly be a need in the world, and so we invite the audience to look at how we believe we can best fulfil that need. This is not just in the qualities of the product or service, but in the qualities of the company. It is on this basis that we build a fairer and more just society as well as value in its various forms for all stakeholders. The strategy here of unifying the cultural touchpoints to provide engaging stories will offer a logical and practical way in which people, as employees, suppliers, customers or investors, can assess the business and in turn commit to playing their part in the overarching direction of the business, even if that is just a purchasing decision.

We in the business of crafting communication solutions need to be capable of ensuring that there is a strategy to contend with these issues. More than anything, this need reflects the fact that the promotion of a human-centric purpose within business is a leadership imperative and cultural must. If we ask ourselves why businesses and their leaders get it wrong, we believe it is because they don't really understand why it is so important and don't therefore develop the personal skills to manage it, or they choose in their ignorance to try to maintain a status quo of how they always operated, because of their own vested interest. Both these illustrate a lack of the 'right stuff' to manage businesses in the VUCA2.0 world, as such behaviour drives nails into their brands and reputations, potentially destroying businesses or at least taking years to rebuild.

So how does one have a strategy around communicating corporate culture? Well, just before we give you our five key attributes of brand preservation, let's just remind ourselves of the sheer range of responses we have seen in one short period, because it is these situations that we in our profession are in effect either trying to manage, going to promote, or are picking up the pieces from.

In this last year alone, we have seen a holiday chain become notorious for callously laying off and evicting its staff from its hotels at the start of the COVID-19 pandemic. We saw global businesses call for government handouts at the same time as suggesting they would still pay senior bonuses and dividends. We saw price hikes on certain goods, reminding us of World War II racketeering, and hedge funders celebrating making billions, as masses became unemployed and the economy tanked. We saw a sportswear retailer suggest his shops were vital to the nation's health, dismissing the risk to the health of his employees. We saw tweets from companies supporting #BlackLivesMatter but who were identified as having funded politicians who had voted against equal opportunities legislation.

We could go on, except that thankfully we have seen much more positive leadership to counterbalance some of these examples. So we saw bonuses being paid by the Aldi supermarket chain not to its senior management, but to its hardworking staff going the extra mile to keep shelves stacked (Pratt,

2020); Iceland, the value food retailer, initiating special hours for elderly shoppers (Winchester, 2020); BrewDog switching production to hand sanitizer and giving it away (BrewDog, 2020); Morrisons supermarkets setting aside £10 million of groceries for food banks (Smithers, 2020); Uber paying for 300,000 free trips for NHS staff (Uber Newsroom, 2020); and various major company CEOs slashing their pay or taking themselves off the payroll altogether (Melin, 2020). Of course, many more smaller, often owner-led businesses were also making tremendous localized efforts, having a significant impact on people at risk. It is looking at these exemplar behaviours that one can see leadership around values driving reputational advantage. These are what you will be looking to foster and promote.

There are five key attributes to developing a strategy to both encourage and reflect the positive internal culture necessary to achieve success in the purposeful age. By this stage we hope you won't be surprised by the following:

---

1 Have a clearly defined human-centric reason why the business exists: **Purpose**.

2 Have a relationship-focused approach to how communication happens: **People**.

3 Encourage great behaviours through a model to suit your business: **Passion**.

4 Capture good news, create engagement and ownership across teams: **Plan**.

5 Develop a unifying theme and then empower your voices: **Prominence**.

You don't need us to tell you how to write a strategy, but if you turn the above into a thought process, it can help craft it. We believe you build brand **prominence** via a **plan** which unleashes the **passion** of **people** for the business's **purpose**. These people can be employees or customers who care about why you exist and how you deliver on that why. You turn them into enthusiastic fans using their own channels and influence to extol the values of the business and celebrate the behaviours they witness.

Malcolm Devoy, the Chief Strategy Officer at PHD, a global communications planning and media buying agency network, is clear on the significance of this. When asked who he felt should own purpose in a business, he replied, 'It is often the case that brands with a strong purpose have a spokesperson to communicate through. This might be a founder or a spokesperson, but it might be a celebrity endorser, or it might be through a third party such as a cause the business works with'.

It is perhaps worth pressing pause slightly here and being clear that all the above is really written on the premise that the organization you will be working on behalf of has a great culture, with fully committed people around a clear purpose, etc. However, this may not be the case of course. Although this book isn't primarily about building the culture, but rather about recognizing its impact on your communications capabilities, we can highlight certain key thinking if things are not as sound as one might hope for.

Keep in mind that some of the most effective changes in corporate behaviour and the illustration of how values matter, can result either through the actions of a single individual or through a small group. Throughout recent years, this has been illustrated by such people who have highlighted poor corporate values and have set out, often against incredible odds, to change what may have seemed to be impossible. Some of these have been great social issues as well, but the point here is that with passion and purpose, the CEO, you, a business unit manager, a group on the factory floor, can take up a leadership position on any aspect of the weakness or strength within the corporate culture. Nothing is immovable, nothing is above change and adaptation if the culture becomes strong. That is why we go back to the famous quote at the top of the chapter about culture eating strategy for breakfast. Just make your strategy the culture.

Opportunities

Historically, the culture of a business didn't often feature in the public consciousness or have much of a role to play in the reputation of the brand unless it affected the quality of the product. That was of course a missed opportunity at the very least and something which now is entirely the opposite, given that customers want to know the values and behaviours behind businesses and the products they buy. Taking away the potential of simply mitigating the negative, the real opportunity for business is where such values become drivers for brand loyalty and the growth of market share. What hasn't happened so much to date is where different scenarios can offer the strength of such internal values and behaviours as a means to be part of the key messaging of a business.

In certain scenarios, the CEO will need to take responsibility for being the mouthpiece of the business, unless they themselves happen to be the story, in which case the board will often assume the role. However, for the sake of argument, let us assume it is the CEO and agree a new definition for those initials: Chief Encouragement Officer. In this role, the CEO's primary opportunity is to represent the best for the business by encouraging which-ever necessary audience to understand the circumstances behind the announcement and hopefully then support it.

Launching a strategy or product

It is always critical to ensure confidence in the leadership of an organization, particularly from external audiences such as the media or investors, when a new direction or strategy might be being announced. The ability to illustrate the strength of the business, employee engagement and successful manage-ment credentials will be seen as more credible if there is a proven track record of human-centric thinking, where others rather than the 'official' spokespeople of the business speak spontaneously and authentically of it and its reputation.

Of course, when there is a significant announcement, it is necessary that the chief executive make it and in so doing, lead the way both in terms of the message and the *way* it is made. It will carry more weight and sense of authenticity if the way in which it is done typifies the human truth purpose, the values and respected embedded behaviours. This may take the form of talking about the new direction's credentials in terms of sustainability or its ability to meet the identified human need, but in essence, absolute alignment of message, means and motivation being in step with the purpose of the business will build confidence.

Brand ambassadors, principles and cultural compliance

Every company should have them. These are not just those paid to represent the business, or even customers who are fans of your products, but rather the employees who are so passionate about the company and what it does that they are in effect living their own purpose through that of the business. They live and breathe the culture, and internally help others appreciate what the values stand for and which behaviours are part of the culture. These individuals, who can exist at every level of the business, can be powerful advocates because they love the company. They are your most authentic cheerleaders.

In order to manage such ambassadors, either hierarchical or not, it's worth defining some general principles about how they will behave when communi-cating the business and its culture. This is not to stifle individuality, but it should be plain that regardless of which individual might be representing the business, the culture-based values must be consistent across them all. You then need to ensure that anyone representing your business appreciates that they need to adhere to these principles as well. If this presents difficulties, then you will find it hard to create a consistency in how you present the business.

You may be representing a well-established set of corporate truths embedded within a positive corporate culture, or you may be looking to shift existing feelings about the business and its behaviours to align around a new clarity. When a company moves into a newly defined, truth-driven and purposeful space, it needs to be appreciated by those leading the change that not everyone is necessarily going to embrace the new way of doing things in the desired way.

As your human truth and purpose is non-negotiable, it cannot be a matter of choice for your employees to determine whether they are supportive of it or not, in the same way that your values are non-negotiable. By establishing a truth-based strategy and leading how it manifests itself in terms of its messaging and its culture, people will self-determine whether they wish to be a part of it, or if they don't and choose to swim against the tide, you will need measures to enforce compliance.

Ethics

It is important at this stage to just spend some time discerning the difference between values and ethics, something which can lead to confusion for leaders and needs to be clear in your mind. These terms are often and mistakenly used interchangeably, but they are different. The greater clarity you have in your minds and those of your employees, the better able you will be to see them clearly represented in the culture of the business.

As we've seen, the values of a business are a set of beliefs which those in the business apply across all aspects of the way they operate, and recognize as embodying the type of behaviours they wish to encourage. These will therefore be such things as being collaborative, innovative, open, transparent and others we are sure you can imagine. They may represent both an aspiration and a set of accepted norms that are celebrated as helping drive the business in a certain way, which marks them from competitors, builds a certain *way* of doing business, and drives corporate culture.

Ethics are distinct, as they are morality-based guidelines or rules that are formulated by the society within which the business is based. It is not that they are set for a particular or specific country or society, but rather that they are seen as universally acknowledged virtues. This might be, for example, to refrain from lying, bribing, dishonesty, prejudice, or even violence. Ethics are of course normally represented by the positive, such as compassion, honesty, humanity and the like.

Values are often very individual to the business, whilst ethics are more universal across the society in which all businesses operate. In short, if you are involved in drawing up a values list to base your behaviours around, be distinct between the societal norms and the particular *way* in which you hope the corporate culture will manifest itself. The former are ethics, the latter are values.

Culture is communications

If a company has the right culture, great things can happen. People love their work and their productivity and pride rise. This leads to greater reputation and revenues from customers whose loyalty can dominate a market, who buy more and act as brand ambassadors. You will know, though, that critical to establishing this and then maintaining it is how it is communicated. A positive culture and its truth-based strategy requires constant vigilance to ensure everything from protecting brand quality, through to addressing anything which might be contrary to normal accepted behaviours. Pitfalls can arise, not, we hope, as huge scandals, but as small doubts or decisions which in turn can grow into larger issues. Your role in communications actually requires you to have the veracity to be watchful.

Sometimes it is small things which either signal the slippage or can encourage others to go further if the original, albeit minor, infraction is not acted upon. So perhaps a favourite, highly successful individual within the business bends a rule, or – even less rigid than that – simply breaks what is considered a value-based behaviour. If they get away without it being addressed, however minor, it can start to undermine the entire internal respect for those values. Or it might be that leaders are failing to provide sufficient guidance around something of importance to the employees. It may not even be an internal business issue. We have seen in recent times where an external societal agenda has required businesses to express, as corporate citizens, a view, a stance on such an issue. Where companies haven't, it has often been interpreted as not caring, thereby causing what might have seemed to that point a very internal 'caring' culture to be undermined.

What this all means is that communications functions in business cannot be simply reactive when it comes to this set of core business factors. The communications internally and externally should always be seen as two way, and in the same way that you will assess the effectiveness of a particular social media or advertising strategy, you should also be taking feedback, assessing the internal state of affairs, in effect taking the temperature of the culture. Anything less and you will run the risk of simply reacting to a situation when it is far too late or being seen through by employees and indeed customers. As Melanie Norris of BBDO told us:

> Consumers are savvy; they can smell a lack of authenticity a mile off. A strong, healthy, positive internal culture will permeate, dictate and influence perception; it is a critical part of any truth. Internal culture will naturally become very public, especially if it is good, or bad. Leadership is critical, leaders set the tone, they live the culture, they are part of this truth.

Summary

These last two chapters have covered the internal understanding and appreciation of where truth and its purposeful embodiment lie within the business. We have stressed that the stories that will power up your ability to best present the business and/or its products or services, should be evident across all functional areas, facilitated by the culture and how it is manifested by its leaders, values, behaviours and the strategy overall. We can summarize this aspect of understanding truth in your business as both a set of questions to ask yourself – listed below – and a few key pointers you can either identify with or act upon.

First make sure your leadership is committed. You cannot deliver a truth-based purposeful communications strategy unless the senior leadership is committed. Beyond the senior leadership, you will need to ensure that all those responsible for talking on behalf of the business, creating collateral or creative, even if just an internal newsletter, are conscious of the tone of voice and the truth and purpose behind it. Your ambassadors, wherever they are, have influence; make sure they have the right support in taking the message out to their audiences.

Make sure you can define the corporate culture for all to see. Regardless of whether you have written values, look carefully at how people in the business behave, how the leadership interacts, and how the strategy is understood. This is the great opportunity to bring a human face to otherwise potentially bland corporate communications, to celebrate great behaviours such as customer care or environmental management by utilizing real stories of real people, rather than stock imagery or fabricated and often obviously contrived photo opportunities.

Your human-based truth will be a key and defining part of your corporate culture. It becomes the basis of a purpose-powered differentiator, because it places at the core of your communications something that is distinct to you.

Finally, at the root of this must always be to 'Think Human'. This whole book is about a human-based truth. That is not some esoteric, intellectual concept, but something which sits at the heart of the relationship the business has with each of its people and each of its people have with each other. The businesses and, to be frank, the leaders who get this right, are those who put the person, the individual human, at the centre of their day-to-day thinking and their long-term plans. This means they show genuine concern, perhaps for employees struggling with poor health; they understand that an overdue payment by a customer may mean deeply troubling domestic issues; they are careful in the application of rules and regulations, when discretion may be the better decision about how strictly things are applied. There are a host of scenarios where leading companies can simply apply what is universally known as The Golden Rule, to treat people as you would wish to be treated yourself. But we must also never forget that the way a business behaves in such a situation is simply based on the way each of us as individuals behave. It is person to person, human to human, conversation to conversation.

YOUR CHECKLIST

1   Make sure your leadership is committed – without this your job will be very hard.
2   Review your values, if published, and how they link to your truth and purpose.
3   Identify your best voices, regardless of hierarchy, and empower them to speak.
4   Look for illustrative behaviours that can be fuel to your communications.
5   Continually review, assess and nurture the human-centric culture.

References

BrewDog (2020) Brewdog Hand Sanitiser, Brewdog Online Marketplace, https://www.brewdog.com/uk/hand-sanitiser (archived at https://perma.cc/QT9E-4GAM)

Holm, E and Das, A (2014) Buffet reminds his top managers: reputation is everything, *Business Insider*, 19 December, https://blogs.wsj.com/moneybeat/2014/12/19/buffett-reminds-his-top-managers-reputation-is-everything/?mod=WSJBlog (archived at https://perma.cc/TR32-S2GZ)

Melin, A (2020) Executives worldwide slash their own pay in coronavirus crunch, *Bloomberg*, 12 March, https://www.bloomberg.com/news/articles/2020-03-12/executives-worldwide-slash-their-own-pay-in-coronavirus-crunch (archived at https://perma.cc/WVD4-KRR6)

Pratt, L (2020) Aldi rewards store and distribution staff with 10% bonus, *Employee Benefits*, 30 March, https://employeebenefits.co.uk/aldi-rewards-store-and-distribution-staff-with-10-bonus/ (archived at https://perma.cc/T7X6-9E7G)

Smithers, R (2020) Morrisons gives food banks £10m during coronavirus outbreak, *Guardian*, 30 March, https://www.theguardian.com/world/2020/mar/30/morrisons-gives-food-banks-10m-during-coronavirus-outbreak (archived at https://perma.cc/X2TJ-V4RZ)

Uber Newsroom (2020) Uber to support NHS staff with 300,000 free trips and meals, Uber Newsroom UK, 30 March, https://www.uber.com/en-GB/newsroom/uber-to-support-nhs-staff/ (archived at https://perma.cc/WC4P-8FQM)

Winchester, L (2020) Iceland's special opening hours and coronavirus care packs—what supermarkets are doing to help over-70s, *The Sun Online*, 10 April, https://www.thesun.co.uk/money/11181020/coronavirus-iceland-supermarket-food-over-70/ (archived at https://perma.cc/4V2K-5KK9)

06

The how: audiences and stories

So far you have been introduced to new ways to think about human truths within your business and how to address them through a clear sense of purpose. You will understand where such truthful purpose fits within your business and why it matters now more than ever. We have explained how thinking around purpose has evolved over time, reflecting changing societal expectations and priorities, and have emphasized the importance of values, behaviours and culture as the essential power sources for your communications and marketing activity.

Now it is time to look at *how* to tell your truth-purpose story or, more precisely, how it can be reflected in the stories shared about your business or brand. This is explained over the next three chapters, looking first at your audiences and messages (better described as stories), next at what we call moments and context, and finally at understanding and measuring their impact.

According to the 18th-century German writer and statesman Johann Wolfgang von Goethe, 'By seeking and blundering we learn'. Or, as John likes to say, 'we can learn from others' mistakes'. And there is no shortage of companies or brands that have blundered in their efforts to appear 'woke', perhaps too smitten with the glamour or the possibility of going viral, despite significant risks such marketing creativity can present (The Economist, 2019).

For example, when McDonald's flipped its arches upside down to make a 'W' for International Women's Day in 2018, advocacy organizations including MoveOn and Momentum thought the effort would be better spent improving pay and benefits for women workers (Whitehead, 2019). In 2019, the mouthwash brand Listerine launched a rainbow-themed bottle during Pride month, and the LGBTQ+ community was not impressed (Ermac, 2019). Similarly, British retailer Marks & Spencer invited a backlash when a special 'LGBT+' sandwich was introduced (Duffin, 2019) and was poorly received. No doubt all of these superb marketers had the best of intentions with their efforts to tap into a momentary zeitgeist, hoping to cement a bond with their audiences in an emotional, enduring way. The problem was that *none* of these efforts were based on anything their audiences suggested they desired or needed, and this is the difference between purposed-washed and purposeful marketing. The former is based on what a business thinks might resonate; the latter is informed by what its audiences require, told in ways that ring true.

This starts with two principles we hope to establish in this chapter:

> 1 **Your audience points the way**. Rather than passive recipients of information that may or may not be moved to think, act, behave or purchase differently, your audience are your guides, partners and collaborators, especially in this purposeful age.
>
> 2 **Messages are stories, and stories start with human truths**. Data, product features, even price points are elements that can support stories that address human truths, but they are not the stories themselves. Stories can come from anywhere, but the best are built on empathy and come from within.

It's not what you say, it's what they hear

We frequently work with a strategic language consultancy, Maslansky + Partners, to help clients to find and use language that shapes perceptions and changes behaviour, and their entire proposition is based on a truth that should seem obvious: in the process of communications, the audience always gets the last word. Their operating mantra: 'it's not what you say, it's what they hear' (Maslansky, 2020).

The firm pioneered the use of 'dial testing' to organize audience feedback as messages are delivered, enabling participants to turn a dial to match the level of agreement or disagreement, or positive or negative sentiment, in sync with what is being said, rather than afterwards. The technology can be applied to short taglines, 30-second television adverts or much longer media statements, or even political manifestos; the results illustrate precisely when a message is connecting, and where it might go off track. Some clients are surprised at how quickly an audience hears something completely different than they intended to communicate.

'We now use a range of tools to see how information is received by audiences,' the company's president, Lee Hartley Carter, told us. 'But the real work now is understanding why it matters to them in the first place, and that's often complex and based on feelings as much as or even more than facts. That requires careful, attentive probing – sometimes asking four or five times, "so what?" or "why does that matter?" to each version of a message,' she said, referencing a process she details in her 2019 book, *Persuasion: Convincing others when facts don't seem to matter*. It is also worth being reminded that our research revealed that when asked how true their business or brand's communications were to the reality of their publicly stated purpose, commitments and actions, only 27 per cent of survey respondents were able to vouch for them being true. Looking at this from a risk assessment point of view, this is a real challenge. If your public perception fed by your communication is higher than the reality, then there is a significant risk of exposure in some form and a resulting scandal. Equally, if your communications are failing to express the positive aspects of internal values and purpose, then opportunity is lost. There can of course be various reasons for this but our own experience bears it out.

One client, a US healthcare company, long since absorbed into another and another through multiple mergers and acquisitions, had the valid and sincere purpose of improving women's lives through science and innovation. One of its flagship products, a treatment for women with menopause-related conditions, showed promise, addressing a new range of other symptoms related to ageing. We were asked to help women understand the benefits (and risks) of the treatment to aid discussions with their doctors about whether it might be suitable for them. Such communications are and were highly regulated in the United States and elsewhere. Advertising for prescription products was not allowed at the time, but we managed to communicate the science widely through news accounts of the research in general interest media and those focused specifically on serving women.

Women, generally, were not impressed. Through market research at the time, we were able to discern that a significant number of women were aware of the new science and saw its potential. We could also see that there were *fewer* conversations initiated by women with their physicians after the science was publicized; the more widely it was seen, the less likely the topic would be raised. It took a series of focus groups to get at the human truth behind the surprising disconnect between awareness and action; the studies raised questions about conditions most women had never considered, and problems they associated with 'getting old'. Instead of prompting discussions with doctors, the science was putting up barriers. What most women wanted, we were told, was to know how the product could help with the issues that concerned them most at this stage in their lives – how to manage physical and emotional changes and to maintain intimacy with partners – not how to prevent conditions they may not have heard of.

Reaching the audience may have been the objective, but the purpose was to improve women's health. Viewing the audience – women in this case – as the destination was less effective than viewing our conversations with them as a map or guide for reaching our true goal.

On another project to establish local language translations of Western literature in a certain Gulf state, we thought the discussion was about access to the classics; what some government ministers *heard* was criticism of Arabic literature. Or there was the project designed to help military units returning from combat re-enter civilian life; we thought the conversation was about reducing friction in the community, but what local law enforcement authorities *heard* was that a crime wave was imminent. We managed to get back on track in each of these cases and no, not *all* of our work started off on the wrong foot, but we do tend to recall the hardest lessons most easily.

All of which is to say that a strong purpose, even one validated by research and communicated with strong data, isn't effective when it is at odds with human truths. As we have seen, so many companies and brands now earnestly embrace purpose and look for authentic ways to communicate it, bolstered by more data and arguably better insight into customer preferences than ever before.

Gaps such as these, where we think we're saying one thing but our audience is hearing something altogether different, could have been avoided by observing a few basic rules before the conversations ever began:

1 **Acknowledge objections.** Doubts about your commitment, capacity to deliver or your motivation do not have to be valid or 'fair'. They are often not. Maybe they are based on past blunders, mistaken identity or false associations, or what you may consider trivial concerns, but they all must be taken into consideration as you develop the stories around your purpose.

2 **Think emotionally.** People feel strongly about their health, their communities, or their heritage. Data and facts, no matter how logically presented, are unlikely to outweigh the emotions they are bringing into the conversation.

3 Speak candidly. Each of the difficulties in the examples above could have been prevented, or at least reduced, had we started not just with a clear understanding of potential objectives and feelings, but by directly acknowledging any 'elephants in the room' about our own limitations about things we didn't know or could not do.

These rules apply to just about any kind of conversation or exchange in which you are hoping to reach some level of understanding and mutually beneficial outcome, but they are especially important when it comes to communicating purpose. Why? Because a purposeful audience expects more, knows more and can do more to aid or thwart your business or brand than a solely transactional audience.

Your audience is your guide

Now would be a good time to mention something important: thinking, acting, and communicating purposefully through your brand *does not replace* your existing marketing plans. Nothing we are about to suggest negates a product-based strategy, a customer-centric approach, a channel plan, a retail programme, a direct-to-consumer platform or a social media content calendar. These were all developed for a reason specific to your business or those you're advising, and there's nothing about purpose that overrides the basic realities of supply chains, sales or distribution needs. The same goes for your wider communications activity – the corporate reputation campaign, your executive visibility commitments or employee engagement efforts; these stay in place, too, although they are likely to more directly reflect your purpose story. We will look at some of these in more detail in the next chapter.

The point is, purposeful marketing and communications does not replace the hard work that needs to go into market segmentation, pricing decisions, promotional considerations or any of the numerous concerns of a viable business. It does require us to examine our plans and assumptions through a few important filters. Are these plans built on truth? Do they connect in clear, understandable ways in pursuit of the larger business purpose? And crucially, have you let your audience, in the widest possible definition of the term, show you the way?

As examined earlier, the importance of a truth-based purpose to a business has been consolidating over the past few decades around concepts related to integrity and transparency, and more recently, sustainability and equality. This evolution has at times come in reaction to negative events, scandals or economic crises, for example, and at other times in pursuit of the potential financial growth attributed to purpose-led businesses, such as reported by Unilever. In 2018 it reported that its 28 Sustainable Living Brands (those in its portfolio taking action to support positive change for people and the planet) grew 69 per cent faster than the rest of its business and delivered 75 per cent of the consumer goods giant's overall growth (Unilever, 2019).

Whether pushed by scandal or pulled by opportunity, or both, the emergence of purposeful business reflects another evolving concept: that of the audience. Our notions of 'audience' have changed over the millennia, moving in step with the main mode of communications available to humans. The US historian Marshall T. Poe has a rather clever way of delineating ages of humanity in this context, starting with *Homo loquens* (humans in the age of speech) through *Homo scriptor* (manuscripts) and *Homo lector* (print) and on to *Home videns* (audiovisual media) and finally to the present-day *Homo somnians* (the internet) (Poe, 2012).

However sophisticated we consider ourselves to be, it is worth acknowledging that much of our thinking about audiences today stems from earlier ages of humanity, constrained by how far our voices could be projected or how many newspapers could be distributed. In other words, the means of communications, the media used, has defined the audience in terms of size, location, engagement, and others. Poe describes eight such attributes of media over the ages: accessibility, privacy, fidelity, volume, velocity, range, persistence and searchability (Poe, 2012), and together they help form the impressions of the audience. Perhaps they're in a stadium, listening to a speech or political rally, or maybe watching the Super Bowl with 100 million others around the world, separate but sharing an experience. And now, in the age of *Homo somnians*, they're likely engaged with multiple forms of media at the same time and, crucially, creating and sharing it with each other on a global scale. Often without our permission or even knowledge.

If the purpose of human life is to be well, as Aristotle wrote, Poe believes the impact of media has been mixed: positive on material and sensory well-being, less so on spiritual well-being (Poe, 2012, p. 275). But as John often says, 'It is what it is,' and what it is, is a new concept of audience, partly defined by the internet and all that it enables, and partly by changing expectations of businesses and brands, as mapped earlier.

FIGURE 6.1 The purposeful audience

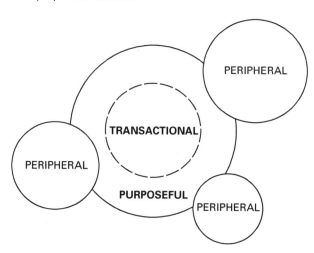

So what does an audience look like today in the age of *Homo somnians*? The purposeful audience (Figure 6.1) includes multiple sub-audiences: individuals and organizations involved a company's regular business transactions (eg employees, customers, suppliers, investors) as well as elements of peripheral audiences that are highly engaged in issues related to the company's stated purpose, regardless of whether they are involved its operations or output.

In the centre is the core, the **transactional** audience: those you are targeting for sales, investment, votes, etc. This can be thought of in the usual marketing jargon – segments, personas, end-users, consumers, etc.

Surrounding this is the **purposeful** audience: inclusive of your core audience but involving a range of other people, organizations and networks that share an interest in your purpose, but not necessarily your business proposition or brand.

And in the outer, adjacent circles we see **peripheral** audiences: those who may have no or little history of engaging with your purpose or product but can insert themselves quickly and sometimes disruptively as the news agenda shifts, issues heat up, and businesses or brands find themselves exposed.

Our main interest is with the purposeful audience, as your core audience will be well known to you and those on the periphery are by definition hard to track or predict, but it's important to understand how all three interact. In fact, we see the majority of 'fails' stemming from confusion about their differences and connections.

Attributes of a purposeful audience

The need to understand our audiences at a transactional level is not changed by intentions to understand them at a purposeful level. We still need data on their demographics, media consumption, buying power and all of the other factors that determine who is targeted, how and where. But if we want to bring purpose authentically into our communications and marketing, we need a wider, more comprehensive understanding of 'audience'. Purposeful businesses interact with purposeful audiences, and we see six attributes about these to consider:

- **Expansive.** As communicators we are trained to be as specific as we can when it comes to identifying our audiences and the pathways to reach them. 'When you speak to everyone, you're speaking to no one,' as the adage goes. True. But purposeful audiences are more expansive than transactional audiences, including not only direct consumers and immediate influencers, but a wider set of stakeholders, including investors, analysts, advocacy organizations, government agencies, even celebrities and media personalities are part of the audience 'ecosystem' you will need to understand.

- **Interconnected.** One reason a purposeful audience is so expansive is because of how highly connected they are online, not to us, necessarily, but to each other. We tend to think of connectivity as a function of our brand's relationship with our audiences, and focus on getting things like the voice, personality and tone or messaging just right, but part of the power of purpose is that it draws people together on a 'higher plane' that may or may not include our business proposition. We need to understand how the many various parts of our audience interact with and influence each other, along with how they want to interact or engage with us.

- **Critical.** Audiences that coalesce around a sense of purpose bring a full tray of sentiments and attitudes to the conversation. On the one hand, in our experience they are often well informed on topics associated with the purpose – say, climate change and carbon tax policies, for example – and therefore knowledgeably critical of the kinds 'purpose washing' tactics described above.

- **Vocal.** As we have seen, reactions to woke ads or management missteps can be swift, cutting and global, thanks to social media. But purposeful audiences are not always tweeting disapproval; much of their power lies in the quiet, daily conversations they are having about your brand, your operations or the management decisions you are making or advising through their own private online discussion forums or, more recently, specific websites and mobile phone apps. These serve information-hungry purposeful audiences in just about every category of consumer goods and services, with two examples being The Good Shopping Guide (covering a wide range of products) and Good On You, which rates fashion brands to let users choose and reward those 'that do good, over the ones that don't'.

- **Authoritative.** Sometimes elements of the purposeful audience speak with literal, legal, regulatory, or industry authority on the content, tone or even the intent of your communications. Government agencies, consumer watchdog organizations, unions and professional or industry bodies all have a stake in your truth-based purpose stories.

- **Contextual.** Societal priorities change over time; sometimes relatively slowly over decades, as we have seen in earlier chapters, and at other times, especially during times of crisis or uncertainty, virtually overnight, as we saw with #MeToo, employee safety and health following the COVID-19 pandemic, and Black Lives Matter. Generally, new or heightened expectations are additive, meaning they don't replace the behaviours already generally established for ethical businesses, such as transparency, fairness or some basic commitment to sustainability, but they're layered on top. With social media news feeds refreshing constantly, we're in constant listening mode.

What are they saying?

Once you have identified the purposeful audience your business or brand serves, one that includes those who purchase or endorse your business proposition and a wider set of interested parties who care about your purpose, but perhaps not about your offer, you can start to listen to what they expect.

In the context of a human truth purpose, we see these expectations as needs and it is worth reminding ourselves of Abraham Maslow's famous hierarchy: physiological, safety, belonging/love, and self-actualization (1943). The premise that our needs progress from the very basic to the more complex helps confirm an important point about communicating purpose: our business does not have to change the world, but it should contribute positively, by understanding where we fit into people's lives, and how we help meet their expectations. It is impossible to list these needs or expectations comprehensively, but in our experience purposeful audiences require a clear response to at least one, often more, of these questions from the businesses and brands that desire their engagement:

- How do you make the future better?
- How do you make the present better?
- How do you make my family/community better?
- How do you make me better?

Your response needs to be realistic, and to be purposeful it needs to be a positive contributor to people and/or the planet. It should not be so remote as to be seen as unrealistic, but it can have ambition. If we remind ourselves of Walgreens Boots' 'Helping people lead a healthier and happy life', it combines both. Critically, such a statement meets some basic criteria: it's honest, it's demonstrable and it's comprehensive.

One way to think about this exchange is that it SHOULD:

State your truthful purpose – your commitment to one of those basic human needs, as this is the market opportunity you are attempting to fulfil.

Honour your commitments – in every aspect of your business and how you communicate about it.

Own the process toward progress – it's okay to acknowledge external barriers or circumstances, but not to use them as excuses.

Understand changes in context – social priorities can shift, intensify or fade.

Listen to questions and challenges.

Differentiate as a true partner with your audience.

In most cases, your purpose actually will line up with a higher-level social challenge or concern, and in these instances it's helpful to know how they are generally labelled or organized in the world, not because there is an established authoritative source on such things, but because this is how your audience will access, organize and share information related to your purpose. This of course helps you listen and process their expectations.

We touched earlier upon the 17 UN Strategic Development Goals, which cover a wide range of issues including poverty, gender equality and climate, and together offer a fairly comprehensive list of aims or needs to which high-level business purposes can be addressed (United Nations, 2015). We sometimes simplify this list into a few wider categories: environment/climate, healthcare, education, youth/ageing populations, science/technology, civil society and media/information. In any case, these kinds of groupings help form the headings or search terms to help define and engage the audiences connected to them.

How to listen

This brings us to a practical set of suggestions to answer *how* you can first listen and then discern some kind of useful signal from the overwhelming, always-on noise that's available, whether we want to hear it or not:

Humans plus humans. Some modes of listening will never go out of style, at least not any time soon, or certainly not for a proposition built on human truths. There is a reason these basic market research tools have been in use for decades: they draw out authentic real-life insights on what people think or believe because they come as close as possible to real-life human conversations. These tools include interviews, focus groups, and facilitated surveys, amongst others, and we have used them all in countless client engagements to glean perspectives on the emotional, cognitive or practical barriers to communicating credible and actionable information.

Humans plus machines. Technology has helped humans process ever-increasing amounts of information for decades and especially over the past decade or two with the spread of mobile telephones and cloud-based technology. We do not need to trace the dramatic increase in tools and platforms using artificial intelligence to understand their usefulness to us as we look through enormous volumes of data to find patterns and insight.

Many of these tools are not nearly as daunting to use as they sound. Twitter, Facebook, Amazon and Google, resources we use every day in our business and personal lives, all offer low- or no-cost analytic tools to help you understand what's happening online with regard to content, searches and traffic. And there is a growing stable of more specialized tools to help harness data for more precise applications. NewsWhip, for example, tracks and predicts the impact of millions of news stories, and Tagger connects influencers and content creators with brands and causes.

There are of course dozens of these kinds of tools, and more launching by the day. The point is not necessarily which to use, but how you complement your human-derived insights and intelligence with tech-enabled data analytics for the best possible understanding of your audience.

What are we listening for?

The final question you must ask about your audiences is what are you expecting to learn from them? Given that we have established that a purposeful audience is somewhat wider than a transactional audience and their input serves a different set of objectives, you should be listening for the following:

- **Validation.** Is the purpose real? Does it meet a human need? Does it link to a larger, established societal concern or opportunity?

- **Relevance.** Does it align with their priorities and interests?

- **Tone.** What kinds of language, imagery and style are commonly used to describe the underlying need or purpose? What is to be avoided?

- **Issues.** What are the driving issues at the centre of the need you're meeting? What are the issues adjacent to it?

- **Opinion.** What are the prevailing opinions and arguments around these issues? Who's driving them? Who or what organization is seen positively? Negatively?

- **Boundaries.** Where do you have 'permission' to operate, and what are the limits to the claims or commitments the audience will accept?

- **Resonance.** And finally, what kinds of stories seem to engage this audience around the need or purpose?

CASE STUDIES

31st State

Careful attention to audiences works for large multinational brands with deep marketing pockets, but rest assured, they also guide start-ups, often more easily as there is less to re-engineer or fewer processes and practices to untangle and they can be led by the founders.

Stephanie Capuano, founder and CEO of the teen male skincare brand, 31st State, jokes that its purpose is to make the world less smelly: 'My boys were at an age when they needed to up their hygiene game considerably; baby soap wasn't cutting it anymore, but I couldn't find products that met my requirements as a mom. I asked other mothers and found I wasn't alone.' They weren't alone because there was surprisingly little on offer to teenage boys; surprising because the market for teen girls was already crowded with products, as was the older male grooming category. 'There just wasn't much on offer for Gen Z guy,' Capuano said. From there she was on a mission, and quickly found she had two audiences: the guys and their mothers, who generally made the purchase.

'We learned a lot through focus groups with both,' she said. 'And while we didn't call it "purpose", we confirmed quickly that we were on the right track. Boys of course want to look and smell nice, and mums obviously want what's best for their families: safe, clean, natural products. But when we dug a little deeper, we found that mums really just wanted to better understand their boys during the turbulent adolescent years.'

Thus 31st State was born (a nod to Capuano's native California) as a brand conceived *for* and *by* Gen Z, and a network of young advisors has 'participated in everything from product development, naming, branding and the social media content around it,' providing, she says 'a window into their interests and issues for mothers, and a platform for them to express themselves.' More than a line of skincare products, the brand has become a way to help mothers and sons connect.

In a few short years, 31st State has become an award-winning personal care brand, now available through a long line of online and retail distributors, including Amazon, Ocado, Liberty of London and Free People, amongst others.

Purpose-led marketing, based on real human truths, works.

King Of Shaves®

A purpose-led strategy can guide a business well beyond the start-up phase, too. Will King, founder and former CEO of the now-famous UK-based toiletries businesses King of Shaves (shave.com), set up the company nearly 30 years ago with a simple premise: to give men a better way to shave, forever.

'I'd studied mechanical engineering, ended up in advertising sales, was made redundant in 1992 and I hated shaving – I had both the time and the motive to introduce something new,' he said. That something new was the world's first natural-oil based shaving oil and an eponymous brand, King of Shaves. 'I realized we could shave more faces with less stuff, and that a natural oil formulation had the advantage of allowing you to see where you were shaving, not what you just shaved off.' That oil, and the entire range of related products that it spawned, reflect a clear purpose, now expressed as 'Clean Shave. Clean Conscience.'

'Audience input was critical to our early success, as it still is today,' he said. 'We were active on social channels from 2007 onwards, and from 2017 onwards, listening to increasing concerns that a clean, natural product was great, but there was an appetite for more sustainable (reduced plastic) packaging.' This led the company to transition King of Shaves from single-use plastic into lifetime-use refillable aluminium packaging in 2020, a shift they call 'Push Out Plastic – #MoveToMetal'.

Purpose achieved? Not quite. 'We know we can deliver better products in more sustainable ways, but there's so much more to be done', King said. 'From our constant dialogue with our audience, we know that pushing out plastic is both possible and expected, but we've got to go above and beyond that, with what we call Code Zero – our mission to develop "100% un-plastic" packaging solutions for toiletries.'

He and his team have been developing a brand-new FM(R)CG proposition – the (R) represents Refill/Recycle/Renew/Reinvent with a new company, Integro Innovations Ltd (Integro is 'to start anew' in Latin) – and a new brand and lifetime use/refillable pack-tech platform, '100% un-petrochemical-plastic' will debut in 2021. 'We're walking the sustainable talk,' he says, 'and others need to join us.' You can follow Will on Twitter at @iamwilliamking.

As shown in this example and other experiences, purpose, when embraced as a business strategy, often evolves with the company, its audiences and the wider world around them all. When we spoke to Interbrand's Manfredi Ricca, he was clear about how they as a business try to capture this sense:

> A customer-focused approach in this way is more than traditional qualitative research or other such formulaic processes; it's an ongoing conversation with people. Charles Trevail, Interbrand's Chief Executive, often refers to how successful brands capture this, as a result of being able to possess a 'customer instinct' – the ability to always capture the zeitgeist and be relevant across different customer communities.

Undoubtedly in our experience, and as in the founder businesses illustrated above, this instinct is a hugely significant factor in success.

Getting your story straight: the truth about messages

Right now, just about every model or framework for illustrating communications and marketing shares the same core components: sender, message, receiver, feedback to sender. There's an elegant simplicity here, encouraging us to assess each part separately and to see the connections between them in a step-by-step linear fashion. However, in our experience these models share a flaw, too, because in real life, interactions between senders and receivers are anything but linear. Feedback happens in real time, messages get lost amongst surrounding social noise, there are fast-moving changes with the news, and senders become the receivers as audiences themselves decide and define what the business or brand's 'story' is about and how it is impacting on their worlds.

Previous models like these miss another point. Much if not most information conveyed about a company or brand is delivered indirectly, through an intermediary. Yes, some audiences will experience your business directly, as a customer, employee or investor. But far more will only have the opportunity to associate your proposition with what they have seen or heard from others, in news reports, through friends on social media, or through an advertisement.

To be fair, technology is rapidly shrinking the perceptions of space or distance between companies or brands and the people they hope to serve, as more and more people move increasingly to digital platforms – websites, social media platforms, and smartphone apps, amongst others – for their news and information. Clever software algorithms intuitively 'guess' which products or brands may be of interest in the moment, popping ads into people's timelines with an uncanny sense of timing. Without doubt, artificial intelligence will continue to bring brands and products ever closer to prospective users, subscribers, investors and voters.

None of this, however, diminishes the importance of your story. If anything, the importance of getting your purpose story 'straight' is greater than ever, for several reasons. For starters, people's expectations of businesses and brands have changed significantly in recent months and years, as discussed in the previous chapters. And the technology that brings ads closer to customers? It turns them into reviewers, too, expanding the commentary exponentially, for better or worse. Moreover, corporate history and ongoing operations are open to scrutiny, leaving the best of intentions subject to analysis and criticism.

On this last point, a number of businesses have learned VUCA2.0 lessons the hard way, especially when it comes to the need to reconcile public statements with what they may have assumed were private realities. With the best of intentions, all kinds of brands rallied to support anti-racist causes and organizations during the Black Lives Matter movement that blossomed in 2020, including Citigroup, the banking giant. The company posted strong statements of support for the NAACP Legal Defense Fund on its social media accounts, along with financial donations to the organization and others committed to civil rights. Sincere and timely commitments toward such sensitive issues weren't the norm for major global brands until recently, and the decision to take a public stand no doubt required courage and internal soul-searching. It also opened the door for a look into other practices at Citigroup, including contributions to politicians through its political action committee, including more than 50 members of the US House of Representatives and 20 senators rated 'F' by the very same NAACP for their poor track record on issues supported by the organization.

People were quick to point out the discrepancy on social media, arguably diminishing any initial positive reactions. Google and Amazon: same discord. Both issued strong statements of support for members of the Black community; both made significant donations to US politicians with the worst NAACP ratings (Legum, 2020).

Political contributions in the United States are (partly) open for scrutiny, but so are other aspects of a company or brand's behaviour. L'Oréal Paris, the beauty brand behemoth, was quick to support the Black Lives Matter movement with a widely distributed image including the phrase 'Speaking Out is Worth It', a play on their famous advertising strapline. Reactions were immediate and fierce, including an accusation of hypocrisy and jumping on the BLM bandwagon from a trans model, Munroe Bergdorf, fired by L'Oréal three years earlier after speaking out on systemic racism in the United States. To the company's credit, Bergdorf was reinstated as a consultant for the company following a conversation that the brand's president, Delphine Viguier, described as 'honest, transparent and vulnerable' (Mody, 2020).

It is tempting to look at these cases as 'damned if you do, damned if you don't' situations, with little possibility of getting it right.

But many brands did in fact get their stories straight, even if after an initial stumble. Netflix, the streaming entertainment business, was quick to acknowledge that its world-reaching platform compelled it to take a stand against racism, and it did so. Equally quickly, observers noted that a film called *The Help* was trending in some regions as its number one recommendation; their rankings are computer generated, but the irony – the film has been criticized for its messages about race in the 1960s American South – wasn't lost on outspoken viewers, who also noted the lack of content on the platform produced by or featuring Black talent. The solution: a whole new genre on the platform called 'Black Lives Matter', featuring content that highlights 'powerful and complex narratives about the Black experience', according to the company (Hibberd, 2020).

And for at least one brand, 2020 was a year of redemption. Nike's support in 2018 for Colin Kaepernick, the American football player who since 2016 has knelt on the sidelines before games to call attention to racism and police brutality, has been widely hailed as a milestone in purpose-driven marketing, standing out both for its social commitment and its commercial success, despite a backlash that effectively knocked Kaepernick out of a job. Two years later, government officials, civil rights advocates and even police officers were kneeling at protests against racism and police brutality toward people of colour, and the National Football League had reversed its policy on sideline protests (Streeter, 2020; BBC Sport, 2020).

Whether a brand stumbled or shined in response to a specific social issue is not our main point, however. We are more interested in how they can thrive in a world in which such upheavals become the norm, not the exception. Models for shaping communications and marketing now need to embrace a number of new or evolved concepts to meet the needs of a VUCA2.0 world, which we believe will continue to disrupt business (and other parts of life, too) for years to come.

Some we will address further in the book, including the use of data, the role of culture and the selection of channels or moments for engagement. For now, it mainly comes down to trust. As Paul Lindley, the organic food entrepreneur we heard from in the previous chapter, told us:

> Consumer brands live or die because of trust. Once established, a business ought to do everything possible to maintain, build upon and protect this vital, very human, asset that can take years to build and seconds to destroy. Trust is a complex phenomenon, so difficult to define, but undoubtedly a key aspect is belief – does the consumer believe what you say about what you and your product or service do for them? And why they should buy them and why you want to sell them.

Stories are better than messages

'Storytelling is on every marketer's lips now as a novel way to think about communications and to frame the content we produce for commercials or websites, but of course the principles of storytelling have been around since the stone age. What is new is the way we use technology to tell stories effectively,' says Petra Sammer, a creativity and storytelling consultant based in Munich, Germany.

Storytelling is in vogue, Sammer believes, because it's a more useful way to think about how people really communicate and find common ground to cooperate – or not. 'People connect with brands like Apple, whose purpose is to challenge the status quo, or Patagonia, which is in business to save our home planet, because the stories around them ring true, and we're invited into the conversations about them.'

We encourage those we work with to think in terms of stories rather than messages for a similar reason: they are human. They create a natural, easily understood framework to convey the roles played by a business or brand, the consumer, and various other parties, to solve a problem or realize an opportunity. And because we are cognitively hard-wired to think this way (Harari, 2011), stories are more memorable, relatable and repeatable than messages or facts alone.

A classic example that stands out in our minds is the Christmas campaign from British grocery retailer Iceland in 2018, which illustrated the impact of palm oil harvesting on rain forest wildlife. Richard Walker, managing director of the company, explained to us the potency of purposeful storytelling:

Our Rang-Tan ad, which became the most watched Christmas ad of all time (even though it was banned!), was a great purpose-led storytelling example. It featured no product, prices or promotions, just a cause that we cared deeply about...

...Storytelling is increasingly being recognized as a uniquely powerful business practice. There is certainly more attention being given to personal narrative by business leaders, which gives authenticity to strategic purpose. The rise in purposeful brands and belief-driven consumer purchases has also seen a definite upturn in this kind of storytelling within marketing activity.

...However, for every purposeful, believable story I have seen, there are many more that exploit the trend with a tenuous grip on truth. We have to accept there is some way to go before we see a mainstream move from the hype and spin that can dominate product and service promotion. But this is where businesses need to take great care. By faking or exaggerating truth-based storytelling they run the risk of exposure that will quickly disenfranchise not just customers, but all of their audiences.

Purpose story types

In Chapter 4 we explored sources for true, resonant stories within a business, inside the operations, with product innovations, people policies, and finance and we emphasized a belief that purpose stories need not be confined to external advertising campaigns or PR stunts. In fact, these may not always be the best vehicles for communicating purpose at all, but every situation is different, and we will cover this in further detail in the next chapter.

There are any number of ways to source, develop or classify purpose stories and one system we rather like suggests 5 P's: planet, purpose, people, process and product (Flashman, 2020), as we appreciate alliteration as much as anyone. We also find it a little vexing, as it's hard for us to imagine purpose as somehow one of many kinds of authentic story, rather than as the steeple of a structure built to support it, but that doesn't have to diminish the thinking it prompts.

Other ways to think about purpose stories can be helpful:

- **Founder** stories. The 31st State case is the story of a founder whose personal experience as a mother striving to both take care of her Gen Z sons and better understand them led to its creation. Tom's (the shoe brand) and Warby Parker (eyewear) are also good examples, where personal experience prompted their founders to launch.

- **Ambition** stories. Setting out to solve enormous problems in David vs Goliath terms almost always resonates. Think of Tesla's commitment to accelerating the world's transition to sustainable transportation.

- **Disruption** stories. Uber ('setting the world in motion') and Airbnb ('belong anywhere') are the classics, with entire new business models invented to democratize transport and hospitality.

- **Challenger** stories. Oatly, the oat-based dairy alternative, made its case with the 'It's like milk, but made for humans' campaign that prompted a lawsuit from the Swedish dairy industry (Gustafsson, 2015).

- **Listening** stories. Iceland, the UK value food retailer, had huge reputational and recognition lift after commissioning the narrated animation around displaced Orangutans we mentioned above. A case study in itself, it simply told the story of why they were changing their policy, but did so in such a way that the film itself became a cause (Hickman, 2018).

- **Redemption** stories. Quaker Oats announced plans to change the name and logo of its long-criticized Aunt Jemima brand amidst the wider discussions of race and equality in the United States in 2020, as did Mars with its Uncle Ben's brand (Gabbatt, 2020).

The Purpose Story Framework™

Someone famous – not exactly clear who – once said that there are only two kinds of stories that really hold up over time and around the world: someone goes on a trip, or a stranger came to town. We love the literary elegance of this and believe the story types we've outlined above can be interpreted in the journey or stranger plots. In fact, the King of Shaves case can be seen as a journey of discovery and reinvention, whilst the 31st State case deals with a stranger, male adolescence. But in practical terms, businesses need a less abstract backbone for conveying what they are and how they evolve to fit into people's lives.

For that, we have developed Purpose Story Framework™ (Figure 6.2), which allows you to consider and monitor several factors simultaneously as you consider your truth-based purpose stories and content. Some elements have been covered earlier: purpose describes why the business exists, and truth confirms why it is important to people or the planet. Mission is your specific strategy within a fixed timeframe, and vision is the change you want to see and effect.

Conversations with your audience provide ongoing streams of input and direction as to its expectations and needs, offer a way of thinking about your supporting messages, and form a future-oriented dialogue. These include your achievements (proof points), commitments (statements of measurable intention for continued improvement), and aspirations ('blue sky thinking' on how progress can be pursued collaboratively with your audience).

And at least three kinds of factors in the VUCA2.0 world we operate in today require constant, diligent monitoring, partly to keep you on course, and partly to help you detect and assess changing societal views and priorities. These include reality (honest and ongoing assessment of operational capacity, service delivery and financial performance, amongst others, to pursue your purpose), context (major 'news' developments, rapid changes to business, cultural or political circumstances), and attitude (shifts in opinion, emerging voices and changing public priorities).

FIGURE 6.2 The Purpose Story Framework™

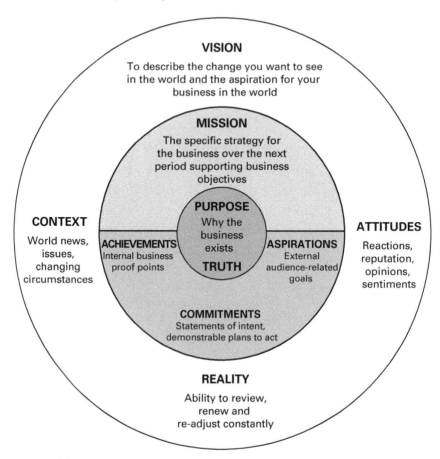

SOURCE **Vision**, **Mission**, **Purpose** and **Truth** are aligned and offer a central, committed perspective. These are surrounded by three fluid streams of conversation with the audience: **Achievements**, **Aspirations** and **Commitments**. Externally, there are three sources of feedback to monitor societal dynamics and possible shifts: **Reality**, **Context** and **Attitudes**. (O'Brien and Gallagher, 2020™)

Summary

This chapter covered a lot of terrain, some of it mapped but much of it still being explored, as businesses and brands expand their experimentation with the potential of purpose-led marketing and communications.

Fresh research shows significant appetite for integrating purpose further into strategic decision making and operations, as well as marketing and communications, from business leaders as well as from those who advise brands as agency consultants or in-house experts. But even as support for purpose-led marketing grows, poorly conceived 'purpose washed' campaigns can contribute to apprehension or cynicism about its potential. Even businesses with good intentions can find associations with social or cultural issues risky in the current volatile environment.

Purposeful communications or marketing starts not with brand promises or product claims, but with a clear understanding of audience needs and expectations and those audiences as humans, people. 'Audience', therefore, is in itself an evolving term, defined in part by the media used to engage them. Communicators can look at their 'purposeful audience' more expansively than traditional core, or transactional, audiences, while minding 'peripheral' audiences whose interests may rise or wane with events. Understanding the attributes of your purposeful audience helps define their boundaries for support and engagement and points the way toward meaningful, engaging communications. There are now both traditional and new AI-powered technologies to help listen, interpersonally and at scale.

Storytelling has emerged as a more compelling and nuanced way to think of messages, reflecting a more human way of communicating that makes information exchanged more memorable, meaningful and shareable. Matched with the human truth required at the core of the purposeful stories, which we have shown can emerge from any corner of a business, this becomes essential for establishing an authentic, verifiable conversation. Although traditional models for story and message structures have been widely used across marketing and communications disciplines for some time, none adequately address the requirement for purpose-led communications as the Purpose Story Framework™ does, as it moves beyond what we want to say and addresses what audiences need and expect to hear in order to believe and engage with our business.

YOUR CHECKLIST

To activate the Purpose Story Framework™:

1 Review and confirm your alignment of Truth, Purpose and Mission or Vision.

2 Confirm the leadership Commitment and resource to act.

3 Map your audiences (core, purposeful and peripheral) and their characteristics.

4 Identify your stories and examples from within your business or beyond.

5 Be clear on your internal Credentials, Achievements and Aspirations.

6 Assess the stories against Context, Reality and Attitudes.

References

BBC Sport (2020) Colin Kaepernick: How the NFL made its U-turn, *BBC News*, 6 June, https://www.bbc.co.uk/sport/american-football/52948942 (archived at https://perma.cc/8USF-MF7J)

Carter, L H (2019) *Persuasion: Convincing others when facts don't seem to matter*, Penguin Publishing Group, New York

Duffin, C (2019) Backlash from shoppers after Marks & Spencer launches LGBT (lettuce, guacamole, bacon and tomato) sandwich for this year's Gay Pride, *Daily Mail*, 6 May, https://www.dailymail.co.uk/news/article-6996097/Backlash-shoppers-Marks-Spencer-launches-LGBT-sandwich-years-Gay-Pride.html (archived at https://perma.cc/C2EZ-8C2F)

Economist (2019) Companies can appeal to workers and consumers with liberal messages, *Economist Business: Bartleby*, 26 January, https://www.economist.com/business/2019/01/26/companies-can-appeal-to-workers-and-consumers-with-liberal-messages (archived at https://perma.cc/QJU9-J3KL)

Ermac, R (2019) Listerine's Pride bottle is leaving a bad taste in people's mouths, *Pride News*, 22 May, https://www.pride.com/news/2019/5/22/listerines-pride-bottle-leaving-bad-taste-peoples-mouths (archived at https://perma.cc/X6L6-5PUT)

Flashman, G (2020) *Content: Using brand journalism to create compelling and authentic storytelling*, Kogan Page, London

Gabbatt, A (2020) Aunt Jemima Brand to change name and logo due to racial stereotyping, *Guardian*, 17 June, https://www.theguardian.com/us-news/2020/jun/17/aunt-jemima-products-change-name-image-racial-stereotype (archived at https://perma.cc/7R3W-9VAN)

Good on you (2020) Wear the change you want to see, https://goodonyou.eco/about/ (archived at https://perma.cc/8LB2-LZQY)

Good Shopping Guide (2020) Ethical Shopping Guide, https://thegoodshoppingguide.com/ (archived at https://perma.cc/KA4T-E6NQ)

Gustafsson, K (2015) Oatly riles big dairy, *Bloomberg Business*, 14 May, https://www.bloomberg.com/news/articles/2015-05-14/swedish-oat-milk-producer-benefits-from-dairy-industry-lawsuit (archived at https://perma.cc/Z8M2-GG2Y)

Harari, Y N (2011) *Sapiens: A brief history of humankind*, Harper, London

Hibberd, J (2020) Netflix adds Black Lives Matter as a new genre after The Help concerns, *EW Entertainment*, 10 June, https://ew.com/tv/netflix-black-lives-matter-genre/ (archived at https://perma.cc/34V5-YAYK)

Hickman, A (2018) Iceland's Rang-tan campaign delivers 65m views, sales and consideration lift, *PR Week News Analysis*, 3 December, https://www.prweek.com/article/1520088/icelands-rang-tan-campaign-delivers-65m-views-sales-consideration-lift (archived at https://perma.cc/4HSR-6M58)

Legum, J (2020) Corporations tweet support for Black Lives Matter. Their FEC filings tell a different story, *Popular Information*, 2 June, https://popular.info/p/corporations-tweet-support-for-black (archived at https://perma.cc/ZX6E-LJK7)

Maslansky (2020) It's not what you say, it's what they hear, https://maslansky.com/ (archived at https://perma.cc/48Q3-7MR7)

Maslow, A H (1943) A Theory of Human Motivation, *Psychological Review*, 50, pp 370–96

Mody, P (2020) L'Oréal Paris regrets how the situation was handled; Fired employee Munroe Bergdorf rejoins after BLM backlash, *Pink Villa*, 11 June, https://www.pinkvilla.com/fashion/celebrity-style/lor-al-paris-regrets-how-situation-was-handled-fired-employee-munroe-bergdorf-rejoins-after-blm-backlash (archived at https://perma.cc/Z32B-4R6N)

NewsWhip (2020) Predictive Media Intelligence, *NewsWhip*, https://www.newswhip.com/ (archived at https://perma.cc/8HJF-L6HP)

Poe, M T (2012) *A History of Communications*, Cambridge University Press, Cambridge

Sammer, P (2014) *Storytelling: Die zukunft von PR und marketing*, O'Reilly Germany, Berlin

Streeter, K (2020) Kneeling, fiercely debated in the N.F.L., resonates in protests, *New York Times*, 5 June, https://www.nytimes.com/2020/06/05/sports/football/george-floyd-kaepernick-kneeling-nfl-protests.html?auth=login-facebook&login=email (archived at https://perma.cc/FKA6-BGCT)

Tagger (2020) The #1 data-driven Influencer Marketing platform, https://www.taggermedia.com/ (archived at https://perma.cc/4YSY-EAV4)

Unilever (2019) Brands with purpose grow – and here's the proof, *Unilever News and Features*, 6 November, https://www.unilever.com/news/news-and-features/Feature-article/2019/brands-with-purpose-grow-and-here-is-the-proof.html (archived at https://perma.cc/Y8GH-TB4G)

United Nations (2015) The 17 Goals, UN Department of Economic and Social Affairs, n.d. Available from: https://sdgs.un.org/goals (archived at https://perma.cc/288Z-NXAN)

Whitehead, J (2019) 8 times 'woke' advertising campaigns misfired, from Pepsi to Listerine, *Independent*, 22 May, https://www.independent.co.uk/life-style/love-sex/men-women/listerine-pride-rainbow-pepsi-mcdonalds-starbucks-social-justice-a8925526.html (archived at https://perma.cc/W5WU-GZQ5)

07

The what: understanding your channels

Now that you have considered where your purpose sits and how it drives your business, and after fully appreciating the human needs and expectations of your various audiences, you should be confident enough to attempt a draft of your Purpose Story Framework™, as discussed in Chapter 6. Having done that, you are now ready to put all of this new-found knowledge and understanding to work. As we keep emphasizing and widely acknowledged research keeps reminding us, purpose-led marketing works and works best when it's truth-based (Barton *et al*, 2018).

Does this mean you are ready to set off and commission a famous film director and creative studio for a short series of films to tell your purpose story to a worldwide audience during the Super Bowl, to explain how your products help save the planet, or how your commitment around diversity increases innovation? Well, maybe, but probably not.

The best opportunities to convey your human truth-based achievements, commitments and aspiration stories, are often those that arise in your business's normal day-to-day operations, or from situations originating externally, from news events or changes in public opinion. A splashy advert may help convey your sense of purpose, and we have seen cases where they have worked well, but as a general rule, there are more authentic situations for conversations with your purposeful audience. In this chapter we focus on *when* and *where* to share these stories.

If one was planning traditional marketing or communications activities, you might consider the when and the where as 'campaigns', waged through specifically identified channels. But whilst the campaign concept remains somewhat useful in the current purposeful age, it falls short of meeting all the needs of our volatile and uncertain realities. We recommend planning and activating marketing and communications work through 'moments', those we can control (not unlike 'campaigns'), and those we can merely anticipate or respond to (like news events). This is best achieved through channels that operate more like communities, with their own norms, rules and behaviours. In this chapter we examine moments and channels (and their communities) and explain ways to help you incorporate both into the strategies that support the drive towards your purpose.

Beyond moments of truth

The word 'moment' is a strangely vague term for a short though unspecific period of time, but it has been generally understood to describe a more precise instance of becoming *aware* of something, an idea, a fact, or a feeling. We experience moments of doubt, bliss, inertia, suspense and, of course, moments of truth.

There is nothing particularly novel about the concept of 'moments of truth' in marketing. Such terminology has been in regular use since at least the 1980s, with comments made by Scandinavian Airlines CEO Jan Carlzon, which have subsequently been expanded upon ever since by great thinkers from some of the world's most successful businesses, including P&G, Google and Apple, amongst others. These moments reflect various inflection points on consumers' journeys as they consider and purchase products or services (and beyond), and how each affects their experience (Hyken, 2016).

The traditional marketing moments of truth are worth summarizing here:

- **Researching** a product or service (reading reviews, asking friends for recommendations).
- **Examining** a product or service (in-store or online).
- **Purchasing** the product or service.
- The **gap** between ordering a product and awaiting its arrival (when the experience may be in the hands of a third-party delivery service).
- Providing **feedback** on the product (including ratings and reviews, often public, as well as 'unboxing' videos shared online, often with commentary).

Such moments, however defined, are useful in traditional transactional marketing activity on their own and in part speak to the wider requirements of a purposeful approach too. The consumer's experience with your product or services will of course need to align with each of these moments. These in turn follow earlier, crucial decisions that reflect just how embedded purpose is within your business, including sourcing, manufacturing, pricing, distribution and every other aspect of how it is run and financed.

We think of these purposeful moments in two ways: internal and external. Internal moments stem from the actual running of the business, and they are often scheduled and planned interactions with audiences. These include earnings reports, sales meetings, employee town halls, annual reports, analyst briefings, product launches, executive appointments, mergers, acquisitions, and a whole raft of similar announcements and disclosures, some required by law, and others seen simply as positive, differentiating news to communicate. Not all internal moments are planned, or necessarily good news; product failures, negative litigation, disappointing financial results, and executive scandals are just a few examples of instances that will require interaction with your purposeful audience. But, good news or bad, all of these moments are opportunities to live and convey your purposeful stories.

The second kind of purposeful moments of truth are what we call 'external', and usually arise from outside the business or brand, somewhere 'out in the world', such as news events or popular culture, amongst other sources. Although it is possible for an external moment to emerge in reaction to a particular company's policies or behaviours, for example a backlash to a scandal, they generally have no direct connection to the business or brand unless that tie is *intentionally* established or, over time, the business is compelled to clarify its position.

External moments of truth can include fixtures on the calendar – holidays, commemorations, sport, elections, and cultural events such as the BAFTAs or Grammys, but they can pop up unexpectedly, too: natural disasters, market crashes, celebrity deaths, or public reactions to government policies, are just a few of the less predictable, externally driven occurrences. These are all capable of igniting social conversations, sometimes with businesses being expected to respond. Again, these may be plannable or not, and positive or not, but they all present opportunities to convey a true brand's purpose. Whether they *should* be the moments you choose to tell your stories is another question altogether, and we will address this after we have briefly expanded a bit further on our two kinds of moments of truth (internal and external) and which kinds of purposeful stories they may or may not lend themselves to (achievement, commitment, aspirational).

Context is everything

Understanding which kinds of stories lend themselves best to different kinds of moments is of course a matter of context, and every business is different, with its own unique track record, culture, and leadership, all of which inform the reputation and credibility attached to it by various audiences. Companies with a history of safety problems or product recalls, for example, may find it difficult to tell achievement stories without making strong, plausible commitments to improve. And brands recognized for consistently meeting business and purpose targets may find it necessary to engage in even bolder, aspirational storytelling to maintain momentum.

Context, in terms of conveying purpose, has in our thinking three main components: audience needs and expectations, as discussed in the preceding chapter; what's happening inside the business and out in the world, as discussed in various places throughout this book; and corporate reputation. There is an abundance of literature and discussion on the importance of corporate reputation and its impact on attracting talent (Auger *et al*, 2013), boosting customer loyalty (Nguyen and Leblanc, 2001), and even adding to the business's market value (Black and Carnes, 2000). We often counsel clients to look to the Fortune/Korn Ferry list of attributes associated with 'most admired companies' as a gauge for their own corporate reputations.

FORTUNE/KORN FERRY ATTRIBUTES OF MOST ADMIRED
COMPANIES

- Ability to attract and retain talented people.
- Quality of management.
- Social responsibility to the community and the environment.
- Innovativeness.
- Quality of products or services.
- Wise use of corporate assets.
- Financial soundness.
- Long-term investment value.
- Effectiveness in doing business globally.

(Korn Ferry, 2020)

A British version of these attributes considers diversity and inclusion (D&I) as a specific metric as well, which we believe is highly relevant to today's operating environment and societal expectation (Management Today, 2019). You may choose to consider specific attributes more closely than others, but it is important to remember these are the things your purposeful audience will consider in their entirety, so it is always best to begin your planning with a thorough and candid assessment of your business's reputation, or that of the brand you are supporting; this is your licence to communicate.

Before we examine some of the moments available to you for purpose-led storytelling, it is worth us explaining more about the kinds of stories discussed as part of the Purpose Story Framework™ in the preceding chapter:

- **Achievement** stories are those that underpin your efforts and successes thus far in your pursuit of your purpose. They are the proof points behind your marketing and communications, aligned with the needs and expectations of your transactional and purposeful audiences, and are often drawn from your day-to-day operations. They are likely to comprise the majority of your purpose-led stories.

- **Commitment** stories are those that reflect an opportunity to collaborate with your audience, or components of it, to either continue progress beyond earlier achievements, or to address setbacks or new developments. These relate to corporate vision and often include partnerships with third-party organizations representing key segments of your purposeful audience. There are likely to be multiple commitments underway at any given time, and we advise clients to develop stories for the good as well as for the not so good.

- **Aspirational** stories set sights a bit further out, usually towards a big, audacious goal. BP, for example, in pursuit of its vision to reimagine energy for people and the planet, aims to be a 'net zero' (commitment to balance any carbon emissions by absorbing an equivalent amount from the atmosphere) company by 2050 – no small pledge for a company that emits 415 million tonnes annually (British Petroleum, 2020). It is unlikely a business will have more than one or two such aspirations at once, and given their size and impact, they can serve as focal points for achievement stories (successes so far) and commitment stories (like progress reports).

With these in mind, let's take a look at some of the moments when purpose-led stories can be exchanged most authentically and meaningfully (and those which perhaps should be avoided).

THE TRUTH, THE WHOLE TRUTH AND NOTHING BUT

First, an important reminder of the importance of truth. It should be clear that in understanding purpose, audiences, the stories we share and the moments we choose for them, they simply form the basis to get beyond limiting assumptions of traditional marketing and communications. The approach outlined still requires the conventions but expands considerations beyond the simple transactional approach. The truthful purpose model should reinforce existing rules for *any* kind of exchange between your business and the wider world in our present purposeful age:

- be transparent with the truth;

- express the truth in terms your audiences can *understand* and *believe*;

- when the truth is less than the audience expects, work with them to *bridge* the gap;

- when you can choose the timing, choose moments where the truth *shines* brightest;

- when you cannot choose the timing (or the issue), avoid over-promising or making commitments you have not had the opportunity to fully evaluate.

The first two of these rules are self-evident: the truth matters and the way in which it is conveyed, on the audience's terms, is crucial. The third may be reassuring, as all businesses will at some point fall short of a customer's expectations, but a purpose-led organization or brand will see those instances as opportunities to regain trust and confidence through collaboration and renewed commitments.

The fourth reaffirms a reality that many brands overlook, which is that often the best, most authentic moments to engage an audience arise in your own regular operations, or at moments when public attention is already drawn to the purpose you share with your audience.

And the fifth rule, jumping on the bandwagon when an issue arises, is tempting, especially with louder and louder calls for brand activism, but research from the Amsterdam-based communications consultancy OPRG NL shows that executives are nervous to jump in head-first (Omnicom, 2019). Rightly so, in our opinion, but this does not mean necessarily not speaking out. Leaders or brands as such can express opinions, we just recommend caution, so listen carefully, get stories straight and tread lightly.

Opportunities, not circumstances

'Real-time agility' and 'shared synergies' are two of those jargonistic objectives that many businesses pursue today, but few seem to fully achieve. In our experience working with companies and brands of all sizes, several realities seem to block them from fully operating with either. Firstly, they tend to operate in silos, with marketing, sales and corporate communications mostly marching to different beats and often in slightly different directions. Secondly, even when activities are centrally planned with every intention of integrated activation, the reality is that they move in different cycles to different tempos; sales synch with purchasing modes, marketing and advertising have production and buying timelines to respect, and communications tends to be guided by corporate financial reporting calendars. And thirdly, it's rough out there. Situations arise, the public mood shifts, and stuff happens – all of which makes it difficult to stick to an annual game plan.

These are real obstacles for any brand trying to stay in step with its audience in a fast-moving, always-on marketplace, and to overcome them we take inspiration from none other than the legendary martial artist, actor and writer, Bruce Lee: 'To hell with circumstances, I create opportunities' (Bruce Lee Foundation, 2020).

One cannot control the circumstances that govern production processes or sales cycles, and much of your effort will need to continue to work within them. But if you allow yourself to look past them, to the moments to engage your audiences that arise every single day, you will see more opportunities than barriers. Clear focus on this will give an elevated perspective to take advantage of the authentic, human-led moments of truth around throughout the year.

We have already described two dimensions of these purposeful moments of truth as internal (relating mostly to how the business is run) or external (relating to external needs and expectations), that may evolve slowly or shift suddenly, depending on events. A second consideration is how plannable or unplannable they are. Some, whether operational or social, are highly plannable; financial reporting, product launches, or new HR policies are all generally plannable operational moments of truth, whereas a product recall, production accident or lawsuit may be less plannable.

On the external side, the calendar abounds with plannable moments: Ramadan, summer holidays, World Cup finals or pronouncements from the World Economic Forum annual meeting in Davos. Less plannable, but no less significant, are the moments associated with natural events: an Icelandic volcano eruption, for example, a global pandemic, or Hurricane Maria, or

FIGURE 7.1 Purposeful and plannable moments

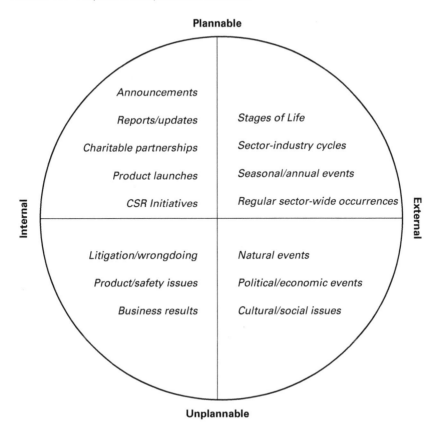

those spurred by cultural, political or business developments, such as a US travel ban on visitors from certain countries, protests against racial inequality, or a declaration of independence by a royal couple.

For illustrative use we have plotted a few kinds of moments in their respective quadrants in Figure 7.1, knowing of course that real life is a bit messier, but believing, as Mr Lee said, that circumstances can give way to opportunity when there is a will and that taking inventory of your available moments of truth is an important step towards exercising that will. What follows is a quadrant-by-quadrant set of moments for consideration as opportunities to convey your purposeful stories, as well as some guidance for each.

Plannable–internal

In our experience the upper left quadrant is the richest territory for finding authentic, credible moments for engaging a business's purposeful audience, and with good reason: it covers the areas we know best, and with the fewest levels of uncertainty, two factors that combine to raise the likelihood for success whilst reducing risks for miscues and mistakes. It also underscores the fact that human-led purpose is a business strategy, not solely a market-ing tactic, and it should be your first port of call for planning your communications.

Virtually every single day of the year presents plannable operational moments to share meaningful stories, but some will be more powerful or easier to convey than others, and some will lend themselves more or less readily to explicit references to purpose. Each of these are instances to remind audiences why the business exists and how it is planning and meas-uring its progress toward that purpose. Consider the following examples of activity which may already offer you opportunities:

- **Internal announcements.** Changes to HR policy, new training programmes, workforce changes, vendor or supplier updates – all are opportunities to reaffirm the purpose and establish how their roles support it, and to ensure the stories told inside the company align with those conveyed outside: 'Our purpose drives our people, and our people drive our purpose in the following ways…'

- **Scheduled reports and updates.** Quarterly financial reports, sales meetings, shareholder conferences and regulatory filings are also opportunities to reinforce purpose internally while conveying it externally: 'We are successful because what we do matters and we do it well, as shown by X, Y and Z…'

- **Product/service innovations and launches.** Attention usually focuses understandably on how new or improved features will benefit the customer, but these are also opportunities to tie them to the larger purpose: 'We share common aspirations with our customers, and this is another important step in our journey together, as shown by…'

- **Charitable, philanthropic or community commitments.** These are some-times confused with purpose itself, or predicated on sufficient levels of financial success, but they are more powerful when associated clearly with the business's purpose: 'Our success requires close partnerships and alliances with organizations that share our sense of purpose, which is why we are committing to 1, 2 and 3…'

In general, these kinds of standard, almost daily activities, offer credible moments to convey purpose and establish its guiding presence throughout the enterprise, do not require significant investments of time or money to effect, and happen frequently enough to offer the benefit of repetition. They require only that you think about purpose and how they connect to it with every piece of planned content or activity, and they typically lend themselves to any of our three story types – achievement, commitment, and aspirational.

Unplannable–internal

Every business will encounter surprises that could not have been foreseen. Sometimes the surprises are good news such as a technological breakthrough, unexpected windfall, or a major new customer. But often the surprises are the kind that the company would have preferred to avoid, like a major accident, litigation, or a blown forecast. In these cases, the business would usually rather not discuss them at all if possible, and would not see them as moments to associate with their purpose. But these unplannable–internal moments should not be immediately swept under the rug and might even offer opportunities to be stronger in the affirmation of the business's purpose.

In good news surprise scenarios, these moments can be treated as those in the quadrant above, as opportunities to connect success with purpose. In situations where the unplanned event was not as positive, they should still be addressed, unless legally constrained, with your audience's needs in mind and against your purpose. These kinds of unplannable–internal moments can include the following:

- **Product/service safety issues.** Accidents, product defects, etc are often less damaging to a company or brand's reputation than the inability or unwillingness to take responsibility and commit to change. A clear connection to purpose points the way: 'We are in the business of helping people, not harming them, and we will work with A, B and C to get back on track and make sure this does not undermine our purpose again in the future...'

- **Litigation/corporate wrongdoing.** Negative lawsuits, compliance breakdowns and other instances of unintentional or even criminal events are a reality in business today. Purpose stories cannot wash them away, but they can illuminate a recovery strategy if offered sincerely with clear actions and milestones: 'We have fallen short of our purpose and will work with A, B and C to achieve 1, 2 and 3 and restore the confidence of all of our partners and stakeholders...'

- **Disappointing business results.** It happens. Sales fall unexpectedly, earnings dip, forecasts are missed. The reasons will vary, as will the required corrections, but none should be seen as a reason to back away from the organization's sense of purpose. 'Our purpose guides our business strategy, but our execution has fallen short, so we are taking the following actions to get back on track.'

In general, these kinds of events should be neither ignored nor used to dilute a company's pursuit of purpose. However, we have to accept that purpose stories cannot magically make them go away. But used as a compass, a company or brand's purpose, supported by a story framework developed in collaboration with its audience, can help restore credibility and reputation when *unplanned* operational moments arise. These situations often call for commitment stories to convey an intention to collaborate and improve.

Plannable–external

Even in today's current ambiguous, uncertain environment, much of life moves in predictable patterns throughout the year. Holidays are planned, families prepare for school, historical anniversaries are commemorated, the seasons turn, and the world seems to offer an almost infinite number of social moments for a brand to engage its audience. This quadrant is attractive for purposeful storytelling because it includes moments that are already in the collective imagination or actual plans and activities of the public, and they can be anticipated and planned for in advance, like those in the opposite operational quadrant. There are hundreds of such plannable–external moments for a company or brand to utilize and determining which are appropriate will depend on the nature, sector and objectives of the business. Some of the more common kinds of moments in this quadrant include:

- **Seasonal/annual observances.** The coming of spring, back to school, tax day, or even Boxing Day lunch are all moments for positive, authentic stories about a business's purpose and its efforts to realize it: 'At this time of year, we are reminded of the importance of X and the need to reaffirm our commitments to Y and Z to see it into the future...'
- **Sector/industry-specific cycles.** Fashion weeks, auto shows, technology events and the like present opportunities to differentiate a brand or product with key audiences through positive, purposeful storytelling: 'As part of our commitment to A, we are proud to share a progress report/ new set of commitments to achieve it...'

- **Stages of life.** Human experiences shared throughout the year can be imagined as moments for purposeful storytelling, too. Pregnancy and childbirth, young families, coming of age, weddings and funerals – the list goes on – offer especially powerful opportunities because they are so fundamentally human, shared and understandable: 'In our pursuit of X, we understand this crucial stage and the challenges/opportunities it presents, which is why we are committed to 1, 2 and 3...'

In general, plannable–external moments have the inherent advantage of being part of the local, national or global zeitgeist, making them natural, credible opportunities for businesses to engage audiences with stories of shared purpose. By their nature – seasonal, cyclical or ongoing – they can be planned collaboratively with audiences, utilizing any of our main story types.

Unplannable–external

This quadrant is in some ways the danger zone for purposeful communications and marketing, inhabited by moments that arise unpredictably and potentially spread uncontrollably. These externally spawned moments – outrage over a social injustice, for example, or the COVID-19 pandemic and associated public health interventions – generate a public roar that is hard to direct and almost impossible to be heard within.

This is not to say there are no opportunities created by unplannable–external moments to engage audiences authentically; in fact, as we have seen in earlier chapters, brands with established, purposeful stories have managed to shine in the midst of these tumultuous moments. But many others, as we have also seen, have stumbled, often either because they chose to associate with moments that were disconnected from their purpose, or because the stories they chose to tell did not align with what the audience believed or knew about them. By definition, unplannable–external moments are difficult to categorize completely. From John's military past and training comes the old adage that no plan survives the first shot and so a military approach is to ensure that when the unexpected happens, there is a framework they can apply to any scenario which allows them to 'grip' the situation. Perhaps a standard set of appreciation principles can then offer some recourse. Looking back over recent years, we can group them into a few kinds:

- **Natural events.** With the possible exceptions of solar eclipses or passing comets, natural events that capture the public's attention are generally negative: earthquakes, storms, wildfires and pandemics, amongst others.

They can, however, provide opportunities for positive engagement by businesses with the right sets of capabilities and commitments: 'Because we are committed to X, and because our people/customers/communities need us more than ever, we are delivering Y during this time of shared crisis...'

- **Political/economic issues.** In an increasingly polarized world, it can seem that everything is becoming political. An Irish referendum on marriage equality, the French yellow vest protests, Brexit in the UK, MAGA in the US – it is hard to find much in life that has not been reduced to political, partisan terms. These and other issues are lightning rods for heated, emotional feedback, and whilst the number of moments they create for interaction is almost infinite, the quality of those moments is hard to know in advance. We advise clients to exercise extreme caution before weighing in on these discussions, and to discuss their purpose at the highest possible level when they feel compelled to do so: 'Because our purpose of X rests on opportunity/equality/democracy etc, we are committed to 1, 2 and 3...'

- **Cultural/social trends.** Closely related to and often overlapping with political and economic events are the cultural and social developments that suddenly take on a sense of urgency in public discourse. These can include the Black Lives Matter and MeToo movements but also less specific topics of discussion and debate, such as diet and lifestyle, diversity and inclusion, immigration and refugees, international conflicts and climate change. Here again, we tell clients to let their audiences be their guides, to make sure their 'inside realities' align with their external stories, and to tread lightly: 'Because we exist to do A, we are striving to understand and improve our capacities to address the issues and opportunities associated with it in the lives of our people/customers/communities...'

In general, recent events have promoted unplannable–external moments to the top of the shared public agenda, and purpose-led businesses justifiably feel compelled to be attentive; brands are striving to become what the consultancy Wolff Olins describes as 'conscious' – conscientious, responsive and responsible (Wolff Olins, 2020). We of course agree, but we also recommend choosing these moments very carefully, and only when your stories, likely a mix of achievement and commitment messages, add up to address them fully.

And with that, it is time to look at *where* to share your purpose stories.

Choose channels that work

There is a saying amongst the cynics of our industry that half of all advertising spending is wasted, it is just not clear which half. We do not share the cynicism, but we fully appreciate the necessity of evaluating return on investment, and in the next chapter we will take a closer look at some of the ways in which the impact of human-focused, purpose-led marketing and communications can be measured. For now, we want to examine some of the more common channels for delivering these stories, and one of the simpler, cleaner ways to think about these is PESO (paid, earned, social and owned) media channels, a model credited to the US consultant and author, Gini Dietrich (2014).

There is of course a great deal of overlap among these four kinds of channels, and more ways to mash them up emerging every day as people expect brands and content to follow them where they are, across two or three (or more) different devices, rather than hoping to find them or drive them to a particular channel (Johnston, 2014) but it remains a useful way to consider channels in broad strokes:

- **PAID** media includes adverts delivered through traditional (eg television, radio, print, outdoor) channels as well as digital platforms in the form of pop-up, banner or display content. Placement and timing of the content is secured by payment.

- **EARNED** media includes information conveyed, stories told, or opinions offered about the business, brand or its products and services through a news article, a review or a third-party expert or independent endorser. The placement is earned through the judgement of the journalist or endorser.

- **SOCIAL** (sometimes called shared) platforms enable users to post and share content they create themselves, or from other channels, including paid, earned and owned.

- **OWNED** properties include the business or brand's websites, blogs, online catalogues or shops, some of which stand alone whilst others are hosted on social media platforms (Bailey, 2019).

Ideally your stories will be told across some combination of, or all of these channels, engaging your audience on their own terms, seamlessly and unobtrusively connecting with them as they scroll down their social media feeds, browse their favourite media apps and listen in to their favoured news.

In reality, this happens less than we might like, due to causes we have discussed (siloed nature of businesses, different cycles and tempos of planning and production, or simply missed opportunities to make ideas work across channels, amongst many others), but we are confident that purpose-led businesses will have an advantage for integrating their marketing and communications for one simple reason: purpose is fundamentally a unifying agent. Aligned to human needs and told in relevant, meaningful moments, purposeful stories hold together in ways that separate, disconnected advert campaigns, PR programmes or sales initiatives simply cannot.

Interestingly, our quantitative research showed strong views on the fact that purpose was seen as applicable across the business overall, rather than just across the communication activity. This inevitably meant it was also seen to influence how a story was told, in that it was a necessity to thereby use multiple channels. Significant numbers consider purpose is applicable or should actively be helping to create core communications and within this, 95 per cent of respondents believed purpose was universally helpful in creating and driving all aspects of how the story was presented. Sixty-nine per cent felt that it should always be reflected in marketing and communications activity.

Misinterpreting facts

The downside of any marketing or communications model, including PESO, is that they can inadvertently lead to the (mis)interpretation of activity that happens separately or independently from the business's core operations. In a purpose-led enterprise, however, these areas are part and parcel of the same overarching commitment. This means that virtually all communications and marketing should be led by truth aligned to purpose and (almost as a contradiction to convention) the most compelling messages are not as such 'marketed' in a traditional sense but are actually illustrated through the true behaviours of the business. This creates real, accountable, transparent and authentic communication that can contrast greatly with more contrived, however seemingly 'clever' campaigns. Two examples come to mind.

The first involved a client in the pharmaceuticals sector, producer of a medicine popular with prescribing physicians and the public alike. Sales were climbing, patient outcomes were improving, and the product practically marketed itself. It was almost too good to be true. Then a prestigious medical journal alerted the company to data emerging that suggested there could be safety issues, which they would be relaying in an upcoming article.

The numbers were small compared to the overall rates of successful use, and no doubt other businesses would have argued to challenge the data, or to explain the relatively low risks to prescribers. In a noisy conference room crowded with medical experts, statisticians, lawyers, and PR people, the CEO listened briefly to the various courses of action available and then called for quiet.

'We're in the business of making people healthier, not sicker. We'll suspend sales now and work with the authorities to get to the bottom of this,' he said, or words to that effect. It was an expensive decision and was followed by inevitable litigation, but it left no doubt amongst the business's wide set of stakeholders what its true purpose was.

The second example is a bit more personal. Dozing on take-off of a routine, short-haul business trip a few years ago, David was jolted awake by a loud bang and the shouts of a few fellow passengers. An engine cover had blown off during the take-off, leading to a small fire and a sudden, dramatic return to the airport, broadcast on national television. There were no serious injuries beyond a sprained ankle or wrist from the bounce down the emergency exit slides, but it was a blow to the airline, a respected national carrier with an outstanding safety record. Their response, following the routine debriefings by the border authorities, local police, air travel authority and airline safety officials, was remarkable. Every passenger received periodic calls from mental health consultants to discuss any related stress or trauma, and all were offered a generous package of travel benefits (which may sound counterintuitive, but what better signal of confidence for inspiring future loyalty?), as well as periodic updates on the investigation into the accident itself. Some may dismiss this as the difference between marketing and communications, or simply basic customer relations, but for David and many of his fellow passengers he stayed in touch with, it was a demonstration of commitment to purpose, and re-establishing broken trust. And it worked.

In these two unplannable–internal examples, businesses allowed their truth-based purpose to guide business strategy, and for communications to convey it. To be sure, there were protocols in place (and regulatory and statutory requirements) to guide the activity, but the decisions around them were driven by the business's sense of purpose, and how best to express them.

But what about those moments when it is advantageous to intentionally build purpose into marketing, when the reality of what you do and how you operate speaks authentically to your purposeful audience?

According to Jon Harris, Senior Vice President and Chief Communications Officer for Conagra Brands, the key is to keep listening to your audience and to stay in the moment (that word again) with them as their circumstances change:

> As a food company, we've always focused on helping people eat great food at home, so solution-based marketing and communication was not new for us. We have a website that is regularly updated with recipes and articles based on what foods consumers are searching for on Google and other platforms. During COVID-19, we pivoted to helping consumers with the current situation – showing how brands like Duncan Hines could serve as a replacement for flour or pancake mix if they couldn't find it and offered tips from Orville Redenbacher's for throwing a great at-home movie night.

No doubt many brands have found purpose-led moments to connect with audiences in recent times and we have touched on a few earlier that managed to do it well, as well as some that did not. But the truth is, it does not require a pandemic to find ways to creatively and authentically connect with audiences. In fact, it should not.

Truth inspired

There are dozens if not hundreds of good examples of businesses finding the right moments to share meaningful stories to inspire your own thinking. Some are examples of how to make use of paid channels, whilst others make more use of earned content or social platforms. Selected below are a few to illustrate the possibilities of how truth-led, purpose stories play across multiple channels:

- **Essity** is a global manufacturer of feminine hygiene products, marketed under the Libresse and Bodyform brands. Over the past few years the company has released a series of provocative adverts, films, songs and social media memes to challenge the taboos associated with female genitalia, menstruation and reproductive health. These pieces of content speak to a widening discussion of gender equality, with paid placements greatly amplified on social media and news coverage (Petter, 2020).

- Specs maker **Warby-Parker** was 'founded with a rebellious spirit and a lofty objective: to offer designer eyewear at a revolutionary price, while leading the way for socially conscious businesses.' The company sells directly to consumers, online and through a few brick-and-mortar retail outlets, giving a pair of eyeglasses to someone in need for each pair sold.

Their purpose-led strategy requires constant innovation and novelty in their marketing and communications in order to hold attention, as exemplified by the 'Spinnies' project, with US comedian and talk show host Jimmy Fallon introducing a new range of eyewear that spins at the temple (for people who like to twirl their spectacles, apparently). The paid spending was low, as the content benefited from a celebrity endorser and was widely shared on social platforms, owned channels and through news coverage (Warby Parker, 2019).

- Car manufacturer **Volvo**, with a purpose of 'providing freedom to move in a personal, sustainable and safe way', launched the award-winning Equal Vehicles Initiative, a play on the equal rights initiative to amend the US constitution, to draw attention to the fact that women are more likely to die in car crashes, partly because crash-test dummies are based on men. As part of the programme the company released its own crash data, going back decades, to encourage the whole industry to improve design. The content was compellingly newsworthy for earned exposure, with interesting visuals to share on owned and social platforms (Volvo, 2020).

- British retail bakery **Greggs**, committed to 'great-tasting, freshly prepared food that customers can trust at affordable prices', launched a new vegan sausage roll in a nod to a growing audience for meat-alternative products. That launch, supported by Apple-spoof ads on its own YouTube channel, mock iPhone packaging and a spat with celebrity journalist Piers Morgan on social media, earned enormous exposure for both the product and the company's commitment to staying in step with customers (Robertson, 2019).

- Occasionally a brand finds itself on the back foot with regard to its purpose. The chicken chain **KFC**, committed to providing food that is 'always craveable' and 'to ensure that every guest leaves happy', found promises impossible to keep when it ran out of chicken. Other brands might have chosen to lay low or pass the blame, but true to its purpose, KFC took out full-page ads in the *Sun* and *Metro* to apologize for the lapse, depicting the famous bucket and the name re-arranged to spell FCK – an unambiguous apology and commitment to set things straight. The paid ads were a clear statement of seriousness, and the creative imagery guaranteed it would be shared on social media and written about in the press (Oster, 2018).

- Toymaker **Lego** has a clear purpose: 'To inspire and develop children to think creatively, reason systematically and release their potential to shape their own future.' The company's Small Builds For Big Conversations initiative helps kids and families work through questions and issues associated with online safety through its own website, featuring a series of challenges to prompt important conversations (Lego, 2020).

- And back in 2011, in what has become a classic example of 'walking the talk', outdoor apparel brand **Patagonia** paid for a full-page ad in the *New York Times* with a simple message, *Do Not Buy This Jacket*, as part of an appeal to reduce unnecessary consumerism around the 'Black Friday' spending frenzy (Patagonia, 2020).

- And finally, sometimes a brand actually finds its voice, if not its purpose, in the midst of a crisis. **Steak-umm**, a US frozen meats brand, found a lot of support with consumers during the earlier days of the COVID-19 crisis by using its Twitter account to reduce misinformation about the virus. Summarizing their position, one tweet said: 'As a company, our end goal will always be selling product, but rather than promoting ads overtly crafted to sell during this crisis, we are committed to: 1) providing factual, helpful information, 2) bridging our cultural polarization, 3) helping people who are helping people' (Di Placido, 2020).

CREATIVE FOR GOOD

There are many examples of creative, purpose-led solutions to real problems and opportunities that brands and the creative industry more widely can help address with their audiences. A few years ago, we piloted a project with the World Economic Forum, the Ad Council in the United States, the global communications consultancy Ketchum, and the Cannes Lions festival to help match brands and creative teams with social, educational and environmental causes. Interest was high, but at the time the technology was not available to create the 'matchmaker' proposition we had hoped to introduce. Perhaps conversations we hope to stimulate with this book can reinvigorate something similar in the future? (Conlon, 2013.)

One such innovation can be found in Good-Loop, an organization founded in the UK by Amy Williams and Daniel Winterstein, who were keen to see a way in which engagement with adverts could be enhanced through a cause-related mechanism that helps online ad viewers direct funds to charitable causes, some of the money that would have otherwise gone from the advertiser to the online platform without the content ever being watched, simply by engaging with the ad (Good-Loop, 2019).

Choosing the right mix of channels and content is part of the art and science of marketing and communications, and no single combination is right for every business or brand. As you have seen, investments in paid advertising can be helpful, but they are not always required. Often, it is what you say on your social media channels, or what is written about it in the news media, that pops up first when your audience is looking into who your business is and what is being said about you. This is only partly driven by marketing activity.

A journalist's perspective

Much of the purpose content we have discussed thus far is paid, from the world of advertising and marketing, but a premium is often placed on the earned coverage afforded by the attention of a prominent journalist from a respected media title for the simple reason it has passed muster with a discerning gatekeeper. The added credibility comes with a price: no tolerance for corporate flannel.

We asked Tim Race, a former colleague and now an advisor to multinational companies, for a view:

> Before I started a second career in corporate narrative development, I spent more than a quarter-century as a business editor and writer for the *New York Times*, working in New York, Paris and London. The *Times* assumes that its audience – even for much of the business coverage – is the literate generalist. And so, for a business story to resonate with that audience, the story must be relevant to the public conversation.
>
> What's more, you don't get to work at the *New York Times* or other major news organizations if you don't have a fully functioning bullshit detector. *Times* editors and reporters approach the business world with a healthy scepticism, and they typically find more news value in exposing problems, misdeeds and hypocrisy than in celebrating a company's noble purposes.

Taking the *Times* as an example of the high media bar a company must clear to communicate its purpose, Race said two key facts need grasping. First and most important, 'Corporate sincerity can't be faked,' he said. And second:

> Marketing messages are not something most journalists pay attention to, unless it's a business reporter whose beat is covering the marketing profession. Or unless it's to ridicule the aromatherapy opportunism of the ad campaigns that too many companies produce in the wake of natural disasters – or global pandemics.

Given these facts, what does it take for a company to authentically tell its 'purpose' story? Simple, Race said: 'The story must ring true. And that can happen only if it is true.'

We obviously wholeheartedly agree.

Every conversation counts

There is literally nothing said within your business or the brand you are advising, or about it by others on the outside, that cannot be guided by your truth-led purpose. Nothing that is not at some point potentially a factor that could be considered by your audiences as they weigh your commitment towards your purpose. As you plan for those internal and external moments discussed above, or imagine scenarios for the unplannable instances, there are other essential channels to add to your inventory:

- **Internal relations.** HR professionals and internal communications special-ists are essential for shaping the direction of policies related to talent and daily business operations, essentially internal relations. As such, how to communicate them through normal channels, hierarchies and rhythms is key, and the importance of purpose must come unambiguously from the top, and embed itself in every internal memorandum, intranet post or departmental meeting. As Julietta Dexter wrote in her 2020 leadership book, *Good Company: How to build a business without losing your values*, 'Make REALNESS you superpower'. Well said. We would add, 'And make purpose how you apply it'.

- **Media relations.** Much of what we understand, or believe we understand about a company or brand, comes not from its advertising, but from what we have experienced ourselves or, even more likely, what others have written or said about it. In our lengthy experience, journalists are out for news, not your friendship. Make sure your stories add up and check out, as if your employers, suppliers or even your competitors were being asked to validate them, because they very well might be.

- **Investor relations.** As described earlier, investors and the analysts who advise them are increasingly interested in non-financial information about businesses in order to assess the company's longer-term strategy, resilience and capacity to achieve it. Occasionally this is described as Purpose and is drawn from ESG (environmental, societal, governmental) reporting, but the main concern for investors is how the business model supports the long-term aims and how, according to Fabrice Baron, head of the financial communications consultancy OPRG Financial in Paris, the metrics are used to demonstrate success. Long-term vision is another important aspect, he says: 'It's one thing for a company to report its ESG achievements over the past six months, 12 months, and its targets for the next two to three years, but what investors really want to gauge is the relevance of these metrics and how they fit with the sustainability of the company over the long run.'

- **Government relations.** In our experience with policymakers over the years in Washington, London and Brussels, purpose stories are more compelling than long analyses and stacks of statistics (although you may need these too). A US member of Congress, very early in David's career, said the best way to brief his colleagues was to 'tell them what you're hoping to achieve, brag a little about what you've already done, and lay out what you're willing to commit to in exchange for support.' Sounds a lot like our Purpose Story Framework™.

- **Influencer marketing.** As mentioned in some of the cases above, the use of influencers, paid or not, to connect audiences with brands and causes has become an increasingly important resource and investment. According to Scott Guthrie, a UK expert, consultant and commentator on influencer marketing, 'Purpose helps establish and reinforce a real, meaningful connection between a brand and a consumer. Influencer marketing helps reinforce this bond because people really buy into people's stories, not brands' stories.'

Real purpose in real life

The Purpose Story Framework™, as introduced at the end of the previous chapter, helps you organize your thoughts, inventory supporting points and identify gaps, but people normally do not speak to people in frameworks. We use the acronym PACA (Figure 7.1) to help to boil down purpose stories in human terms:

- PURPOSE: 'We help people... (truth-led, human or planet benefit).'
- ACHIEVEMENT: 'So far, we have accomplished A, B, and C on this journey, in collaboration with 1, 2 and 3.'
- COMMITMENT: 'There is always more to be done, and we are committed in the near-term to delivering D, E and F in partnership with...'
- ASPIRATION: 'In the long run, we want to see... as measured by...'

FIGURE 7.2 Purposeful flow

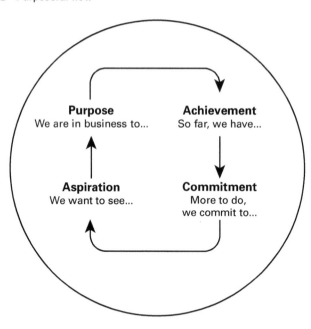

Purpose
We are in business to...

Achievement
So far, we have...

Aspiration
We want to see...

Commitment
More to do,
we commit to...

Summary

Traditional marketing and communications, planning and activation cycles are being compressed to ever-shorter periods of time by social media, mobile technology and other factors. For purposeful communications to succeed, it is instructive to think of these as 'moments' in time of shared awareness of an idea, fact or feeling, some of which arise from inside the business, others externally. We have illustrated the importance of context for choosing and activating 'moments of truth', a phrase drawn from traditional marketing which we have expanded to address moments of purposeful communications.

Moments of truth, whether internal or external, can be plannable (ie on predictable schedule) or generally unplannable (less predictable), and when plotted in quadrants provide a helpful set of points to prepare marketing and communications content and activity.

Selecting which moments will engage the audience is partly the decision of the brand, and partly of the audience, and many of the best moments in terms of authenticity are drawn from day-to-day operations that substantiate the business's sincerity and progress towards its purpose. Other moments are created, either in response to unplanned events, or intentionally through planned and activated marketing or communications activities. Both can be effective means for conveying purpose, and we discussed the PESO (paid, earned, social and owned) model as a way to describe different available channels.

There is ample inspiration for finding creative ways to communicate purpose through combinations of the various channels. Other channels, not always explicitly linked to PESO, are also important, and these are briefly described: internal communications, investor relations, government relations and influencer marketing.

Finally, a useful acronym to help summarize purposeful stories in human terms is PACA (state your business Purpose, substantiate Achievements so far, confirm Commitments for progress, and establish a longer-term Aspiration).

YOUR CHECKLIST

1 Have you mapped and prioritized your plannable moments, internally and externally?

2 Have you anticipated unplannable moments that might require a purpose-affirming response?

3 Have you assessed the business's reputation to establish where it has credibility to communicate purpose?

4 Have you begun to plan different creative approaches and the supporting content and channels to communicate purpose?

5 Have you mapped all of the opportunities in non-marketing areas of the business to reinforce your purpose stories?

6 Can you deliver a simple PACA summary of your purpose, achievements, commitments and aspiration?

References

Auger, P *et al* (2013) How much does a company's reputation matter in recruiting? *MIT Sloan Management Review*, 19 March, https://sloanreview.mit.edu/article/how-much-does-a-companys-reputation-matter-in-recruiting/ (archived at https://perma.cc/K87L-78PE)

Bailey, R (2019) Briefing: PESO, Public Relations Academy, 16 September, https://pracademy.co.uk/insights/briefing-peso/ (archived at https://perma.cc/8X27-D6JS)

Barton, R *et al* (2018) From me to we: The rise of the purpose-led brand, *Accenture Media*, https://www.accenture.com/_acnmedia/thought-leadership-assets/pdf/accenture-competitiveagility-gcpr-pov.pdf (archived at https://perma.cc/Q64K-BHVA)

Black, E L and Carnes, T A (2000) The Market Valuation of Corporate Reputation, *Corporate Reputation Review*, January, https://www.researchgate.net/publication/233665799_The_Market_Valuation_of_Corporate_Reputation (archived at https://perma.cc/9USW-TPLM)

British Petroleum (2020) Reinventing Energy, BP Global Corporate, https://www.bp.com/en/global/corporate/who-we-are/reimagining-energy.html?gclid=CjwKCAjwmMX4BRAAEiwA-zM4JnHltXyYt6lPKM35Iss14amRiWr_PWNpAXBS_SReWDC5RKstCQ9ZuxoClgsQAvD_BwE (archived at https://perma.cc/5BMM-KULR)

Bruce Lee Foundation (2020) #74 To Hell with Circumstances, Bruce Lee Foundation, https://brucelee.com/podcast-blog/2017/11/28/74-to-hell-with-circumstances (archived at https://perma.cc/6EBK-5WZ4)

Conlon, P (2013) Advertising as a force for good, World Economic Forum: Global Agenda, 24 June, https://www.weforum.org/agenda/2013/06/advertising-as-a-force-for-good/ (archived at https://perma.cc/GY9S-8ZA9)

Dexter, J (2020) *Good Company: How to build a business without losing your values*, London: Atlantic Books

Di Placido, D (2020) The strange saga of the Streak-umm Twitter account, *Forbes*, 15 April, https://www.forbes.com/sites/danidiplacido/2020/04/15/does-steak-umm-represent-the-next-mutation-of-brand-twitter/#39a675e710b7 (archived at https://perma.cc/3CTF-QCRU)

Dietrich, G (2014) *Spin Sucks: Communication and reputation management in the digital age*, New York: Pearson Education

Good-Loop (2019) The Good-Loop Story, https://good-loop.com/our-story (archived at https://perma.cc/7TBG-PVR7)

Hyken, S (2016) The new moment of truth in business, *Forbes*, 9 April, https://www.forbes.com/sites/shephyken/2016/04/09/new-moment-of-truth-in-business/#476ddb0538d9 (archived at https://perma.cc/44QW-QWD7)

Johnston, S L (2014) Media: How to prepare for a media-convergent future, *Campaign Live*, 28 August, https://www.campaignlive.co.uk/article/media-prepare-media-convergent-future/1309739 (archived at https://perma.cc/9N6N-EBEL)

Korn Ferry (2020) World's most admired companies, FORTUNE Magazine, https://www.kornferry.com/insights/articles/fortune-worlds-most-admired-companies-2019 (archived at https://perma.cc/3P74-3NNN)

Lego (2020) About Us, https://www.lego.com/en-gb/aboutus (archived at https://perma.cc/N5D5-QZA6)

Management Today (2019) Britain's most admired companies 2019: Criteria, *Management Today*, https://www.managementtoday.co.uk/britains-admired-companies-2019-criteria/reputation-matters/article/1667530 (archived at https://perma.cc/Y2YM-3EW3)

Nguyen, N and Leblanc, G (2001) Corporate image and corporate reputation in customers' retention decisions in services, *Journal of Retailing and Consumer Services*, 8 (4), https://www.sciencedirect.com/science/article/abs/pii/S0969698900000291 (archived at https://perma.cc/W4Z6-6Q9T)

Omnicom PR Group (2019) CEOs reluctant to participate in public debates, even during the corona crisis, https://www.omnicomprgroup.nl/agency-news/ceos-reluctant-to-participate-in-public-debates-even-during-the-corona-crisis/ (archived at https://perma.cc/2D6S-N29N)

Oster, E (2018) KFC responds to UK chicken shortage scandal with a timely 'FCK, We're Sorry', *Ad Week*, 23 February, https://www.adweek.com/creativity/kfc-responds-to-u-k-chicken-shortage-scandal-with-a-timely-fck-were-sorry/ (archived at https://perma.cc/QC5P-WJ4G)

Patagonia (2020) Don't Buy This Jacket, Black Friday and the *New York Times*, https://www.patagonia.com/stories/dont-buy-this-jacket-black-friday-and-the-new-york-times/story-18615.html (archived at https://perma.cc/URC6-ZUPQ)

Petter, O (2020) BodyForm advert hailed for tackling menstruation taboo endometriosis, infertility and miscarriage, *Independent*, 3 July, https://www.independent.co.uk/life-style/women/bodyform-womb-stories-periods-taboo-stigma-advert-a9599346.html (archived at https://perma.cc/9C4T-MAX9)

Robertson, J (2019) Greggs: How its vegan sausage roll stormed social media, *BBC News: Business*, 11 January, https://www.bbc.co.uk/news/business-46809868 (archived at https://perma.cc/SYS5-JCM4)

Volvo (2020) The E.V.A. Initiative: Cars should protect everyone, https://www.volvocars.com/uk/about/human-innovation/future-of-driving/safety/cars-safe-for-all (archived at https://perma.cc/REX8-S5LH)

Warby Parker (2019) The Birth of Spinnies, *YouTube*, 6 December, https://www.youtube.com/watch?v=Ta47pKFpK3M (archived at https://perma.cc/EXZ2-EESG)

Wolff Olins (2020) Conscious Brands: The race to make a better brand, https://www.wolffolins.com/views/wolff-olins-conscious-brands/ (archived at https://perma.cc/V6KW-NRWU)

08

The wow: how to measure success

In the previous chapters, we have shown how a truthful purpose can identify great storytelling potential and drive successful audience engagement across multiple channels. That is all good and well, but we still face the conundrum facing all marketing and communications professions: how does one measure success? Well in a very simplified way, we could say it is if you create a 'WOW'!

The **'WOW'** factor is a commonly used business term that normally defines what a business does to go above and beyond customer expectations. In our world, delivering this *Wow*, applying it to just one stakeholder isn't sufficient. The business of being purposeful requires you to deliver a delight, a *Wow* across all stakeholders and society at large. In these times, for the reasons we have laid out across the previous chapters, if you aren't *Wowing* across the board, you aren't *Wowing* at all. Achieving this requires the broader outlook on your role that we have promoted throughout the book and is nothing less than instilling in your various stakeholders an appreciation that your purpose is contributing positively to life generally, through all you do. This is not just how you *Wow*, but it's how you build long-term, deeply held reputational collateral.

Wow happens, of course, when what is seen as normal, the expected, the ordinary, is turned into the extraordinary. For customers it will be the experience of the product, but in this day and age, we know wider society is looking for exceptional behaviours, far beyond the customer experience, or in instances where an extraordinary proposition is based around a product. What can then be seen as an ordinary experience if you buy one product from one company can be seen as an extraordinary experience, statement, endorsement, if you purchase a similar product from another. Your aim will be to create such an appreciation in the widest range of audiences possible. It is how you then turn customers into raving fans, suppliers into partners, employees into ambassadors and more besides.

If you consider how this will then manifests itself, it can require multiple different processes to help see attributable and measurable results. In which case, just consider some of what you may be looking to achieve through establishing such a *Wow*:

- Awareness generally of your business, its purpose and how it is achieved via your products.
- Enhanced societal reputation and trust in your business and its products.
- Improved specific opinions from specific audiences, customers, employees, suppliers.
- Greater employee engagement, performance and advocacy for your business.
- Increased customer loyalty and advocacy for your business.
- Rise in share value of the business through enhanced performance.

In a more insightful manner, we all know that you cannot manage something unless you can measure it, and that what gets measured gets attention. This is as true (indeed probably more so) in the purposeful age and VUCA2.0, where cynicism is rife, budgets are diminished and leaders often struggle to know how best to respond to the type of influences we have discussed previously.

When it comes to purpose-driven communication, it can be challenging to see what metrics might best reflect the impact of your activities and across which areas of impact. There are an array of tools and advisory processes, some emerging out of national ESG/CSR/sustainability movements, some from global frameworks such as the United Nations' Sustainable Development Goals or the Global Reporting Initiative. Others have been created from within the marketing and communications field itself. Undoubtedly, all of these can be useful, but depending upon your own circumstances, size of business, role, (either in-house or advising), won't necessarily always be appropriate to measure what we describe as the *Wow* of your work. This chapter brings our key learnings and those of other experts in the field to help you find an approach capable of measuring and influencing your strategies.

Return on investment (ROI)

We all know that measuring return on investment (ROI) has been a bugbear for our profession ever since it emerged. Many will know the attribution to John Wanamaker (1838–1922), although perhaps not know him. He was a US businessman who opened one of the first and most successful department store chains, which became part of Macy's. He is credited with the phrase, 'Half the money I spend on advertising is wasted; the trouble is I don't know which half'. Today, with analytics and data traffic measured by clicks and customer acquisition, this perhaps isn't as true as it might have appeared then, but when it comes to measuring the impact of the new type of communications we advocate, not everything can be measured so easily. As we have seen, other stakeholders can rapidly affect your licence to operate, far beyond simply those who purchase from you (Bradt, 2016).

So, the first thing we need you to consider is actually what you currently do. How do you measure your existing ROI? You are likely to have existing data, coming in from various sources, delivering some degree of consistent measurement across your various channels and possibly across different geographies, products and services. In addition, it is worth looking to see what is being measured elsewhere around the business. For example, HR might well have indicators on numbers of job applicants, diversity of the workforce and other relevant supportive data that you wouldn't normally capture in the marketing and communications functions. Finance will certainly be monitoring aspects of financial performance as well as (if applicable) ESG data and shareholder reputation. All these could help support your efforts in being able to demonstrate the impact of your work and may save both time and money by not requiring you to capture information yourself.

A key indicative opportunity is of course to utilize such various methodologies to compare performance against your competitors and market norms. This methodology has already shown the positive aspects of purpose-driven strategies, as part of building up the case for what we advocate.

Measurement without understanding is pointless

First things first. The value of measuring and understanding what you have measured has one prime purpose. It is to provide you with insight into the way in which you and your leadership can have confidence in making the next decision, the next investment of effort, which in turn will have a practical and positive impact on your business's performance. It shapes decision making, not so much around the truth and your purpose, which should be well defined and established, but around its connectivity, significance and successful application into specific marketing and communication activity.

Knowing, therefore, *why* you are measuring something, allows you to be better prepared in analysing and understanding the resulting implications. In finding these answers, possibly from comparative analysis like that shown above, will still require you to ask yourself even more questions. These include:

- How much real insight is actually being contributed by your current reporting mechanisms to your planning and decision making?
- How much of your data is capable of showing distinction around your purpose agenda?
- What are you not currently measuring which might be an agenda that society will expect you to be accountable on?
- If you are inhouse, do your media partners, ad agency colleagues, PR advisors or others really understand what results you are looking for from a purpose perspective over and above what might be described as 'normal' matrices?
- What other proof points can you build in to measure broader society-wide reputation?

These sorts of questions almost certainly will require specific pre-planning around market research questions asking about societal impact issues different to those surrounding products or services. You may even wish to create new metrics that measure awareness around a third party, cause or issue, if you are seeking through your communications to support a particular stance. By way of example, how did the awareness of deforestation issues rise in UK society when value food retailer Iceland ran a Christmas advert on that issue? It didn't necessarily increase, or even aim to increase Christmas sales, but it wanted to raise awareness of a third-party issue. Societal shifts in thinking would need to be measured to indicate whether such an investment by Iceland had been worthwhile or could be equally so in future.

Define what is what

Various definitions are used by different organizations to define the parameters of measuring the impact of your efforts. One thing we find, however, is that regardless of the definitions, there is often a tendency for people simply to gravitate towards reporting on what is easiest. This inevitably means saying how much is invested and what is done, so 'we spent so much and created this advert which ran on these channels over this period'. The trouble with this, as we all can appreciate, is that it shies away from demonstrating the real impact of any effort and therefore is useless in helping to determine future courses of action. Reminding ourselves that the point of this is to drive forward future interventions, to inform the picture, is only partly shown if the impact remains unreported.

Although you will find different terminology used in different ways, our simple way of ensuring people understand what we are looking for is based on the following definitions:

Input: What is invested, both financially, in terms of time, other resources, the total value invested.

Output: What is undertaken, produced – an advert, campaign, celebrities engaged, etc.

Outcomes: What effect upon your target audience(s) in terms of raised awareness, brand recognition.

Impact: What resulting action, increased footfall, sales, reputation, opportunities.

Input and output are not outcomes or impact

We accept that *input* and *output* analysis is understandably the start point of measurement for anything you should be considering, but it simply must not end there. This really isn't enough, as the only true value for understanding the effect of your communications is the outcomes and ultimately the impact. Although many agencies concentrate on providing support around the first two, or at times three, this is primarily because they are easy. You can measure the numbers of tweets, column inches, referrals etc, increasingly of course via low-cost algorithms, but measuring, assessing impact – now there is the issue.

The challenge with this is that if you wished, you could convince yourself you are being successful when all along, nothing is really having an effect on your business. An example occurred with John in 2012 when he was leading a major campaign associated with the Queen's Diamond Jubilee, to engage as many people in the UK as possible to support a particular call to action. At one point, the agency coordinating its social media got terribly excited because they had managed to get a member of the world-famous boy band One Direction to re-tweet the call to action across his multi-million followers. This in turn was re-tweeted and liked at a level previously unprecedented within that campaign. When data was presented to John, the enthusiastic agency highlighted this and made a great show of the power of their own efforts to drive awareness of the campaign.

That all sounds good, except that at the same meeting two other items were reported. First, somewhat negatively, neither website visits nor the registration of individuals into the initiative had registered any exceptional increase in activity as a result of the One Direction tweet. As far as the campaign registered, the tweet had delivered nothing. The social media agency was adamant that this activity would bear fruit, but what John and others could see was that the followers of One Direction were not the type of audience likely to engage in this specific campaign. So, to all intents and purposes, the highlight of the agency's efforts was a misfire at the wrong demographic. They had convinced themselves that the outcome proved their effort a success, but there was no impact.

The second item on the agenda which illustrated an entirely different outcome and impact was that John had secured a media partnership with the UK magazine *Hello!* They had covered the story with some celebrities in an edition which a reader had then sent to her sister in New Zealand, thinking it would interest her. On reading it, that individual was inspired to mobilize others in New Zealand and within four months there were 40,000 participants on the other side of the world. There was a specific input, which led to a magazine article, which led to it influencing the right target audience with a resulting impact which, although perhaps unexpected, was certainly measurable and attributable.

A universal approach

We identify certain examples of supporting frameworks and mechanisms in the rest of this chapter, which you will be able to assess, alongside others you may already know about, be using already, or researching yourselves. However, at this stage we want to share with you our top tips to get you in the position to progress putting something in place to help you measure impact. They will help discussions around which tools you might choose to support your own efforts, and also ensure you have the necessary grounding within the business and in your own mindset as to what you are looking for. In our work and in conversations with others, it became clear to us that these are the six factors you should consider – we call them the 'Get & Go'.

1 **Get a start point**. Start by clarifying your baseline and the various means you have chosen or will choose to get your story across. These could include the current take-up on your marketing channels, followers on social feeds, interactions, media coverage, etc. You cannot measure progress and impact unless you are clear on your baseline.

2 **Get others on board**. Ensure whoever you are answerable to and any other internal important stakeholders (your team for example, executive or the board) understands why a process is important, your start point, what you hope to achieve, and how you will measure impact. Getting buy-in at this stage will engage them in the process and make them more interested in results.

3 **Get specific**. As definitions of success will vary and depend on many variables, clarify your agreed KPIs straight away, ensuring no misunderstanding on what you will derive from future data and how you will interpret it. This will include measuring investment in order to show ROI across all your activities and needs to be understood by those collating results for you.

4 **Get thinking 'Rialto' (the wider world)**. As we explained in Chapter 1, you need to constantly have a wider view on the world you occupy. What are your competitors measuring? What are they doing that appears successful? What are people talking about? What trends do you see? If possible, set these as a backdrop to the data and measurement when reporting.

5 **Get social**. One advantage of today's social media world is that you can see what people are saying about your efforts, instantly. Engage with it, understand it, become at one with it. This can provide snapshot quotes, anecdotal narrative to support statistical results.

6 **Get aligned**. Research those who are well established as providers of measurement support in your sector, those institutions who have publicly available market comparators and have a reputation in this space. Build a trusted, truthful relationship with them and the data in order to afford benchmarking against others and external scrutiny.

Complementary resources

A key component to our ethos is 'not reinventing the wheel' and throughout this book we have attempted to signpost useful additional links, approaches, research and supportive resources where they may add to your understanding and ability to activate truthful purpose. In this regard, when we considered the challenge in the measuring of impact, we saw the need to identify processes that could be easily followed, worked across previous silos, and could encompass the broadest set of channels – paid, earned, shared and owned. We looked closely at who we had previously worked with, our own client offerings, and those of competitors in the marketplace.

What we found was that there are some solid, considered frameworks to measuring different activities related to purpose, marketing and communications, but no single one-size-fits-all solution. In reality, businesses will need to consider several complementary approaches to registering the results of their efforts in the areas of most interest.

Below are a number of such frameworks or methodologies and resources that overlap somewhat but generally focus on either specific areas of activity or business impact. The first few help assess the impact of communications and marketing activity overall, but do not specifically address 'purpose', at least not directly; these are frameworks fit for evaluating any kind of marketing or communications exercise. Another addresses purpose in terms of how it is understood by employees, and how their engagement and subsequent culture drives business performance, and we also look at a new way to measure the overall impact of a business. Finally, we look briefly at shifting sources of public trust in various institutions worldwide over the past two decades.

Working across PESO

A good starting point is that of the International Association for the Measurement and Evaluation of Communication (AMEC, 2020). In 2016, AMEC introduced the Integrated Evaluation Framework, an interactive online tool that guides users through a process of establishing the necessary objectives to aligning a plan, setting targets and then being able to measure the effect. This was updated again in 2017, and in our opinion, affords a compelling and user-friendly process which users can follow in order to frame both inputs and eventual impact. It can be used to plan a programme in advance, assess its performance as it's running, or to evaluate its performance after the fact.

Importantly, it works across the PESO channels described in Chapter 7, giving a common language and taxonomy to professionals that in the past have often worked towards different and increasingly antiquated metrics, including 'reach' and 'recall' for paid activity and, bizarrely, the 'advertising value equivalency' (AVE) for earned content. How odd that some market-eers insist on assigning an arbitrary value to earned content based simply on the price of a similar placement of paid material.

One of the chief differentiators of the AMEC framework, in addition to being free and a 'live' and customizable tool, is that it draws from fields beyond marketing and communications to include public administration, performance management, and social psychology, amongst others.

Richard Bagnall, AMEC Chair and CEO of Europe and the Americas for CARMA, the global data media company, explained the framework's origins to us in an interview:

> Since 2010 AMEC has been responsible for a number of global educational initiatives designed to bring the PR and communications industry forward to better measurement and evaluation. We had created the Barcelona Principles – seven statements of what a good measurement programme should – and should not – include. We had created the valid metrics frameworks and had also recently released the social media measurement frameworks. By 2016 it was clear that there was an ongoing challenge. The whole direction of travel in PR and communications was towards integrated communications, yet AMEC didn't have a single recommended approach to measure comms across each area. So the idea behind the integrated evaluation framework was born.

It is already in wide use, Bagnall said:

> More than 2,000 organizations all over the world are using it as a basis for their approach to evaluation, as it is designed to work for organizations of all sizes and with any budget, working across any objective. The key thing to remember is that it is a customizable process and not a prescriptive tool that solves every problem. It is designed to guide communicators through the thought process that needs to happen to link communications objectives and goals to realistic targets, meaningful measurement and insightful evaluation. Global take-up has been phenomenal, with it being translated by volunteers into over 20 different languages.

Listening externally

Another interesting and complementary model was developed by Jim Mac-namara from the University of Technology Sydney (UTS), who collaborated with the Public Relations Institute of Australia (PRIA, where he is a fellow) to develop further guidelines with the aim of filling in some of the gaps left by existing frameworks while borrowing some of their better features. This model (see Figure 8.1), while not yet available in an online interactive format, does align in principle with the AMEC framework and, as the illustration shows, makes a few important additional points worth considering, especially when evaluating purpose-driven communications:

- It shifts objectives from being largely internally driven toward goals developed with consideration for the views, needs, and interests of stakeholders, publics and society.
- It recognizes that different stages of a programme are overlapping and contingent, rather than linear.
- It reflects the interactive, two-way nature of communications between the organization and its publics.
- It shows that all stages of communications are conducted within internal and external contexts, and these need to be monitored throughout.
- It recommends that the unintended impacts should be measured along with those created by design.

Macnamara explained to us that he was writing his book, *Evaluating Public Communication: Exploring new models, standards, and best practice* (2018) and at the time was working with AMEC as Chair of its Academic Advisory Group. He explained:

> The PRIA wanted to update its evaluation advice to members and AMEC was supportive. So, we worked together and the PRIA adopted a beta version of the 'Integrated Model of Evaluation' that has since been published in a book and academic journal articles.
>
> Of all the elements highlighted in the Integrated Model of Evaluation, the arrows representing information flow are probably the most important. They show that insights gained through formative evaluation and monitoring must be fed into the organization during planning at the input stage, as well as at the outcome stage to identify audience response to communication (Macnamara, 2018; Public Relations Institute of Australia, 2020).

Measuring multiple factors

One of the thornier challenges facing communicators or marketeers trying to prove the impact of their work is understanding the relationship between

FIGURE 8.1 Integrated model of communications

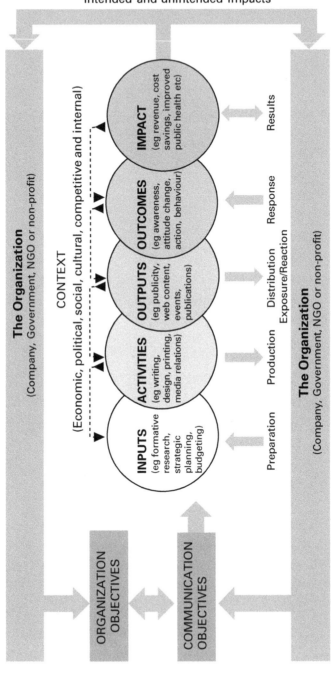

Intended and unintended impacts

The Organization
(Company, Government, NGO or non-profit)

CONTEXT
(Economic, political, social, cultural, competitive and internal)

INPUTS
(eg formative research, strategic planning, budgeting)

ACTIVITIES
(eg writing, design, printing, media relations)

OUTPUTS
(eg publicity, web content, events, publications)

OUTCOMES
(eg awareness, attitude change, action, behaviour)

IMPACT
(eg revenue, cost savings, improved public health etc)

The Organization
(Company, Government, NGO or non-profit)

Preparation

Production

Distribution
Exposure/Reaction

Response

Results

ORGANIZATION OBJECTIVES

COMMUNICATION OBJECTIVES

Reproduced with permission.
SOURCE Jim Macnamara, UTS, 2017

two or more variables of interest – after all, most marketing programmes will involve multiple inputs, activities and outputs, all of which combine differently to affect outcomes and impacts in myriad ways. Did the launch publicity generate the most web traffic? Or was it the advertising? And which landing pages produced the most purchases? And did any of it do anything that a sales force alone couldn't have done? The process of assessing which factors matter most and how they can be optimized is called regression analysis, and recent developments in the space have proven very exciting.

One of the most sophisticated software platforms delivering regression analysis we have seen on the commercial market is from Proof Analytics, a US company with clients around the world. At the heart of the Proof proposition is a fully automated 'Universal Marketing Optimization' platform that Proof calls a 'GPS' for marketing and communications. Harnessing automated data flows and automated regression analytics, Proof reveals the network effect of the multitude of factors that are causing or inhibiting outcomes. This is more far more realistic than the one-to-one correlation processes limiting most other models, as we learned in a conversation with Proof's CEO, Mark Stouse:

> What Proof has done is to take the long-proven Marketing Mix Modelling methodology introduced by Procter & Gamble and dramatically enlarge its scope while making it much easier to use and understand. In addition to assessing which variables were most important (or not) in delivering a programme's results, Proof enables you to dial up or dial down the variables to project future effects – manna for leaders looking to get the most back from their investments, and a big part of why we have found major supporters in companies like Salesforce, Deloitte, PwC, Samsung, Oracle, United Healthcare, and Johnson Controls.
>
> Historically, the use of regression modelling has been very accurate, but also very expensive, slow and hard to scale. We saw the opportunity to upend these challenges by automating most of the technical pieces, including data aggregation, cleansing, and harmonization – all of these are very tough hills for companies to climb without help. When we paired those advances with automated regression analytics, we found that the system worked almost exactly like a GPS, enabling you to see exactly how you are moving towards your goal and what is accelerating or slowing your progress. And just like the GPS in your phone, Proof shows you when you should be 'arriving' at your destination, whether you need to change your route, and what a change might mean in terms of delayed effects.

Can Universal Marketing Optimization help refine a business's purpose story framework, as described in Chapter 6? 'Absolutely,' says Stouse:

> The beauty of the algorithms is that they are completely scalable and subject-matter neutral. As such, you can evaluate the impact of any number of variables on the business outcomes most important to the company or brand, including the areas that historically have been considered 'intangible', like brand impact, audience sentiment, employee confidence, and customer trust.

Minding the authenticity gap

One theme we have touched upon frequently in this book is authenticity, and the need for companies and brands to ensure their deeds are as good as their words. FleishmanHillard, the global consultancy we have drawn from in previous chapters, has developed the Authenticity Gap methodology (see Figure 8.2) 'to help companies understand and proactively manage the gap between audiences' expectations and actual experiences with a company or brand. The insights allow organizations to create true relationships with their audiences – authentic engagement that drives progress and opportunity' (FleishmanHillard, 2020).

As Stephanie Bailey, Managing Director of the consultancy's UK corporate practice, told us:

> Walking the line between having a distinctive point of view and coming across as disingenuous is becoming increasingly more difficult for companies, particularly in today's changeable and charged environment. Using the nine drivers of authenticity allows us to establish what your audiences expect against their actual experiences of the brand. That means being able to create communications that are shaped by your different audiences and the channel you wish to use to engage with them. So, by doing this we focus on what actually matters and bridge the gap between experience and expectation to create an expression of who a brand really is, what it truly stands for (its purpose) and why it is different.

The nine drivers she mentions fall into three sets of behaviours, benefits or outcomes:

- management behaviours – doing right, consistent performance, and credible communications;
- customer benefits – better value, customer care, and innovation;
- society outcomes – care for environment, community impact, employee care.

FIGURE 8.2 Bridging the authenticity gap

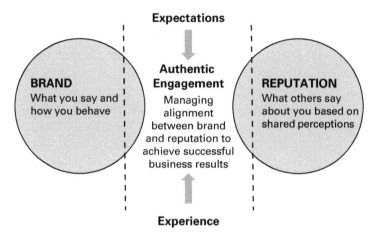

Reproduced with permission, FleishmanHillard, 2020

Building purpose from the inside

While start-up businesses have the opportunity to build first their operations and later their communications around purpose, legacy brands and established businesses must sometimes start from scratch, or at least work their way outward from some internal starting point. Ketchum, a leading global communications consultancy (where David served as UK and European Chief Executive for nearly a decade) has an inside-out, five-step purpose planning process for organizations keen to get it right, as explained to us by Jessica Mendelowitz, Managing Director, Purpose:

- Perspective: audit goals, practices, policies and protocols to identify opportunities and challenges.
- Purpose: articulate platform based on perspective that reinforces belief system.
- Partner: identify communities, internal and external partnerships to support, drive, authenticate and measure purpose.
- Programme: craft strategic plan with immediate and long-term roadmap to accelerate engagement.
- Performance: monitor, measure and evaluate to assure goal achievement and to gain social permission to proceed.

Mendelowitz went on to tell us established brands are beginning to listen more closely to their audiences:

> Purpose is moving from the executive level and making its way to the brand level, as CEOs are counting on brands to deliver ambitious corporate commitments. Even just 10 years ago, we saw brands dip a toe in purpose projects, but quickly turn away if they didn't see the return on investment, but now it's exciting to help 25-, 50-, even 75-year-old brands that are beloved by consumers find better ways to connect through a renewed sense of purpose.

Bringing purpose mainstream

Porter Novelli, a global consultancy we both work with around the world, was a pioneer in the United States in social marketing, the concept of achieving 'social good', and has been a leading advisor in the business purpose space for more than five decades. We asked Kate Cusick, the firm's Chief Marketing Officer, what they have learned over those 50-plus years:

> It sounds cliché, but the one constant we have come to expect is change. Our journey as an agency has coincided with some of the most volatile events of our lifetime, not least the 2020/21 global coronavirus pandemic and the financial crash of 2008, events that have forced businesses to change focus and behaviours. The other constant has been that companies who have responded to these challenges by prioritizing purpose have thrived – they just haven't always received credit for their commitments and for behaving in a values-driven way. It took time for the business lexicon to catch up but in 2021, at the start of the decade of delivery for the UN Sustainable Development Goals, it feels purpose has finally gone mainstream.

For business, the lesson is that there is no returning to the way things used to be, she said:

> There is this unprecedented push for corporations to build a new type of economy that is coming from stakeholders – your stakeholders. Our own research shows that 55 per cent of US adults are looking for companies to innovate solutions to create a 'new normal'. It's clear that recent events have fundamentally changed the business environment – as well as the role of business in society – and that there is more urgency than ever before for business to be a leading player in solving critical global issues.

The firm has a dedicated practice for integrated purpose communications, and produces the Porter Novelli Purpose Tracker, a rich and frequently updated source of data on consumer opinion and expectations of business on issues ranging from social justice to climate to employee safety, as well as insight into views from specific generations (Sheehan, 2020).

Measuring purpose's impact on business performance

Another approach we examined looks beyond the return on communications and marketing activity, to help make the case that purpose-driven businesses perform better overall. Organizations, now more than ever, need robust, reliable and actionable metrics to ensure firstly that purpose is authentically lived internally, and secondly (and demonstrably) so for an external audience of critics from consumers to journalists to regulators. Metrics that help the company shift from simply having, to *living* purpose and track progress in real time. After all, as discussed in Chapter 3, the great benefit of Milton Friedman's focus on the profit motive is that it can be easily measured and benchmarked, as profit gives one number to aim towards and one number to measure success against. But there is no such universally accepted measure for purpose. Even in July 2020, Blueprint for Better Business stated, 'Purpose cannot be measured directly and evaluating social outcomes and the quality of human relationships is difficult' (Blueprint for Better Business, 2020).

It was to address that deficit that Contexis, a B Corps organization, and researchers from Cambridge University came together in a four-year research programme that has resulted in the Contexis Index of Purpose Performance. The Index measures purpose and provides one single number to aim towards and measure success against. But unlike profit, this is a single measure at *source*, not at an outcome. It is a lead indicator of organizational performance, not the result of it. The Contexis methodology is unusual in focusing not on externalities but on the impact of purpose on the culture of the organization itself.

Specifically, the Index measures a specific set of human behaviours that are known to result in enhanced human and, critically, business performance. It then assesses organizational purpose and the extent to which it is impacting these positive performance behaviours. Central to the methodology is the insight that to have any impact, purpose must be *activated*, and what activates purpose is a highly specific set of cultural characteristics. These tend to be alive in agile, entrepreneurial businesses, but suppressed in most large, legacy-driven organizations. It is these characteristics, and not just purpose itself, that it suggests are behind the startling performance gains of the best purpose-led organizations. The Contexis Index uses this insight to create a measurement methodology that provides the hard numbers to answer two questions. To what extent is purpose driving performance in my organization? And how and why is it working and where is it blocked?

Contexis Index CEO John Rosling says:

> The real value of the Index is not just in the numbers that measure the authenticity of purpose and its impact on human fulfilment and business performance, but in the detailed analysis by Cambridge and ourselves that shows companies how purpose is working in each community in their global business and helps them to understand what is really driving their cultural strengths. It gives leaders the levers to pull to remove blocks and maximize cultural performance through highly focused interventions, and to track the performance of these initiatives over time. Our work funds further research whilst providing detailed analysis and recommendations to the company. We have successfully measured major organizations across the globe but are keen to work with more – in fact with any business that wants to bring its purpose to life.

Analysis has been conducted on businesses in over 20 countries on every continent (bar Antarctica) to date. So what is this significant data set revealing about purpose and its real impact on people and business across cultures?

According to Rosling:

> Getting purpose right is only the start. Bringing it to life requires a real focus on consistently and authentically living it in the strategy of the business, building radical levels of trust, and encouraging a culture of ownership for all. And that means a change in how most leaders lead. But the rewards are remarkable. We see companies who bring purpose to life seeing extraordinary leaps in human and organizational performance with real and measurable outputs in terms of commercial return.

Measuring real impact

Under today's accounting rules, companies can show healthy profitability without reflecting their actual costs or contributions to the environment. Researchers Ronald Cohen and George Serafeim from the Harvard Business School are hoping to usher in what they call the 'age of impact transparency' through a study of the costs of the environmental impact of 1,800 companies in their Impact-Weighed Account Initiative (IAWA), which launched in

July 2020. Future reports will evaluate the costs of product and employee impacts, too, to give a fuller view on the impacts that companies create.

Under the IAWA lens, some industries would see their profits eliminated or greatly reduced, the researchers wrote in the *Harvard Business Review*, while others can find a competitive advantage from benefits brought by product or employee impacts. Greater impact transparency can lead to some significant changes in how business is conducted and performance evaluated, they wrote, including:

- **Fairer corporate tax policy.** Rather than universal taxation to remedy negative impacts, governments can tax companies directly for harm or damage, or provide incentives for those that provide positive impact.
- **More accurate investment pricing.** Investors can price the environmental and social costs of companies directly into their investment analyses.
- **Better alignment with customer and employee values.** Individuals, other businesses and employees can all better evaluate their purchasing or career choices.

More profoundly:

> Impact transparency will reshape capitalism. By shifting the pursuit of profit away from negligently creating problems to purposefully creating valuable solutions for the world, it will redefine success, so that its measure is not just money, but the positive impact we make during our lives (Cohen and Serafeim, 2020).

A word on trust

Edelman, the world's largest public relations firm, has produced its Trust Barometer™ annually since 2000, examining shifting levels of trust and confidence placed by the people around the world in four major societal institutions: government, media, business and non-profits. Useful both longitudinally and with each year's report as a weathervane for gauging slowly forming patterns and sudden lurches of public opinion on who to trust, and how much.

Amongst the trends emerging over the past decade, several stand out as instructive for the VUCA2.0 age, including a widening 'mass–class' divide in which trust within the 'informed public' has soared whilst plummeting among the masses, new expectations for business and leaders to speak out on issues, and a 'battle for the truth', as social media hands content over to individuals and away from expertise.

Chief executive Richard Edelman boiled it down to this:

Throughout 20 years of studying how trust is won, violated and lost, we have learned that the two essential elements of trust are effectiveness and ethical conduct. These qualities have always been critical to any trusting relationship. What has changed profoundly are the expectations for what institutions must do to meet promises before people trust them (Edelman, 2020).

Summary

This chapter has highlighted the need for measurement, to successfully understand the impact of your efforts, in order to inform future decisions. We have focused on illustrating some practical ways to consider the challenge and some of the existing matrices we utilize, as well as complementary frameworks that can be combined for a solid starting position.

We recognize that this particular focus requires additional resource, but it is undoubtedly important if you are to move the conversation forward from the risk of being seen as esoteric, to that which can be illustrated to all across the business, namely measured, managed, and appreciated as a key component to future business success.

We also appreciate that while purpose resonates globally on a human level, it is interpreted and activated differently around the world, reflecting sometimes significant variations in culture, business history and social expectations, and these are obviously important considerations when working across borders.

By way of conclusion, before we bring all the component parts of *Truth Be Told* together in our final chapter, be sure to consider our questions below.

YOUR CHECKLIST

- Have you clear objectives, specific by audience?
- Have you detailed what Input, Output, Outcome and Impact mean in your particular case?
- Have you identified and do you have confidence in the means to measure the above?
- Have you made clear with delivery partners the distinction between quantity and quality?

- Have you identified other areas of the business that may have existing indicators?
- Have you established clarity with your key stakeholders as to why you are doing this?
- Have you consulted national or local resources for insights into important cultural, historical or business drivers or constraints related to purpose-driven communications and marketing?

References

AMEC (2020) AMEC's Integrated Evaluation Framework, https://amecorg.com/amecframework/ (archived at https://perma.cc/5MBG-9DG7)

Blueprint for Better Business (2020) Business as a force for good, https://www.blueprintforbusiness.org/ (archived at https://perma.cc/X2X8-KUUL)

Bradt, G (2016) Wanamaker was wrong—the vast majority of advertising is wasted, *Forbes*, 14 September, https://www.forbes.com/sites/georgebradt/2016/09/14/wanamaker-was-wrong-the-vast-majority-of-advertising-is-wasted/#2526c58e483b (archived at https://perma.cc/UM83-NRUX)

Cohen, R and Serafeim, G (2020) How to measure a company's real impact, Harvard Business Review, 3 September, https://hbr.org/2020/09/how-to-measure-a-companys-real-impact?ab=hero-main-text (archived at https://perma.cc/WF5F-FB5T)

Edelman (2020) 20 years of trust, https://www.edelman.com/20yearsoftrust/ (archived at https://perma.cc/K5WG-U45C)

FleishmanHillard (2020) Authenticity Gap, https://fleishmanhillard.com/products/authenticity-gap/ (archived at https://perma.cc/AU6F-896G)

Harvard Business School (2019) Impact-weighted accounts, 9 July, https://www.hbs.edu/impact-weighted-accounts/Pages/default.aspx (archived at https://perma.cc/3MBE-YP6T)

Macnamara, J (2018) *A Review of New Evaluation Models for Strategic Communication: Progress and gaps*, Taylor & Francis Online, 31 January, https://www.tandfonline.com/doi/abs/10.1080/1553118X.2018.1428978 (archived at https://perma.cc/78YA-YHHS)

Public Relations Institute of Australia (2020) Measurement & Evaluation Framework, https://www.pria.com.au/education/measurement-evaluation/measurement-evaluation-framework/ (archived at https://perma.cc/SXD9-KDDY)

Sheehan, D (2020) Introducing the Porter Novelli Purpose Tracker: The business imperative for social justice today, *Porter Novelli*, 18 June, https://www.porternovelli.com/intelligence/2020/06/18/introducing-the-porter-novelli-purpose-tracker-the-business-imperative-for-social-justice-today/ (archived at https://perma.cc/M3DQ-H84P)

09

Activate NOW

Making change happen isn't easy. For many of us change can be uncomfortable, even alarming. For those with vested interests in maintaining the status quo, it can be a threat, so we know that what we advocate and practise is neither easy nor always welcome. However, our experience is that what is challenging can be most rewarding and where success is achieved, the conversion of doubts to celebration is part of the joy of such success. We have challenged you in this book to think differently, dramatically, about your role in your business, the role of marketing and communications generally and the position of your business within the world. Converting such thinking into actual action is the final challenge ahead of you and a challenge that should not wait.

Before we end the book and you start writing your own personal chapter, let us just consider this. Many great ideas never happen; many great reads never manifest themselves beyond the pages of a book. Those that do rely upon several factors, not least a level of luck, perhaps a receptive audience or environment, but at the core, in our mind are four critical factors:

1 The 'Idea' resonates in the mind of an individual.
2 The 'Individual' is capable of imagining such change.
3 The 'Imagined' change provides a rewarding impact.
4 The 'Impact' extends the idea so it resonates with others.

Before you know it, the radical idea is universally adopted, moving from the peripheral to the mainstream, as has happened with everything from organic food, alternative therapies, climate change, e-commerce, the sharing economy and video calls to name just a few. The critical part in ensuring that the individual can turn the imagined into the impactful is a clarity of thinking and a matching process which they can then use their own leadership and personal characteristics to simply 'make it happen'. This is what this chapter is about.

They say the best time to plant a tree was yesterday and the second best is today.

So, the best day to start activating your truth-based marketing and communications strategy is today. As we have seen in the previous chapters, the world has shifted into one of ever more complexity and expectation. A desire for a more human, truthful and purposeful way of doing business and communicating is now generally accepted and it is purely understanding how to turn such sentiment into deliverable reality, that is the purpose of *Truth Be Told*. This chapter is designed to compress all the learning we have imparted into an overarching methodology to help you activate and start your own truthful journey today.

It may seem strange to quote Arthur Schopenhauer, the 19th-century philosopher who is often considered a frightful pessimist, but his approach gave us this:

All truth passes through three stages. First, it is ridiculed. Second, it is violently opposed. Thirdly it is accepted as being self-evident.

Although there may be individuals still caught in the first two stages, the majority of people consider both the business purpose approach and the need for a human truth to be self-evident. The obstacle now is simply understanding how to approach winning with it, rather than needing to know how to convince people of it.

Follow a plan

To successfully activate the thinking in this book, it is necessary to be absolutely clear how the various stages build into one clear and managed process. This allows you the chance to advance the thinking and methodologies of questioning yourself in order to achieve the best results with continuous experimentation and agile decision processes. Performance must be flexible and have real-time components

To digest the entire book and find a path, a summary is here. We have illustrated the process in one flow diagram in Figure 9.1 and grouped the chapters into four key stages to assist you in the practical activation of your truth strategy. The flow diagram takes each chapter and, where appropriate, groups some into defined activation groups. These are:

FIGURE 9.1 Truth be told process

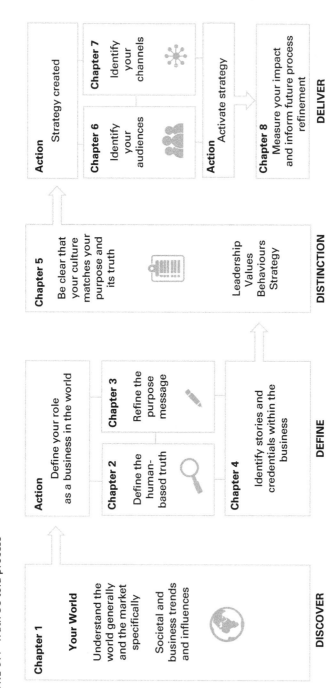

Chapter 1

Your World

Understand the world generally and the market specifically

Societal and business trends and influences

DISCOVER

Action
Define your role as a business in the world

Chapter 2
Define the human-based truth

Chapter 3
Refine the purpose message

Chapter 4
Identify stories and credentials within the business

DEFINE

Chapter 5
Be clear that your culture matches your purpose and its truth

Leadership
Values
Behaviours
Strategy

DISTINCTION

Action
Strategy created

Chapter 6
Identify your audiences

Chapter 7
Identify your channels

Action
Activate strategy

Chapter 8
Measure your impact and inform future process refinement

DELIVER

Discover: where you will discover your business's place in the world.

Define: where you will define your human truth and refine your purpose message.

Distinction: where you will appreciate your distinct credentials to support your messaging.

Deliver: where you identify your audience, your channels and how you measure success.

This chapter provides the necessary summary questions and reminders of the key indicators to ease you through from adopting the thinking, to its successful application.

Discover

To kick start your Discover phase, reminding yourself of what we understand as *The Purposeful Age* – people seek greater purpose in their own lives and the organizations they work for and purchase from. As you embark upon activating your own strategy, you need to be bold in reimagining the way in which you view the business and its relationship with the wider world and much broader stakeholders. Remember BP's Lord Browne and his phrase taken from Shakespeare, 'What news on the Rialto?', ensuring a knowledge of the wider world. This is the world far beyond simply the market you are operating in, or your direct customers; this is what you now need to start considering.

Remember, this approach requires you to combine your specialist knowledge in marketing and communications with an important general knowledge, which we have described as *informed empathy*. As a start to this, ask yourself these questions:

- Are you ready to lift your awareness of the world beyond the business?
- Are you clear on how to be aware of trends?
- Are you confident that you can interpret such trends to shape your strategies?

Once you know you are capable of making this broader assessment you can move onto the true discovery phase, by exploring – perhaps individually, but we would suggest at a minimum with your team – these following questions. Designed to be expansive and flexible, but capable of concentrating your ability to think differently, as we say, *further away* from the business-specific, this exercise will allow you to interpret your own business position from the wider world.

EXERCISE
Three sets of questions

Society

- What is society currently concerned about?
- What is government currently concerned about?
- What trends are we seeing in the environmental space?

(These are in effect environmental, social and governmental [ESG] questions, which we explain more about in Chapter 3.)

Marketplace

- What trends are we seeing in our rivals?
- What trends are we seeing in suppliers?
- What trends are we seeing in customers?

(These are essentially standard market assessment questions.)

Business

- What trends are we seeing in our employees?
- What trends are we seeing in our leadership?
- What trends are we seeing in our culture?

(These are essentially standard internal management questions, which we talk more of in Chapters 4 and 5.)

Having successfully completed these questions, you will be able to move into phase two, the Define stage, which requires you to define your truth, refine your purpose language and look into the business for the collateral, the stories and foundation on which your messaging will be based.

Define

This phase brings together the critical steps of defining your human truth, refining your purpose language, and then identifying where your credentials are.

Human truth

From your discovery phase, you now know the place of your business in the world – now you need to find the human truth that is at the core of it. To meet this, you should try to define how your business 'helps people and or the planet'. Sounds simple, doesn't it? But be reminded of the need for succinctness, ease of understanding and something, which when spoken, seems natural.

This human need, when it rings true, should come to be seen in your business as an undeniable truth. Make sure you approach your thinking around people, not customers. You may remember we used a verbal analogy based loosely on John F Kennedy's famous statement of 1961 – 'Ask not what your country can do for you...' – but as 'Ask not what you sell to someone, ask what you solve for someone'.

Being human means being emotional, empathetic; it means uncovering people's needs but also understanding both the rational and the emotive influences your messaging will directly address. From a person's perspective, you want to make sure you can illustrate the truth as the business believes it and that such truth, through its products and services, addresses their needs. Try and stand in your audience's shoes and ask yourselves key questions. Does the business brand appear trustworthy? Does the product perform as it says it should? How does the experience make me feel? The following questions are the triggers through which you should be able to determine your human truth:

- Are you clear on what the human truth is that resonates with you and your proposition?
- Are you clear on how your business purpose meets that human need?
- Are you confident in the truth of how you operate?
- Are you confident on the qualities of your product or service?
- Envision the effect of you aligning all of the above.

Purpose

This brings us swiftly onto defining your purpose, indeed if done correctly, the likelihood is that it will emerge from the process of questioning and the creative and critical input of the people you involve. In refining your language, be clear in the distinction between Purpose, Vision and Mission and as shown here:

Purpose: WHY the business exists, contributing something positive to people, and or the planet. This should be short, memorable and aspirational.

Vision: WHERE the business is heading, with a view of the world envisaged as being created by being successful in its purpose. This can be both a vision of the world and a vision of where the business is within that world.

Mission: WHAT the business will do to achieve its purpose over a specified period of time.

You now recognize that in today's business context, *purpose* is defined by fusing two dictionary definitions: firstly why something exists, and secondly the values and ethics on which it stands. In this define phase you also need to be clear of the values on which your proposition is based, even though they will be specifically a focus of analysis in the distinction phase, next. However, in the forefront of your mind, in bringing all the truth and purpose thinking together, must be that the words need to be reflective of the reality within the business; this needs you to consider where your purpose is best illustrated already, in effect, where the examples and areas of the business are which you will draw upon. Consider these questions:

- Have you reviewed and defined existing activities as CSR, Philanthropy, Sustainability?
- Can you put into perspective the evolution of these activities in your own business?
- Are you clear on the distinction between your Vision, Mission and Purpose?
- Have you an ability to define or refine any existing language used in the above?
- Are you confident that others in your team or business understand the above distinction?
- Start to think about the clarity such understanding could bring to your people.

The Define phase has allowed you to bring together the foundation blocks on which the strategy will be built. In short, you now know the place of the business in the world, what human truth sits as a driving rationale to your purpose, how you describe it, and where the evidence is already in place in terms of where illustrative messaging will be created. The next phase is to ensure that the leadership, culture, strategy and supporting values and behaviours all are capable of at least meeting scrutiny and, to a more positive degree, powering up your business-wide commitment in advance of external activation.

Distinction

In the previous phase, you will have identified where examples of your human-based truth and purpose sit within the business. You will be reminded that beyond the functional areas, there sit at the heart of any business four core attributes – values, behaviours, leadership and strategy – which influence how it is perceived, inside and out. They hold such an important position because they reflect the way in which the business is operated and how a human, truthful purpose manifests itself tangibly and empowers an authentic story to be told. In the Distinction phase they create the 'way' your business operates, its culture and what could be described as its character.

This character is how your human truth lives in the business, how it forms the consistent approach to your strategy and all other activity within a purposeful business. You will need to ensure that within your corporate culture and character, your identified human truth is free to manifest itself fully and energize your activities.

As a reminder, but also as a practical activity, take a dictionary definition of the words 'Corporate Culture' along the lines of 'The beliefs and ideas that a company has and the way in which they affect how it does business and how its employees behave' (Cambridge University, 2011). Then think about summarizing this sense of the business in your own words and as a litmus test, be clear to appreciate the existing 'beliefs' and the 'way', to ensure they are aligned to the work you have done previously. If they lack something , then this must become a priority for you before progressing, but hopefully to have reached this stage, the authentic alignment of these with your truth and purpose will already be in place.

1   **Beliefs and ideas**: What generally the people involved in the business think. This is a collective sense, the values and the ethics on which they are based.

2   **The way**: How it does business, how the leaders serve the business through their strategy, and how its employees behave internally and externally.

Finally, at the root of this must always be to 'Think Human'. This whole book is about a human-based truth. That is not some esoteric, intellectual concept, but something which sits at the heart of the relationship the business has with each of its people and each of its people have with each other. The businesses and, to be frank, the leaders who get this right, are those who put the person, the individual human, at the centre of their day-to-day thinking and their long-term plans. This means they show genuine concern, perhaps for employees struggling with poor health, or they understand that an unusual overdue payment by a customer may mean deeply troubling domestic issues, or they are careful in the application of rules and regulations when discretion may be the better decision about how strictly procedures are applied. There are a host of scenarios where leading companies can simply apply what is universally known as *The Golden Rule*: treat people as you would wish to be treated yourself. But we must also never forget that the way a business behaves in such a situation is simply based on the way each of us as individuals behaves. It is person to person, human to human, conversation to conversation:

- Make sure your leadership is committed – without this your job will be harder.
- Review your values, if published, and how they link to your truth and purpose.
- Identify your best voices, regardless of hierarchy, and empower them to speak.
- Look for illustrative behaviours that can be fuel to your communications.
- Continually review, assess and nurture the human-centric culture.

Deliver

The Delivery phase is the point at which your thinking, your internal interpretation of purpose, your credentials checking, your story identification, culture and leadership go from being part of your preparation, to being a

FIGURE 9.2   The Purpose Story Framework™

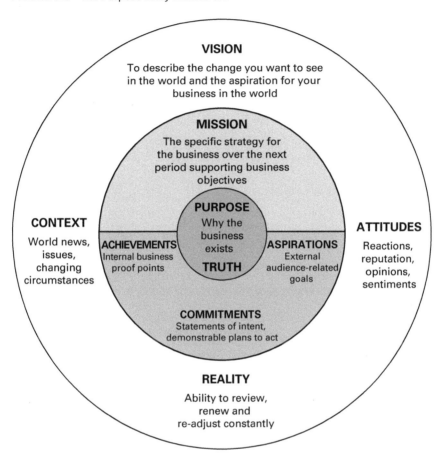

strategy to purpose-power your marketing and communications. It is at this point that we remind you of our Purpose Story Framework™ diagram (Figure 9.2) as the lens through which you will achieve alignment and ensure that each heading triggers the necessary thinking to help you craft your strategy.

Given that you will have already determined your message, etc, your strategy will focus on being absolutely clear on the stories you wish to tell, your audiences and your channels. As a reminder, let us take you through the questions and influences you should be considering. First start with these two key principles:

> **1 Your audience points the way**. Rather than being passive recipients of information who may or may not be moved to think, act, behave or purchase differently, they're your guides, partners and collaborators, especially in this purposeful age.
>
> **2 Messages are stories, and stories start with human truths**. Data, product features, even price points are elements that can support stories that address human truths, but they are not the stories themselves. Stories can come from anywhere, but the best are built on empathy and come from within.

You then will need to ensure the following:

> - Review and confirm your alignment of Truth, Purpose, Mission and Vision.
> - Confirm leadership Commitment and resource to act.
> - Map your audiences (transactional, purposeful and peripheral) and their characteristics.
> - Identify your stories and examples from within your business or beyond.
> - Be clear on your internal Credentials, Achievements and Aspirations.
> - Assess the stories against Context, Reality and Attitudes.

Having reached this point, make sure you break down your audiences as we described in Chapter 6, between the **transactional**, the **purposeful** and the **peripheral**. Given that your strategy should focus on the purposeful audience, you will have already worked out your human truth, how you 'fit' into people's lives, and how you will help meet their expectations. You won't meet all of these, but which will you be suggesting within your strategy and its stories?

> - How do we make the future better?
> - How do we make the present better?
> - How do we make your family/community better?
> - How do we make me better?

Once you have completed this, then you are ready to engage internal or external creative support, start to explore ideas, etc, but it is at this point that we also need to flag up the risk that comes with this activity. It is the risk of being seduced by the creative at the expense of the truth.

We have cited examples of where creative thinking has actually led people into telling stories which backfire because they are far removed from the truth. Sometimes this may have been deliberate, on other occasions it will have happened simply because enthusiasm and raw ideas run away from the reality. Whatever the reason, this needs to be avoided.

It should be clear to all that in understanding purpose, audiences, the stories we share and the moments we choose for them, truth must prevail. The truthful purpose model should reinforce existing rules for *any* kind of exchange between your business and the wider world and so hopefully natural checks and balances will control such a risk. However, you can stay alert:

- Be transparent with the truth.

- Express the truth in terms your audiences can *understand* and *believe.*

- When the truth is less than the audience expects, work with them to *bridge* the gap.

- When you can choose the timing, choose moments where the truth *shines* brightest.

- When you cannot choose the timing (or the issue), *avoid* over-promising or making commitments you have not had the opportunity to fully evaluate.

Determine the channels

Put simply and using broad strokes, you need to determine which of the following and in what measure form part of your strategy:

PAID media: adverts via traditional (eg television, radio, print, outdoor) channels as well as digital platforms. Placement and timing of the content is secured by payment.

EARNED media: information conveyed, stories told, opinions offered about the business, brand or its products and services via articles, reviews or a third-party expert or independent endorser. The placement is earned through the judgement of the journalist or endorser.

SOCIAL media: shared platforms enabling users to post and share content they create themselves, or from other channels, including paid, earned and owned.

OWNED properties: the business or brand's websites, blogs, online catalogues or shops, some of which stand alone whilst others are hosted on social media platforms.

Selecting which channels alongside the moments with which to engage the audience is the key component of your thinking and the resulting strategy. Use the acronym PESO (paid, earned, social and owned) and consider other channels not always explicitly identified, such as internal communications, investor relations, government relations and influencer marketing.

Finally, a useful acronym to help summarize purposeful stories in human terms is PACA (state your business Purpose, substantiate Achievements so far, confirm Commitments for progress, and establish a longer-term Aspiration). Ask yourself these questions:

- Have you mapped and prioritized your plannable moments, internally and externally?
- Have you anticipated unplannable moments that might require a purpose-affirming response?
- Have you assessed the business's reputation to establish where it has credibility to communicate purpose?
- Have you begun to plan different creative approaches and the supporting content and channels to communicate purpose?
- Have you mapped all of the opportunities in non-marketing areas of the business to reinforce your purpose stories?
- Can you deliver a simple PACA summary of your purpose, achievements, commitments and aspiration?

Activation and monitoring

You will determine how you have chosen to monitor the success of your strategy, and in Chapter 8 we highlighted various mechanisms and tools to assist in this. This of course brings us to the final major aspect of delivering, namely that of managing to measure the impact, the *Wow*. We highlighted the fact that to successfully understand what the impact of your efforts have been, you must put in place some form of measurement, as without an ability to manage and illustrate the value of such work, you won't be able to inform your own decisions, or those of others to whom you are responsible.

We acknowledge that this may require additional resources but it is undoubtedly important if you are to move the truth-based impact of your work forward. Remember, there may well be existing processes in use elsewhere in the business which may support your efforts, the key being to consult widely with others who can be encouraged to share data to support your efforts.

We also explained that although purpose resonates globally on a human level, it is interpreted and activated differently around the world, often illustrating particular cultural variations or social expectations. These all need to be appreciated when working across different territories.

To assist you, this summary checklist raises what you need to consider:

- Have you clear objectives, specific by audience?
- Have you detailed what Input, Output, Outcome and Impact mean in your particular case?
- Have you identified and do you have confidence in the means to measure the above?
- Have you made clear with delivery partners the distinction between quantity and quality?
- Have you identified other areas of the business that may have existing indicators?
- Have you established clarity with your key stakeholders as to why you are doing this?
- Have you consulted national or local resources for insights into important cultural, historical or business drivers or constraints related to purpose-driven communications and marketing?

Summary – activating YOU

There will of course be times where issues and challenges that are beyond your control affect your ability to progress through the ideas and model within this book. We accept these; after all, we haven't reached our positions and stage in life without suffering some pretty hefty setbacks and failed efforts along the way. However, the one thing we all have to acknowledge is that often the barriers to successful implementation of an ambition do not lie outside but rather lie within us. The factors that are strongest at stopping us following through, are those personal doubts, distractions and dalliances which drain our energy, divert our thinking, dissipate our energy and waste our time. Time, of course, is the thing we have a limited amount of and when in business there are added expectations of activity; it can be too easy to adopt the expected path rather than put extra effort into a new one. Ideas, great ideas and work die a death here, not of one great blow, but of a thousand little cuts, the nagging niggles, the challenged comments, the doubtful look, which we ruminate on and in so doing let grow to the point where we ourselves cease to believe.

Being purposeful and having the ambition to drive purpose into this, our world of advertising, marketing, PR and general communications, requires something more of you. It needs a single-minded determination to challenge the doubters. It requires an intellectual reach to illustrate the wider world's influence on your business. It requires an enhanced bandwidth through which to understand not just your own specialism in the business, but its culture, its finance, HR, leadership, product innovation and all else, in order to truly understand the purpose of the business. This is where, whether you walk alone or lead a team who look to you for direction, your personal qualities, the characteristics of a purposeful leader, will bear fruit. Not least because you will see, as we have, an emerging band of thinkers and believers who are on the same path.

They will be global CEOs who are transforming their businesses to become the most positively impactful and far-reaching businesses in the world. They are the founder entrepreneurs who have chosen to take their drive and energy not into politics or non-profits to change the world, but into pioneering purposeful businesses and social enterprises. They will be matched by longstanding family businesses who, across multiple generations, have embedded values and ethics reflective of their own family values, as the driver of their business. And finally, you will see the non-profits, government organizations and society generally, looking for the skills and values to tell their stories well.

This, readers, is the purposeful age; this, readers, is your age.

References

Cambridge University (2011) Corporate Culture, *Cambridge Business English Dictionary*, n.d. Available from: https://dictionary.cambridge.org/dictionary/english/corporate-culture (archived at https://perma.cc/7YNC-BJMS)

Janaway, C (2008) Arthur Schopenhauer, *BBC Radio 4*, http://www.bbc.co.uk/radio4/history/inourtime/greatest_philosopher_arthur_schopenhauer.shtml (archived at https://perma.cc/7BKJ-YR3G)

The Stanford Encyclopedia of Philosophy (2017) Arthur Schopenhauer, Stanford University Centre for the Study of Language and Information, 11 May, https://plato.stanford.edu/entries/schopenhauer/ (archived at https://perma.cc/L9SW-UME5)

INDEX

9 781398 600164